The Point Is To Change It

D0947742

MODERN AND CONTEMPORARY POETICS

The Point Is To Change It

Poetry and Criticism in the Continuing Present

Jerome McGann

THE UNIVERSITY OF ALABAMA PRESS
Tuscaloosa

Copyright © 2007
The University of Alabama Press
Tuscaloosa, Alabama 35487-0380
All rights reserved
Manufactured in the United States of America

Typeface: Baskerville

∞

The paper on which this book is printed meets the minimum requirements of
American National Standard for Information Sciences-Permanence of Paper for
Printed Library Materials, ANSI Z39.48-1984.

Library of Congress Cataloging-in-Publication Data

McGann, Jerome J.
The point is to change it : poetry and criticism in the continuing present /
   Jerome McGann.
       p.   cm.   (Modern and Contemporary Poetics)
   Includes bibliograhical references and index
   ISBN-13: 978-0-8173-1551-1 (alk. paper)
   ISBN-10: 0-8173-1551-9 (alk. paper)
   ISBN-13: 978-0-8173-5408-4 (pbk. : alk. paper)
   ISBN-10: 0-8173-5408-5 (pbk. : alk. paper)
   1. American poetry—20th century—History and criticism. 2. Experimental
poetry, American—History and criticism. 3. Modernism (Literature) 4. Poet-
ics. 5. Criticism. I. Title.
   PS323.5.M395 2007
   811'.509112—dc22

                                                            2006024306

For Charles and Johanna

We detest these depthless pretenses—these present-tense verbs, expressed pell-mell. We prefer genteel speech, where sense redeems senselessness.

—Christian Bök, *Eunoia*.

Contents

Acknowledgments

I wish to thank the editors of the journals who first published some of the materials that appear in this book. In the last two sections I have lifted and reworked parts of the essay "Contemporary Poetry, Alternate Routes," *Critical Inquiry* 13 (Spring 1987): 624–47. The following essays are reprinted here more or less exactly as they originally appeared:

"Truth in the Body of Falsehood (Clark Coolidge's Poetry)," *Parnassus* 15 no. 1 (1989): 257–80.

"Marxism, Romanticism, and Postmodernism: An American Case History," *South Atlantic Quarterly* 88 (Summer 1989): 605–32.

"The Alphabet, Spelt from Silliman's Leaves (A Conversation on the American Longpoem)," *South Atlantic Quarterly* 89 (Fall 1990): 737–59.

"Charles Bernstein's 'The Simply'," in *Contemporary Poetry Meets Modern Theory,* ed. Antony Easthope and John O. Thompson (Harvester-Wheatsheaf: London, 1991), 34–39.

"Art and Error: With Special Reference to the Poetry of Robert Duncan," *Modern Language Studies* (special issue on "The Problem of Beauty," ed. Lisa Samuels) 27 no. 2 (Summer 1997): 9–22.

"From Sight to Shenandoah," *The Bellingham Review* 20 (Spring 1997): 38–43.

"The Apparatus of Loss: Bruce Andrews Writing," *Aerial* 9 (1999): 183–95.

"Looney Tunes and Unheard Melodies: An Oulipian Colonescapade," *Descant* 133 (Summer 2006): 111–30

Chapter 12 reprints a conversation I had with Johanna Drucker that was originally published in *Textual Practice* 18.2 (2004): 207–219.

The Argument

> It is a privilege to see so
> Much confusion.
>
> —Marianne Moore, "The Steeple-Jack"

This book is about the ancient quarrel between philosophy and poetry. When the dispute involves a claim to critical thinking, the question is usually decided in favor of philosophy. Poets, after all, "are such liars, / And take all colours, like the hands of dyers" (Byron, *Don Juan*, canto 3, st. 87).

A certain line of versemaking—Byron is part of it—challenges this customary priority. Its most celebrated members include the Greek dramatists, especially Euripides; Ovid and Lucretius; Dante and Pope. This kind of writing was energized in the early twentieth century when philosophy took its "linguistic turn," which made the scene of writing itself the source and end and test of the art of critical thinking. The result for philosophy was Wittgenstein and Derrida—arguably, with the possible exception of Nietzsche, the greatest poetic philosophers since Plato: truth as an endeavor of thinking rather than as a system of thought.

The most significant poetry after 1848, and certainly much of twentieth-century poetry, has been consciously language oriented (as opposed to content driven). McLuhan's famous proverb—"The medium is the message"—defines this aesthetic orientation, which began a comprehensive exploration of its resources in the late twentieth century. Nowhere was that self-study more rigorously pursued than in the line of experimental verse known as language writing, where the poetic field is less a vehicle of thought than an environment of thinking. That event is the central focus of this book.

While the book pivots around a localized event in the history of contemporary poetry, datable more or less from 1971, its proper subjects are more general. The case studies given here argue that contemporary language-oriented writing implies a marked change in the way we think about our poetic tradition, on one hand, and the way we might engage a critical practice, on the other. In this frame of reference, the book takes Walter Benjamin and Gertrude Stein as important intellectual resources. Both approach the history of poetry as an emergency of the present rather than as a legacy of the past.

The emergency appears as a poetic deficit in contemporary culture, where values of politics and morality are judged prima facie more important than aesthetic values. But in Benjamin's view—assumed into this book—culture wars are simply a mug's game unless measured by what power judges least important to its social interests and purposes. Hence the fundamental relevance of the aesthetic dimension, and the special and specifically *contemporary* relevance of cultural works of the past.

The experimental move in contemporary poetry is an emergency signal that flashes for readers and critics as much as it does for writers and poets. For this book, the signal calls us to rethink the aesthetics of criticism. The interpretation of literary works has been dominated by Enlightenment models—the expository essay and monograph—for almost two hundred years. With the emergence of new media, and of digital culture in particular, the limitations of those models have grown increasingly apparent. This book offers examples of alternative critical methods and procedures that are inspired by some of the most imaginative critical works of the past hundred or so years—Poe, Swinburne, Wilde; Wittgenstein, OuLiPo, Stein—as well as by ancient dialogical models.

Poetry and the Privilege of Historical Backwardness

> Literary works, primary as well as secondary, are each named
> 'Angelus Novus.' They are angels looking as though about to move
> away from something fixedly contemplated. Their eyes are staring,
> their mouths are open, their wings are spread. This is how one pic-
> tures the angels of history. Their faces are turned toward the past.
> Where we perceive a chain of events, they see one single catastro-
> phe which keeps piling wreckage and hurls it in front of their feet.
> The angels would like to stay, awaken the dead, and make whole
> what has been smashed. But a storm blowing in from Paradise has
> got caught in their wings with such a violence that the angels can
> no longer close them. The storm irresistibly propels them into the
> future to which their backs are turned, while the pile of debris
> before them grows skyward. This storm is what we call progress.
>
> —Walter Benjamin, "Theses on the
> Philosophy of History, IX" (variant text,
> possibly spurious)

I

Benjamin's "Theses on the Philosophy of History" stands to twentieth-
century Western culture as its inspiration, Marx's "Theses on Feuerbach," stood to the nineteenth. From their outset both documents
proved essential points of departure for reflecting critically on the relation of intellectual work to the condition of society at large.

Benjamin remains especially relevant—in the presumption of this
book—because he refashioned Marx's theses along a specifically aesthetic line. In this respect Shelley is Benjamin's closest English-language
forebear. Both had what Shelley called "a passion for reforming the
world" ("Preface" to *Prometheus Unbound*). Unlike Marx, however, Shelley and Benjamin were men of letters, not social scientists. Because
they engaged the relation of aesthetic work to social conditions from
an inner standing point, their positions are at once more trenchant
than Marx's and far more troubled. (For Marx, art was "not among

the ideologies"—a simplistic view that seriously weakened his discussions of art and society.)

Reflecting critically on Shelley's work a generation later, Matthew Arnold famously described him as "a beautiful and ineffectual angel beating his luminous wings against the void in vain" ("Preface" to *Byron's Poems*). Arnold's judgment has in mind a contradiction he saw between Shelley's exquisite and often difficult verse, and his reformist passion. This contradiction is nakedly exposed by Shelley himself in his "Preface" to *Prometheus Unbound,* where he gives a brief and lucid summary of his poetic program and its relation to society.

> For my part I had rather be damned with Plato and Lord Bacon, than go to Heaven with Paley and Malthus. But it is a mistake to suppose that I dedicate my poetical compositions solely to the direct enforcement of reform, or that I consider them in any degree as containing a reasoned system on the theory of human life. Didactic poetry is my abhorrence; nothing can be equally well expressed in prose that is not tedious and supererogatory in verse. My purpose has hitherto been simply to familiarise the highly refined imagination of the more select classes of poetical readers with beautiful idealisms of moral excellence; aware that until the mind can love, and admire, and trust, and hope, and endure, reasoned principles of moral conduct are seeds cast upon the highway of life which the unconscious passenger tramples into dust, although they would bear the harvest of his happiness.

"The more select classes of poetical readers": observing the acute changes that industrialization and capitalism were visiting upon English social conditions, Arnold judged Shelley's a doomed program. In its place he offered a project of general education to bring culture down from the mountain. His answer to class war and social dislocation was the "sweetness and light" that would follow the acquirement of culture.

That Arnoldian ideology began collapsing in Europe around 1914, and by 1945 it was in ruins. But in the society of what Benjamin called "the victors"—that's to say, in the United States—the ideology continued to thrive well past 1945 in programs of general education—the "Great Books" programs founded and augmented over some forty years at Harvard, Columbia, and Chicago, and the reading methodologies sponsored by the New Criticism.

Written just before his death in 1940, Benjamin's "Theses" addressed the crisis of European culture that he was living through. But at that point the dark meditations of a scholar trained in European philological traditions had no special urgency for most American artists, writers, scholars, or critics.

However, when Hannah Arendt's translation of the *Illuminations* essays was published in the United States in 1968, the situation had changed. Benjamin's declaration that "there is no document of civilization which is not at the same time a document of barbarism" (Thesis 7) captured in a single apothegm the shocking question his work raised for the Arnoldian project. For the scholar and critic, Benjamin's next sentence is even more devastating: "And just as such a document is not free of barbarism, barbarism taints also the manner in which it was transmitted from one owner to another."

The Benjaminian challenge would grow a dominant one for the next academic generation, and even yet it has lost little of its relevance, particularly in the United States, as one readily sees when Benjamin speaks about "the danger [that] affects both the content of the tradition and its receivers." So far as works of culture are concerned, "the same threat hangs over both: that of becoming a tool of the ruling classes." "In every era the attempt must be made anew to wrest tradition away from a conformism that is about to overpower it. The Messiah comes not only as the redeemer, he comes as the subduer of Antichrist. Only that historian will have the gift of fanning the spark of hope in the past who is firmly convinced that even the dead will not be safe from the enemy if he wins. And this enemy has not ceased to be victorious." (Thesis VI) After World War II, "this enemy" shifted its home base from Europe to the United States, the great power that, un- *nonsense* beknownst to J. R. R. Tolkien, was rising more formidably in the West than it was in the East. The widespread appeal of Benjamin's work in America from 1968 indexes the struggle between Benjamin's Messiah and Antichrist over the "cultural treasures" (Thesis VII) handed down from the past.

II

Out of scholarship comes the advancement of learning, out of criticism, its arrest. Of course scholarship would be worthless if it had no critical conscience, and criticism without what Emily Dickinson called "the scholar's art" would be empty.

Still, the two are different acts of reflection with different emphases. This is primarily a book of criticism. And its focus on Gertrude Stein's "continuing present" is a critical not a scholarly focus. It approaches contemporary cultural practice—in this case, the writing and reading of poetry in our time—much as Shelley and Arnold and Benjamin approached it, as a "state of emergency in which we live" (Thesis VIII). Benjamin's "Theses" resonate powerfully through the dark backward and abysm of time: "In every era the attempt must be made anew to wrest tradition away from a conformism that is about to overpower it." This is at once the privilege and the obligation "of the now" [Jetztzeit] (Thesis XIV). *Jetztzeit* is Benjamin's fleeting "moment" of emergency. In the "fight for the oppressed past" (Thesis XVII), such moments must be seized before they "disappear irretrievably" (Thesis V) because, "as a model of Messianic time, [they] comprise the entire history of mankind in an enormous abridgment" (Thesis XVIII).

Some will judge it mildly ludicrous to investigate cultural practices like the writing and reading of poetry as a social emergency. Because Benjamin's "Theses" themselves measure social crisis in cultural terms, they are scarcely regarded outside academic circles. Inside our tight little island, the "Theses" have been sacred writ for nearly a half century.

But is Benjamin's *Angelus Novus* the ineffectual angel that our age demanded? As we know now only too well, even the rhetoric of a "redeemed mankind" has not been safe from expropriation by "the victors." In our recent culture wars we seem to witness the combat of Benjaminian warriors with conformist adversaries. But to many—some of whom appear in this study—the culture wars were largely a dispute about the division of spoils. Books of Virtue and Books of Culture—"the best that has been known and said"—are equivalent conformisms in the following perspective: "A chronicler who recites events without distinguishing between major and minor ones acts in accordance with the following truth: nothing that has ever happened should be regarded as lost for history" (Thesis III). Benjamin extended the mission to "save the appearances" (Barfield) beyond the limits of conformed tradition and managed culture.

The academic movement to cultural studies gave special honor to that declaration when it nailed Benjamin's "Theses" to the door of its Castle Church. But in the case of literary studies—philology—the protest movement against Arnoldian culture had unforeseen consequences. These register most acutely in the world of aesthetics and especially poetry. Art and architecture trade in fully capitalized economies, as does film, popular television, even fiction. But poetry, once the prince of cultural production, is deboshed. You trade in junk bonds if you trade in verse.

All aesthetic work involves an element of gratuity and uselessness, beauty and ornament. Shelley's "idealisms" and Arnold's "best" reference this crucial element, which is likewise acknowledged in Marx's thought about art. In contemporary cultural studies, however, the critical investigation of this aesthetic element was largely set aside (dare one say "marginalized"?) in order to examine social formations and ethical problems as they were reflected in aesthetic representations. These political and moral emphases licensed sharp engagements between what was seen (on all sides) as a "radical" academy on one hand and on the other a conformist culture most deeply invested in traditional religious institutions. In the event, Shelley's ineffectual angel reemerged as that devalued security: poetry.

III

What Trotsky called "the privilege of historical backwardness" has been one of the great intellectual legacies of modern critical thought. It is in fact a memorial reconstruction. Pervasive through Benjamin's work, the idea traces its legacy to Jewish and Christian messianic thought, perhaps most famously expressed in the teachings of Jesus. The outcast, the meek, the unprivileged: these shall inherit the earth. When their redemption translates to their victory—a sobering outcome foreseen by ancient fatalist historiographies—we observe the critical limit set upon all messianic commitments. Nonetheless, that limitation—which Benjamin understood—does not cancel the redemptive privilege of recessive and backward forms.

Nothing illustrates this privilege better than "The Moment of Language Writing," whose emergence may be dated from the first issue of the small magazine *This* (1971–82). As poetry and the work of individual poets were growing less relevant to scholars turning toward ideology critique and cultural theory, a verse practice was developing with virtually identical critical interests. But there was a significant difference. Because language writers were pursuing these interests as a poetic rather than as a scholarly or philosophical practice, the writing went virtually unnoticed among academicians for a dozen and more years. In the 1970s and 1980s, questions about verse style and poetic method did not compel the scholarly community. Dwelling among untrodden ways, these poets set the practice of poetry in North America on an entirely new footing.

More important still, the work made possible new avenues for thinking about critical and scholarly practices themselves. For nearly two hundred years a "new philology," born in late eighteenth-century Germany, had carefully assembled a set of interpretive and analytic procedures for accessing and studying cultural work, and most especially poetical work. So powerful were these tools that writers in the 1890s—Wilde, Jarry, and Hofmannsthal most notably—began to think and write against that grain. Their antithetical practices would continue at the margins of the academy throughout the twentieth century, from Pound's earliest *Cantos* and *ABC of Reading* to Graves's *The White Goddess* and the work of OuLiPo. Frederick Crews was perhaps the first card-carrying academic to suggest—in his exquisite 1964 parody *The Pooh Perplex*—that literary studies was growing dull, programmatic, *uncritical*—that is to say, un*self*-critical. Then came the moment of language writing and with it bpNichol's and Steve McCaffery's Toronto Research Group, Ron Silliman's *The Chinese Notebook*, Susan Howe's *My Emily Dickinson*, Alan Davies' *Signage*, and Charles Bernstein's *A Poetics* and *My Way*.

From a scholarly vantage, two things are especially important about these kinds of work. First, they clear paths for rethinking and reconceiving what Benjamin called "the fullness of the past" (Thesis III). None of these works approaches "tradition" as a repository of "cultural treasures" (Thesis VII) but as a set of exemplary practices for the emergency that defines Jetztzeit. Second, they demonstrate that scholars as much as poets are obligated to transmit a living tradition. The demonstrations come as a passage of style, an aesthetic procedure validating whatever content—Dante called it *ragionamento*—may be drawn out of the work. These stylistic passages locate the writing's Jetztzeit where we are persuaded that the work is reporting, is *undergoing*, a cultural emergency.

Criticism that does not practice self-criticism stands apart, illusioned in enlightenment, paring its fingernails. Scholarship may and should hypothesize enlightenment for itself. Criticism ought not.

IV

Such at any rate is this book's point of view. Although it has proposed for its immediate object contemporary poetry, not the literary archive, the latter is also my concern, as I hope the initial section, "Philological Investigations," will make quite clear. The point is to change it: the Archive, our thinking about the Archive, the ways we write about it. The several writers taken up in this book made that obligation for change a central issue of their work. By casting their arguments in poetical forms, they plunge their work deep into their writing surfaces, exposing it to what Laura Riding called "the common risks of language, where failure stalks in every word" (*The Telling* 66–67). That is Benjamin's "real state of emergency" (Thesis VIII). It is real because it puts itself at the risk of its own cultural complicities. This is the fate of poetry. It is also the obligation of criticism.

Critical thinking "that avoids any [sense of its] complicity" with "our accustomed ways of thinking" will have, Benjamin warns, "a high price to pay" for setting that privilege upon itself (Thesis X). This danger carries a special threat for those whose vocation is to recreate and sustain our cultural traditions. So professionalized has the academy become in the past fifty years, particularly in the United States, that we academics can and do fashion our lived time not as Benjamin's *Jetztzeit* but as a disciplinary field. In that institutional practicality, all of culture—immediate as well as inherited—joins the "triumphal procession in which . . . the spoils [of the victors] are carried along" (Thesis VII). In that kind of situation—prevalent since 1968—the great gift that poetry hands over to criticism is its naked address. The emperor of ice cream has no clothes.

The emperor's ministers may aspire to a similar privilege. For that reason I have not updated the core of early critical essays around which this book has been constructed, as would be expected for scholarly essays. Like science, scholarship advances, continually working to improve the estate of human knowledge. Criticism, however, like poetry, does not move that way. Thinking, not knowledge, is the object of criticism.

Written between 1985 and 1996, each of these essays was originally conceived as a polemical work to explore verse writing then of little account in the culture at large. I did not originally approach such writing as a scholarly project but as a critical investigation—even, for me, an emergency. The writing seemed important for the ways it implicitly, sometimes explicitly, sought to reimagine our entire cultural inheritance. Misplaced or selectively remembered as my scholar's mind could see, that past was being called back to a new life by this writing. Because reimagining the practice of criticism was part of its cultural agenda, I read it as an urgent call to stop and think what we all should be looking for now (and then) in the practice of both scholarship and criticism.

In their once upon a time, this book's early pieces were therefore also exploring critical methods that might escape some of the limitations of our inherited academic models. Now they have a story to tell about the case they once brought on behalf of critical thinking. They have become part of our "pestilence stricken multitudes," the "dead thoughts" that Shelley insisted should go to "quicken a new birth."

Thinking always comes in that kind of continuing, ephemeral present, the vantage from which we study and try to learn from the household gods we carry with us.

But the gods are crazy, as we know now. So we have to begin again with our crazy gods. Klupzy Girls for crazy gods, playing Leonard Cohen: "There is a crack in everything, / That's how the light gets in."

Like scholarship's advancement of learning, the arrest we know through criticism remains a distinct pursuit, worthy in its own right. Indeed, it may now be something more imperative—a demand still laid upon us by Walter Benjamin's angel of history, whose back is turned toward the rising winds blown from paradise.

The Point Is To Change It

1

Philological Investigations

1

Forty-eight constellations once populated the heavens. Then, at the end of the sixteenth century the navigator Pieter Keyser traveled to the East Indies and discovered in the southern sky twelve more to add to Ptolemy's canon. Today eighty-eight have been officially recognized. But we know that those "infinite mountains of light" are in fact numberless. We know too that they are, as Blake knew, for ever "falling, rushing ruining! buried in the ruins, on Urthona's dens."[1]

Suppose we start again, this time from the ruins of Poe and not Paumanok, from Swinburne instead of Browning, from Stein and Riding rather than Pound and Eliot. Suppose we start by imagining the protest Robert Burns would make against any *Lives of the Poets* written to the measure of *Lyrical Ballads*. Would not he have justly cried: "Before Wordsworth was, I am"?[2]

"Are there not other gods for other loves?"[3]

For all the gods undergo shocking changes in their historical passage, as the pestilence-stricken Coventry Patmore shows. There is more in those ruins than "The Angel in the House."

What rumour'd heavens are these
Which not a poet sings,
O, Unknown Eros? What this breeze
Of sudden wings
Speeding at far returns from interstellar space,
To fan my very face,
And gone as fleet?[4]

That verse marches to a drummer we have forgotten to our cost. Constructed, like the verse of Poe, from an articulated thinking on itself, Patmore's theoretical clarity and innovation create the solitude upon which this verse is brooding, like a god out of time.

> Say, should the feet that feel thy thought
> In double center'd circuit run,
> In that compulsive focus, Nought,
> In this a furnace like the sun;
> And might some note of thy reknown
> And high behest
> Thus in enigma be expressed:
>
> "There lies the crown
> Which all thy longing cures.
> Refuse it, Mortal, that it may be yours!
> It is a Spirit, though it seems red gold;
> And such may no man, but by shunning, hold.
> Refuse it, till refusing be despair;
> And thou shalt feel the phantom in thy hair."
>   —"The Unknown Eros,"
>   1–7, 48–52, 62–75

In our own day Robert Bresson would find his way in just this kind of ruined Roman Catholic dialect. For Patmore as for Bresson, there is a poetical Comfort of the Crucifixion as well as a Comfort of the Resurrection.[5] A *poetical* comfort—reading itself in a passion of refusals, always dark, often comical. And this comfort has assumed other, secular identities: postmodern, anti-aesthetic, simulacral.

"In a dark time, the eye begins to see."[6]

Which is true. But with the dawning of that light, what then? We go on to other wonderings:

> God appears, and God is light,
> To those poor souls who dwell in night,
> But does a human form display,
> To those who dwell in realms of day.[7]

And if the days are lost in translation, what forms might those human forms take?[8] Monsters? (Hal Hartley) Philandering butterflies?

(William T. Vollmann) Glorious whores, poets are the unacknowledged legislators of the underworld, dancing in the dark.

2

"What's past is prologue"?[9] If Shakespeare has it so, then it must be so. On first looking into Keats's *Endymion,* what do we discover?[10] (About ourselves.) (Every looking is a first looking.)

> A thing of beauty is a joy for ever:
> Its loveliness increases; it will never
> Pass into nothingness; but still will keep
> A bower quiet for us, and a sleep
> Full of sweet dreams, and health, and quiet breathing.
> —*Endymion,* bk. 1, 1–5

Does this sentence tell the truth? Not if we think it references the quotidian world where "we live and move and have our being."[11] In that horizon each of these four (or is it five, or six, or seven?) Keatsian assertions will trigger various dubieties in an attentive reader.

—But poetry has special licenses. It doesn't speak the language game of information.

—Then what language game *does* it speak? Or do poets speak each her own language? What is Keats's language game? Perhaps if we read on he will explain.

> Therefore, on every morrow, are we wreathing
> A flowery band to bind us to the earth,
> Spite of despondence, of the inhuman dearth
> Of noble natures, of the gloomy days,
> Of all the unhealthy and o'er-darkened ways
> Made for our searching: yes, in spite of all,
> Some shape of beauty moves away the pall
> From our dark spirits. Such the sun, the moon,
> Trees old and young, sprouting a shady boon
> For simple sheep; and such are daffodils
> With the green world they live in; and clear rills
> That for themselves a cooling covert make
> 'Gainst the hot season; the mid-forest brake,
> Rich with a sprinkling of fair musk-rose blooms:

And such too is the grandeur of the dooms
We have imagined for the mighty dead;
All lovely tales that we have heard or read:
An endless fountain of immortal drink,
Pouring unto us from the heaven's brink.

"Therefore"? But since the first sentence itself needs some shape of beauty (or truth?) to move away the pall it cast on our thoughts, how *therefore*? Or does Keats's language game stand aside from reason as well as reference?

—Perhaps we should take the first five lines as a hypothesis. A kind of propositional imagining whose consequences unfold in the rest of the passage. The o'er-darkened ways of the first five lines were made by Keats for our searching.

—Or re-searching. Only when the first passage gets recalled does the hypothesis about deathless beauty gain the beginning of a rationale.

And still Keats seems whistling in the winds he has himself stirred up.[12] For all of this is, by its own self-insistence, thoroughly unreal, a flowery wreathing that binds us to no natural earth. Dark spirits and shapes of beauty are alike the creatures of this waking dream.

—The passage itself illustrates the thing of beauty it imagines for itself.

—But what does *that* mean? That things of beauty are momentary in the mind but immortal in the flesh of language?[13]

Things of beauty. That raises a problem, perhaps *the* problem. As if there were such things, like pots made by that puttering artisan of the Bible.[14] Keats's view seems more primitive: "Therefore . . . are *we* wreathing / A flowery band to bind us to the earth." This polytheistic "we" references (I take it) the visionary companies of poets and artists, whom Keats's soul selects for its society. But the company is also here imagined—in the entirety of this scene of earthbound imaginings— as the *we* we meet (again) at the close of the passage: ourselves, readers and listeners, not poets and makers. Is Keats one of that company? Certainly he seems to be listening to these words he is even now, apparently, writing. Listening to what he says, as if he were making up what he means as he goes along. (He sings a solitary song / And whistles in the wind).

We will have to think more carefully about what kind of beautiful things this Keatsian text has summoned.

—But that's not all we have to think about. However we judge those *things,* only on this special Keatsian account can we say, or believe, that they are joys forever, or that their loveliness increases, or that they bring pacific pleasures.

—We have to suspend our doubts about the imaginative hypothesis; we have to read in the horizon of another hypothesis: "With the same spirit that its author writ."[15] Which must be hypothetical since that spirit is inaccessible to us, only something we may surmise and then seek to share with others.

—Yes. But then are we also to forget that we have willingly suspended our disbeliefs? Is this *expected* of us by the act of reading itself?

—And what can it mean to speak of Keats's intentions or reading expectations? Of course we imagine that he must have had them. But to speak of them now, to hypothesize them, is surely a rhetorical move by the reader—made, presumably, to persuade *his* readers to join what is being represented as a select reading company (one including the poet himself!)

3

"A thing of beauty is a joy for ever." The nominatives on both sides of the copula are uncertain; and they discover their uncertainty in being joined at the copula, which defines an identity that, in this case, also presents itself as a problem. Note the special character of the uncertainty, that's to say, the patent condition of its apparent untruth. So brazen that we may be teased out of our critical certainty (our certainty of the untruth of the statement) and begin to wonder if there might not be some special case where the statement could be said and could be true. And at that point we begin to interpret, to go a journey in quest of this special case of truth.[16] We interpret the assertion in order to remove that uncertainty of meaning.

The journey toward meaning proceeds through the remainder of the text, where fresh uncertainties and arresting moments emerge to make the journey more complicated and interesting.

—Because Keats's poem has been widely read, a meaning-consensus has developed. Many hypotheses have evolved a general theory of the poem, which encompasses this opening passage as well. *Endymion* (we say) is a Romantic poem. It operates on principles of imaginative desire. Or as Keats's friend Leigh Hunt observed, it gains its objects by its desire for them. The poem's opening statement is in the optative mood.

"But does this general theory of Keats's poem close down its interesting uncertainties of meaning?" "Clearly not, for people keep reading it." "Perhaps they keep reading it for its *certainties*—for instance, the declared certainty of poetry's joyful permanences." "Reading, in other words, in a state of perpetual hope and desire." "Why not? Would that not be, as Leigh Hunt thought, a *Keatsian* reading?" "But what if readers lost interest in it, lost sight of it?" "Then it would cease to be meaningful." "And its opening passages would cease to be true, even in your Romantic sense?" "That question is a hypothesis about the conditions of the poem's meaninglessness. And it's implicit in the general Romantic theory of the poem's meaning. So I want to answer this way: Yes, it would cease to be true, but not 'even in your Romantic sense'; rather, it would cease to be true *only* in your Romantic sense. That's to say, it would cease to be true for us. Now."

4

But is it accurate to say that "poetry doesn't speak the language game of information"? That its language is rather the language of imagination—that artifice of figurations wreathed, as in a double helix, with its co-dependent strand of informational artifice (syntax, vocabulary, usage). Even nonsense speaks a common language. How else could Alice get so annoyed with Humpty Dumpty, how else could they converse at all?

—But then how accurate can it be to make the distinction in the first place, as if the codes of image and metaphor were noninformational. Besides, those communicating codes are clearly not the only ones at play in the discourse of poetry, as we can see in the conversation about poetry between Alice and the egg:

> "As to poetry, you know," said Humpty Dumpty, stretching out one of his great hands, "I can repeat poetry as well as other folk, if it comes to that—"

> "Oh, it needn't come to that!" Alice hastily said, hoping to keep him from beginning.

"The piece I'm going to repeat," he went on without noticing her remark, "was written entirely for your amusement."

Alice felt that in that case she really *ought* to listen to it; so she sat down, and said "Thank you" rather sadly,

> "*In winter, when the fields are white,*
> *I sing this song for your delight—*

only I don't sing it," he added, as an explanation.

"I see you don't," said Alice.

"If you can *see* whether I'm singing or not, you've sharper eyes than most," Humpty Dumpty remarked severely. Alice was silent.

> —*Through the Looking Glass,* chapter 7

The code of bibliographical inscription brings an added dimension to a textual game—in this instance—"written entirely for your amusement." Alice holds her own in bantering with Carroll's literalist of imagination because she can *see* that he doesn't, in fact, *sing it* at all. "He doesn't write it either. It was written by somebody else, a man with a birth certificate, as we all know and anybody can see. And what should we say about the printing of what was written entirely for our amusement?"

—And how can we speak of a textual double helix? Here are three strands of code operating code-pendently.

5

So we can *see* that Humpty Dumpty is singing, for we see a difference between his prose texts and his poetry texts. The difference is inscribed bibliographically.

—But *the music being sung* cannot be seen. Music is not coded for the eyes. We should see the music, we could aver that, if it were cast in a graphical code.

—Can it then be heard?

—No, not here. It would be heard only if the poem were repeated orally. Recited. Then we should register a fourth strand of code operating in the discourse of poetry, the metrical code. As Alice says, this is a code strand that "ought to" be listened to. The music of poetry can be recoded in bibliographical terms, can then—as in this text of *Through the Looking Glass*—be recoded into another form of expression. But the music itself, its metrical form, is coded for the ears, not the eyes. Alice tells us this and she ought to be listened to too.

6

One strand of code—say, the bibliographical—can encode another strand—say, the metrical. That kind of transformation appears a general feature of all forms of expression. Expressive forms are then not just forms of code—signs and symbols. They are codings of forms that are already encoded. Not just mediations (though mediation is one of the phase spaces of code) but remediations as well, simultaneously.

This multidimensional state of expressive forms comes clear when we test any given form for its constituent parts. Take the verses Humpty Dumpty recites; how do we identify them? "Well, various ways are possible. They are verse, not prose. They are verses Humpty Dumpty recites for Alice. They are also verses that come into this chapter of *Through the Looking Glass*. They are verses written by C. L. Dodgson, perhaps writing as Lewis Carroll. They are one component of a larger textual unit, of verse and prose, that is itself multidimensional (it is a narrative, it is a complex exposition, it is a textual game). They are also one component that is oddly but interestingly divided into several parts, and those parts are themselves open to a number of different kinds of partitionings."

—One could extend this naming of parts indefinitely. Those who devise logical markup schemes for digital texts speak of this phenomenon as "overlapping structure." It seems the feature of language that most clearly sets poetry outside the language game of information.

—All expressive forms exhibit overlapping structure. Poetry appears to be a coding system determined to solicit and exploit the phenomenon of overlapping structure—in sharp contrast to digital markup as normally conceived, which seeks to disambiguate itself.

—Disambiguated language would then be language speaking the game of information. And if so, do markup languages argue that one can't have digital poetry? Clearly not, for we *do* have it. How then do our

imaginary gardens—oral, textual, digital—have real toads in them?
Marianne Moore raised the question but didn't really answer it.
    —Perhaps she did when she argued in her poem that poems are

> important not because a
high sounding interpretation can be put upon them but
    because they are
        useful[17]

and by "useful" she means useful to readers who, "in defiance of . . .
opinion," place the "demand" of usefulness on the poet and the poem.
The language game of information is a subroutine in the language
game of poetry:

> case after case
could be cited did
one wish it

The cases will be cited if the "demand" for them is made. "Business documents and // school-books"? In the abstract, "all these phenomena are
important." It is for the reader to "discriminate" the minute particulars of what is "valid" and "genuine," and it is poetry's part to facilitate
that kind of discriminating demand.
    —So poetry is a coding system that solicits and exploits the special
interests of individual readers. Poems are joys forever because they
lie open to endless rereadings. Those subjective acts subject poems to
further recodings. And not only each new "reading" or interpretation.
Each recitation, as well as each retranscription (any new printing), will
recode Humpty Dumpty's poem, rather the way each performance of
a musical piece recodes the original composition.
    —But then we cannot here speak of "the original composition," for
in any case we can have only whatever set of recodings stand in the field
of attention that organizes the new composition.
    —The idea of original composition is a particular critical formu-
lation, a certain way of coding a work for certain reading purposes.
Shelley's famous remark, distinguishing the poem in its compositional and its inspirational states, seems to the point. "When composition begins, inspiration is already on the wane."[18] The author's act of
composition—-or any act of recomposition—is a certain kind of re-

coding process, as it were, an effort, an initial effort, to map a territory that is known but not yet adequately explored.

7

Then what is the set of recodings that organizes the repetition Humpty Dumpty produces?

—It is the set licensed by the book in which Humpty Dumpty has his conversation with Alice. There he is repeating a poem written by "Lewis Carroll," as the book itself allows us to see.

—But the field of attention is not so restricted, as one may also see if we let Humpty Dumpty's repetition go beyond those first two verses:

> *"In spring, when woods are getting green,*
> *I'll try and tell you what I mean:*
>
> 'Thank you very much,' said Alice.
>
> *"In summer, when the days are long,*
> *Perhaps you'll understand the song:*
>
> *"In autumn, when the leaves are brown,*
> *Take pen and ink, and write it down."*

Here the text explicitly codes Humpty Dumpty's parodic repetition of Wathen Mark Wilks Call's contemporary poem "Summer Days," which begins:

> In summer, when the days were long,
> We walked, two friends, in field and wood. . . .

Humpty Dumpty's poem, we say, makes an allusion to Call's poem. Which means that its various codes, those we've been examining, seem conspiring to gain a level of reference beyond the linguistic or textual level—what scholars call an "intertextual" reference.

"But Humpty Dumpty doesn't *repeat* Call's poem, he makes a nonsense transformation of it." Yes, but in that transformation the poem is called back and, as it were, negatively repeated. To have repeated the poem in the form of a transcriptional (or recitative) copy is but one style or mode of repetition. A minimalist style, like a "literal" or inter-linear translation. Beethoven's Violin Concerto may get repeated in a printed musical score or in a performance by Itzhak Perlman. "But Perlman's would not be a work of nonsense." No, it would be a work of consummate illusion, persuading us (perhaps) that we were hearing Beethoven's music. Nonsense is repetition in flight from the illusion that Beethoven's music might be repeated. "But in flight to other illu-sions." Yes, to illusions—codings—that mark themselves as such. The world of nonsense is the limit case of a world of singularities. That is Humpty Dumpty's demonstrative argument to Alice, first and last:

> So she got up, and held out her hand. "Good-bye, till we meet again!" she said as cheerfully as she could.
>
> "I shouldn't know you again if we *did* meet," Humpty Dumpty replied in a discontented tone, giving her one of his fingers to shake: "you're so exactly like other people."
>
> "The face is what one goes by, generally," Alice remarked in a thoughtful tone.
>
> "That's just what I complain of," said Humpty Dumpty. "Your face is the same as everybody has—the two eyes, so—" (mark-ing their places in the air with his thumb) "nose in the middle, mouth under. It's always the same. Now if you had the two eyes on the same side of the nose, for instance—or the mouth at the top—that would be *some* help."
>
> "It wouldn't look nice," Alice objected. But Humpty Dumpty only shut his eyes, and said "Wait till you've tried."

Why does Humpty Dumpty shut his eyes and then, we are told, take no further notice of Alice? Is his gesture a sign that he is trying to make out a more imaginative view of Alice? So that he'll recognize her the next time they meet? We could decide to think that. But if we did, we would have to understand as well that our reading was an arbitrary choice, a hypothesis. Humpty Dumpty's might be as well a sign of bore-dom or a sign that he is sleepy. Or the sign might not be given any psy-chological significance at all; it might be read as a rhetorical sign (for instance, a signal that chapter 7 of *Through the Looking Glass* is nearing a conclusion). Or it might be nonsensical, which is what (it seems, though we cannot be certain) Alice decides:

> Alice waited a minute to see if he would speak again, but, as he never opened his eyes or took any further notice of her, she said "Good-bye!" once more, and, getting no answer to this, she quietly walked away: but she couldn't help saying to herself, as she went, "of all the unsatisfactory—" (she repeated this aloud, as it was a great comfort to have such a long word to say) "of all the unsatisfactory people I *ever* met—" She never finished the sentence, for at this moment a heavy crash shook the forest from end to end.

But what could be more satisfying—for the reader, anyhow—than a conclusion like this? Alice ends up expressing herself in a prose that rhymes with Humpty Dumpty's verse.

> "You needn't go on making remarks like that," Humpty Dumpty said: "they're not sensible, and they put me out."
>
> *"I sent a message to the fish:*
> *I told them 'This is what I wish.'*
>
> *The little fishes of the sea,*
> *They sent an answer back to me.*
>
> *The little fishes' answer was*
> *'We cannot do it, Sir, because—'"*
>
> "I'm afraid I don't quite understand," said Alice.
> "It gets easier further on," Humpty Dumpty replied.
>
> *"I sent to them again to say*
> *'It will be better to obey.'*
>
> *The fishes answered, with a grin,*
> *'Why, what a temper you are in!'*

I told them once, I told them twice:
They would not listen to advice.

I took a kettle large and new,
Fit for the deed I had to do.

My heart went hop, my heart went thump:
I filled the kettle at the pump.

Then some one came to me and said
'The little fishes are in bed.'

I said to him, I said it plain,
'Then you must wake them up again.'

I said it very loud and clear:
I went and shouted in his ear."

Humpty Dumpty raised his voice almost to a scream as he repeated this verse, and Alice thought with a shudder, "I wouldn't have been the messenger for *anything!*"

"But he was very stiff and proud:
He said, 'You needn't shout so loud!'

And he was very proud and stiff:
He said 'I'd go and wake them, if—'

I took a corkscrew from the shelf:
I went to wake them up myself.

And when I found the door was locked,
I pulled and pushed and kicked and knocked.

And when I found the door was shut,
I tried to turn the handle, but—"

There was a long pause.

"Is that all?" Alice timidly asked.

"That's all," said Humpty Dumpty. "Good-bye."

This was rather sudden, Alice thought: but, after such a *very* strong hint that she ought to be going, she felt that it would hardly be civil to stay. So she got up, and held out her hand. 'Good-bye, till we meet again!' she said as cheerfully as she could.

Here she's only pretending to be satisfied. Humpty Dumpty's poem not only refuses the sense of an ending, it stops and starts for no apparent reason and with all too apparent rhyme.

—And yet what could be more delightful than this? "Certainly not Call's 'Summer Days'?"

—Well, so you may think. But Alice clearly might think otherwise, and at least one reader I know found this doggerel effort the worst poem in Carroll's book—"of all the unsatisfactory."

—"But Carroll was entirely satisfied with all of these nonsensical deviations from sense and orderliness." You may think so, he might have even said so, but we can't be sure. We can only imagine and hypothesize. I may imagine, for instance, that these texts are composed as provocations. Humpty Dumpty's poem needs an ending (so we may decide), and we may then decide to write one for it—this has been done many times—or decide not. Either way leads to a satisfying, or a dissatisfying, conclusion. Either way would be "nice." And in the event, as we know, all those roads have been taken, as well as others, and chapter 7 of *Through the Looking Glass* has remained a joy forever. *Credo quia omnis possibile.*[19]

8

We don't seem to be *getting* anywhere.

9

"Is that what we want then, what we ought to want, when we read? To get somewhere?"

—To get to the end of the book, the end of the story, the end of the poem. "But when we were going the journey of the stories and the poems, if things were going well, we wouldn't have cared about getting to an end at all."

—If not the end in that sense, then the end in the sense of the meaning of the thing. Poetry is often hard to understand, and stories take time to fill themselves out and find their way to finishing. Part of the pleasure in the journey is the sense we get of the ending that the work builds for itself. "But what *is* that sense of an ending? If the ending were achieved, why would we ever want to read the poem or the book again? It's plainly the case that the texts we most love are ones we want to reread or even memorize."

Meaning can't be what matters most in this sense of an ending. Who could possibly tell someone the meaning of *Clarissa*, or *Wuthering Heights*? Or a much simpler story, like *Washington Square*? Not even to speak of the poems, those flagrantly mysterious creatures:

> Poetry is like a swoon, with this difference:
> It *brings* you to your senses.
> —Charles Bernstein,
"The Klupzy Girl" 1–2

There you have it, a stand-up, completely *un*mysterious example of poetic elusiveness, all the more outrageous for its simple declarative form. Or go back to Keats: "A thing of beauty is a joy for ever." Out front, openly stated, the poem's meaning. Right at the beginning. Why go on? If getting the meaning is the point, why play out all those decorative riffs?

—"But what is the point of interpreting poems if meaning isn't the point?"

—What if we say the point lies in the act of the interpreting itself, whose emblem and elemental form is simple recitation. If we have "composition as explanation" on the poetical side of things, may we have "explanation as composition" on the interpretive side?[20]

—Could we otherwise escape that "superstition of proper and correct meaning" investigated long ago by Ogden and Richards?[21]

10

"The philosophers have only tried to understand the world. The point is to change it."[22] The maxim applies to the world of culture as well as the social world.

—But wouldn't "we who love to be astonished"[23] rather want to say, "the point is to preserve it"?

—Or in cultural terms, "to remember it"? —Or in personal terms, to recite it.

—In these living worlds we're concerned with, Shelley's recreation of the hydrogen cycle, "The Cloud," applies: "I change, but I cannot die." Autopoietic worlds that sustain themselves through processes of feedback, of which the rhymes and repetitions of verse are the symbols that stand for themselves, who constitute the process.

A contemporary educator has rewritten that maxim as a thesis for scholars: "The best way to understand how a text works . . . is to change it."[24]

11

Why should the resources of procedural writing remain the privilege of the poets? I can imagine a game, let's call it IVANHOE,[25] where scholars are called in a circle, like fools in *As You Like It*.[26] Their subject is themselves and the cultural inheritance that we're remaking in our own image and likeness. The game is to study our remembrance of things past and present—by taking our thinking apart, setting it alongside other rememberings for contrasts and comparisons, imagining different contexts and different histories, as many as you can, and altering and abusing it for its own good.

> Before the beginning of years
> There came to the making of man,
> Time, with a gift of tears,
> Grief, with a glass that ran.[27]

Who ever read those lines without wondering: why not "Time, with a glass that ran, / Grief, with a gift of tears"? *What's* the difference?

—"Well, write it so and *watch* a difference unfold itself." Or rewrite the last two lines as a riddle—"What is the Time that comes 'Before the beginning of years' "?—and then propose an answer—propose *two different* answers—to the riddle.

—"And observe that one might 'change it' by changing one's self. Imagine you are Aeschylus, or Euripides, brought from the dead to discuss this passage from Swinburne's pastiche Greek tragedy. Imagine you are Huck Finn, or Kathy Acker. It is precisely a superstition to imagine those verses possess a proper or correct meaning."

—So imagine yourself bound by that superstition. How then would you *correct* the poem's meaning?"

12

"*Should* scholars gather in a circle like the fools in *As You Like It?*"
  —"Or like advertisers trying to sell a product?"
  —"In a desolate market, where none come to buy"?[28] Where else?

How can you really care if anybody gets it, or gets what it means, or if it improves them. Improves them for what? For death? Why hurry them along? . . . Nobody should experience anything they don't need to, and if they don't need poetry, bully for them. I like the movies too. . . . As for measure and other technical apparatus, that's just common sense: if you're going to buy a pair of pants you want them to be tight enough so everyone will want to go to bed with you. There's nothing metaphysical about it.
                                    —Frank O'Hara,
                                        "Personism: A Manifesto"

Meditations for scholarship in an emergency.

I
It Must Be Abstract

2

Truth in the Body of Falsehood

At the time Wordsworth published his manifesto against the artifices of eighteenth-century verse—his call for a poetry that would reflect the "language really used by men"—William Blake was already committed to a different set of proposals. Instead of (the artifice of) common speech, Blake invoked the artifice of eternity. He began to take dictation from other worlds, setting down words and sentences that were obscure and unfamiliar, as materially obdurate as the medium in which Blake chose to embody his work:

> Rintrah roars and shakes his fires in the burden'd air. . . .
> *The Marriage of Heaven and Hell*

Part of the shock that such poetry still produces comes from its commitment to what the eighteenth century called "the language of Adam." Because the word "Rintrah" is angelic, this verse declares itself inexplicable in any but its own terms. In this, the opening line of one of the most important English poems of the eighteenth century, we do not confront a language really used by men. Rather, we attend to a statement "dictated" from another world and declaring that "eternity is in love with the productions of time." It is one of those "sentences" that later, in *The Marriage of Heaven and Hell*, Blake said were "now perceived by the minds of men, & read by them on earth" for the first time.

When Clark Coolidge wrote in his *Notebooks* that "there are forms / in words for what is not known" and that "poetry is always using words you don't know" he attaches himself to a tradition that has kept its distance from those Wordsworthian compromises so trenchantly criticized by Blake in his annotations to Wordsworth's poems. The line of descent is quite exact, for instance, in the following *Notebooks* entry by Coolidge:

> It has always puzzled me when a poet, who must
> primarily expend so much energy transforming
> the common language into an irreducible variation,
> then immediately wants to break down what
> he has made into the common tongue again.
> As if fear of the unknown were
> the mother of discourse.[1]

Of course, it is not as if Coolidge had no fear of the unknown—the opposite is the case, as we shall see—but that he means his fear to parent "an irreducible variation" rather than "the common tongue again." Blake held that "Thought is Act" and that poetry is an act of thought demonstrating most clearly the truth of that proposition. In Coolidge we observe the same impulse to collapse the distances between word and thought and thing:

> At a loud report the lines of all the tree
> trunks and smallest branches on the far hillside
> volley across the cold space to become
> cracks in the window glass. The effect
> is utterly precise. Then the fragments
> begin to loosen and to fall into the room,
> the whole pattern bulging to give, revealing
> a blackness of space behind, howling with
> something that wants to get in.
>
> —from *Notebooks*

The passage is uncanny because it defines a series of objectivities and differentials which, while clearly distinguished from each other, do not occupy a "realist" space. "The effect is utterly precise," but it is difficult to translate or redescribe such an "effect." This is a passage to the "irreducible," at once descriptive (but of what? a certain scene, a certain sound?) and self-enacting. It becomes a confrontation with the Other, the god "howling with / something that wants to get in."

If one knows Coolidge's impressive long poem *The Crystal Text* (1986), one also knows that the figure of the house set out in this passage serves *The Crystal Text* as a figure of poetry and of the imagination of poetry. Coolidge's house of poetry is haunted, and that final complex image from the *Notebooks* text might well be taken as an epigraph for all of Coolidge's work, into which something irreducible and other continually fights to get in.

The *Notebooks* text also illustrates some of Coolidge's most characteristic poetical moves. Coolidge has observed in that work that "a sentence, when written, seems to / move backwards to complete its hold / on itself." In the passage above, that effect is unmistakable. Thus, we alternately read the "lines" as a (referential) "report" on a kind of landscape and as an instance of poetical language carrying out a description of its own immediate activity. The lines continually "move backwards" to reorder our perception of what they are saying. Subtle word plays contribute to the multiplication of meaning ("to give" suggesting not only "to give way" but also "to hand over"), as do the turns that hover at the line endings and the parallelisms. "The whole pattern" gets summarized in the final lines, where Coolidge's technique of double exposure is epitomized in the nuanced syntax. The final participle ("howling") operates in two possible structures of modification, and the preposition "with" sketches a figure within a figure: a "blackness" that is howling out of its own desire to "get in," and a howling blackness in possession of "something" else that is possessed of that desire. That figure within a figure is the text's final poetic license to the reader "to move / backwards" with the poem and its recursive structures.

In this kind of writing Coolidge imagines what he has called the "whole poem composed of / the empty space of the first thought / the second thought erased" (*Notebooks*). Absence thereby comes possessed of, and by, a concrete presence, and "empty space" delivers up the secrets of its apparitional emptiness.

> Do you see the part of the hill's open the wind has shattered
> the bolls have scattered at the limbs' encased retreat
> and there's no prong left in the twist of emittance
> the skull turns glass and the orbs to be wind things beat
> > —from "The Blades and the
> > Whiles of During Abutment"

This final stanza from one of the shorter works that comprise *Solution Passage. Poems 1978–1981* is another typical instance of Coolidge's wordmagic. Here the key, the signaling word, is "open." As the first line moves toward it we expect to find a noun in its position, and indeed the syntax finally forces us to read "open" as a noun (modified by "hill's"). But the artificiality of that structure makes us aware at once of another syntax that is cunningly hidden in the movement of the first. According to this second syntax we read "the hill's open[,] the wind has shattered / the bolls." The first line thus keeps itself "open" to a variety of readings, not the least moving of which is the one with the implied ellipsis, where the initial question is left hanging fire, uncompleted—a question interrupted in mid-career by a "statement" ("the hill's open") that breaks open the field of the text.

The energy of this first line is thus seen literally to balance on its (apparently) least significant term, "the" ("Do you see the part of the hill's open . . .") Here is work clearly "composed of / the empty space of the first thought / the second thought erased." And the effect forces us to "move / backwards" as we read further forward—to read, for instance, the hover lying hidden in the very first "the" to appear in the poem (for another sub-syntax is possible, the statement "part of the hill's open").

This type of maneuver—classically, anacoluthon—occurs repeatedly in Coolidge's work, for example, in the opening passage of "I Could Live Here" from *Solution Passage*.

> I could live here, a bed love and a
> table to write, food over there to eat
> and beautiful country out to nevermind
> the truck noise.

Two syntaxes compete (unsuccessfully) for dominance in the third line: We could read it with a dash or an ellipsis after "out to" and thus let "and beautiful country out to" trail off romantically, to be followed by a brief imperative; or we could read "out to" as that American idiom (in this very American scene, perhaps a motel) which allows us to speak of someone being "out to" (i.e., determined to) do something or other—in this case, the "someone" being that "beautiful country" determined to pay no mind to the noise of trucks passing on the nearby highway.

No small part of the pleasure of such a text depends upon its transparent self-referentiality. The "I" of this verse is imagining life "here," in the world of the poem where we encounter "a table to write" in two senses (for that poetic table has to be written, and "I" has "a table to write" for the text). And when that "table" is written, the word itself creates the imperative to fill out (or imagine) a world that is growing so populous with so many things and relations of things. Hence we come to the "food over there to eat" and so forth.

Here are two further examples of Coolidge's reflexive procedures, both from his superb long prose writing *Mine: The One That Enters the Stories* (1982).

Then came again the animals. The aloof snort snail, strumming his glass ear rods to good effect as tweezers. Through the agency of this one, odors could be perceived purely visually. He disappears down the carbon lane, as if a gruff rug were tucked at the end of town. Next comes a lion whose torso is composed of a trembling peach bag, from which bellows a report like audible parsnips. He is erased at the edge of a weed space by a passing glazier hefting his sign. . . . [my ellipsis] Then the lime worms, borrowed from the neighboring town, short themselves into the ground at any point, eking out a labyrinth of passageways of complex extent but such narrowness as to prevent human investigation. Knowing these worms to be tireless in their excavations, and so fearing the collapse of the very earth beneath their feet, the remaining animals hiding in the wings, and there are some fascinating examples such as the Zeppelin Spaniel or the Cleat Hog, have announced their unconditional refusal to appear here on this day. Thus comes to its end yet another world.

In this text we are evidently not very far from those staring series of hard verbal things that make up so much of the earlier poetry—for instance, these from the volume *Space* (1970):

itchy fickles freedom in feldspar, gecko lave
hell bender backs to back, time fray party sample
it's its list & crust soak be slow
bang gravy little its apes a few
the fire on asp street crooning

—"Rights"

And:

> be having
> eight
>
> priate
> via
> iny
>   —"A D"

In the passage from *Mine,* however, the staring series has been mediated by a narrative syntax, so that the text makes the process of mining the imagination one of the products of the imagination's world. Furthermore, that world is wholly verbal in the sense that it is integral to (and as) this text and its "carbon lane" of writing. Those "lime worms" come from their own "excavations," from the "Mine" that the text itself is digging. The phrase "Through the agency of this one," by calling out to the book's subtitle ("The One That Enters the Stories"), reminds us that each individual linguistic thing—each of these "animals"—is prized for its determinate singleness, for its "haecceity." Each "enters" the text sharply, physically defined, and each "enters" as an active agent for the text in two senses: They are beings who might come in, as through a door, and beings who (as it were) copy the text out in their passage through it, "entering" it in their peculiar ledgers or notebooks.

A passage like this from *Mine* can easily recall Ashbery's *Three Poems* or certain surrealist writings. And while I do not doubt that Ashbery's work has had a signal impact on *Mine,* Coolidge's objectivist inheritances make the latter very different from *Three Poems;*[2] Coolidge's animals, for example, are imagined with grit and solidity, for two "mines" have entered the storeys/stories of his work: the "mine" of a subjective consciousness and the "mine" that enters the earth, a thing of rock formed by the quest for rock.

Other passages from *Mine* may at first seem far removed from the early staring series and closer to Ashbery—for instance, this sequence:

> Paper is no problem since someone keeps bringing me more. How do they know the time? They are so prompt. Sometimes I refuse the writing in order to count the number of pages left. Sometimes I want to question them as to . . . But most of my time

passes in reveries of the nerve. The sneak attack which it turns out was known in advance, how was that allowed to happen? Only knowledge itself allows, that is true. No it's not. Some events have no semblance at all in the mind. They strictly occur, vicious word. The animals certainly are thoughtless, and the unpainted walls. A world in which only alien things can be said to be housed. The contents of bodies remains a mystery, no matter what has been laid bare in moments of fear. I am often afraid to open my shoes. The pendulum I can only dimly see through the stained glass of the clock case, what accompanies it in its daily rounds? A vast treatise could be constructed on the aids to interiors.

Here sequence develops through more evidently various procedures: contiguity of idea (through similarities or differentials), assonances and consonances, relations of images, and so forth. Unlike *Three Poems,* however, these sentences are imagining thought as a physical process. The "subject" that has entered this text as one of its ordering principles/principals has an insistent concrete presence because that subject has been completely incorporated into the text's language. Indeed, this work's effort is to shut down all the gaps that might develop (and that do develop) between thought and word and thing.

In such a passage Coolidge attempts to lift the structures of syntax and rhetoric to the same level of objectivity as his words, word strings, and pieces of words had in such an early book as *Space.* When Coolidge finally established, around 1978, his methods for imagining the physique of syntax and rhetoric, he became an important poet. A small but usefully dramatic example may serve to indicate what I mean. Consider the final line of the passage from "The Blades and the Whiles of During Abutment" (quoted above). Leaving aside the inertias that carry over from previous lines, we may be struck by the variety of syntaxes that play about the last twelve words of Coolidge's verse. I want to highlight one of these in particular because it bears so crucially on all of Coolidge's work.

The final line may be (must be) read in the following way (though of course not only in the following way)—as a compound sentence followed by a simple sentence, thus: "The skull turns glass and the orbs to be wind. Things beat." In this syntax "the" transforms into a nominal, the subject of the verb "orbs" (which stands in parallel with "turns"). In another writer, perhaps, such a reading might seem merely clever, or even perverse. But Coolidge has shown himself, particularly in his

earlier works *Space* and *The Maintains* (1974), as committed to the revelation of the materiality, the objectivity, the "thingness" of language.
The very title *The Maintains* involves a remarkably complex word play.[3]
In it, "The" is clearly to be taken as the subject of the verb "Maintains";
but "Maintains" is also to be taken as a nominal, one that plays with
the presence of the word "mountains." The latter is important because
of Coolidge's polemical drive to establish the concreteness and even
the monumentality of every part of language. Thus, *The Maintains* also
gives us (as it were) the "name" of a certain "range" of "Maintains"/
mountains. The range is called (to be called) "The"; and it is properly
so called because "the" *maintains* so much of the bedrock of our language. (If "so much" can be said to depend upon a red wheelbarrow,
how much more depends upon "the"?) Furthermore, this power in
a word like "the" is a function of its inherent syntactical energy. The
whole point of a book like *Space,* where words and pieces of words are
often set down in apparently white isolation, is to emphasize the relational energies that inhere in every piece of language. Artificially (and
fictionally) tortured and isolated, the monstrous fragments cry out toward (and from) the societies and relationships that they only appear
to have lost.

In this context we understand the importance that Stein's and
Zukofsky's work has had for Coolidge. Indeed, in many ways Coolidge
ought to be read as one of Stein's most lucid explicators—much as
Tennyson and D. G. Rossetti are, in their radically different ways, explicators of Keats.

2

In an excellent discussion of Coolidge's early poetry, Charles Bernstein
calls attention to the thingness of the work:

> Take a line. What is it about? What is it referring to? What pic-
> ture can I think of to replace it?

>   "is so
>   of
>   I
>   from"

Bernstein urges the reader to accept the obduracy of such writing Coolidge's effort is not (as it were) to "make sense" but to "make dense": to produce works "with a high specific gravity that weighs them down to earth, keeps them resistant to easy assimilation, lets them hold their particular space through time." In general: "words are not used as references to objects but as concrete objects, themselves, as texture, sound—and the poems more shape than idea or description."[4]

For the reader, the consequence is what Blake would have called a cleansing of the doors of perception. As Bernstein maintains, in Coolidge's "poetry of elimination" the verbal clusters allow for the most extravagant and wonderful fantasy—words building entities wilder (and more hilarious) than our dreams. My favorite is from "Calypso"— "hum over glow trout" and "cog world sigh blimp." One is, after all, left to one's own resources: one can only imagine what these things are.

That description of Coolidge's work—and Bernstein's entire essay about it—remains as pertinent for the later books as for the earlier. Bernstein's remarks on *Space* and *The Maintains*—just cited—apply equally to the following passage from *The Crystal Text:*

A pile of hooted buckets.
A loose laugh spoon.
Miles of adroited pain paper.
Lungs full of glass beads.
A list of nodules knowing of nameless.

But in the writing since 1978 or so, Coolidge has increasingly moved away from (I would not say "moved beyond") his early activist styles into far more reflective and mediated procedures. The passage just quoted from *The Crystal Text* does not stand so nakedly in the poem; it is framed by three introductory lines:

A prosewriter's mind's mass is thought plots
but a poet's is fielded of words.

What do you see when you look out with your language?
A pile of hooted buckets . . .

and by a series of subsequent "meditations" (that is Coolidge's own word) which begin thus:

> These are never only things, just, but the words
> retracked. . . .

It is as if Bernstein's thoughtfulness about Coolidge's work had now become included in the work. The word-as-thing is now seen to be "re-tracked" through the poetry: words not as the dress but as the physique of thought.

The syntaxes examined at the beginning of this essay are the clearest instances of Coolidge's effort to educe a physique of thought from the physique of the language in which it is embedded. The poetry before 1978 might be imagined as part of Coolidge's *Tractatus,* whereas from 1978 until now we are reading his *Philosophical Investigations.* The break is clear and distinct, but so is the continuity between the two periods. We see the continuity very well if we compare, for instance, two random passages from *The Maintains* with a poem like "The Developed World" (from *Solution Passage*):

> conglomerate aldebaran
> still toy in the eye
> off the shadlike stamp
> served hence as a thin loophole
> to the appointed arms in monazite sands
> the hot cup still on the lead look

And:

> ordinate two the tree
> me in shortest azurite
> similar into
> being to come notices
> a wall hanging in bad hence
> cause tude
> aperient aside or bees
> in an otherwise
> choke

And:

> Rangers in complete sheeting
> Deltoid impossibilities
> Rackstraw Downs
> The irreplacement of enviable feet
> Matisse in place of ear rings
> A store in which you can only buy canopies
> Sunken yards of ballbearing skating
> The lab in which Rover got plated
> The stocking of the sausage
> The rating that never got a hearing
> These things are not strange or rare
> They are waiting
> In the warehouse, they are yours

Lines 6–9 of "The Developed World" plainly involve simple descriptive statements (line 7 referring to a peculiarly contemporary phenomenon), and they work back over the first five lines to suggest that there, too, "strange or rare" as the words might initially appear—we are confronting material from developed worlds. Knowing the specific references of each word-string is not necessary (e.g., the location, time or place, of "Rackstraw Downs") and is perhaps even undesirable so far as the poem is concerned, because the wit of such verse entails our perception of an equivalence between words and things.

Neither words nor things are "strange or rare" in this poem, though Coolidge counts on his reader initially registering them as very strange indeed—along the lines of Bernstein's registration of the rarities in *The Maintains*. In this poem, any appearance of strangeness is taken as a sign of an imperceptive consciousness. "The Developed World" is Coolidge's late twentieth-century American version of Blake's "Auguries of Innocence": in each case an angelic imagination has been set free "to see a world in a grain of sand." Angelism in Coolidge, however, requires one to see the developed world in those "sunken yards of ballbearing skating" patronized throughout America by young people with skateboards and to see it as well in the word-string that Coolidge produces as a match for (rather than a mirror of) that world.

Without the final three lines of "The Developed World," however, we would be in a linguistic arena not far removed from *The Main-*

tains. The final three lines completely alter the poetic situation, causing it to turn reflexively. The elemental syntaxes of the earlier work quoted have given way to more "developed" syntaxes and even to that most highly developed of all forms of syntax, an explicit rhetoric. The reader is specifically invoked and imagined in this work ("In the warehouse, they are yours").[5] In addition to offering readers an opportunity to cleanse the doors of their perception, the poem insists upon the presence of the readers' thoughts. Finally, the work uses its angelism to pose a searching ethical problem for a world ("Developed") whose warehouses are a figure not merely for that world's productive goods but for its luxuries and imperial possessions as well.

The poem poses a serious ethical problem for itself, as a poem situated and produced in the developed world. The problem is one that impinges on all of Coolidge's work. In this case it appears through the double wordplay of the title, where certain interesting and critical relationships are suggested between writing and politics. For "The Developed World" may be taken to refer both to a particular trans-global political phenomenon and to "the world" that "develops" through this and every act of writing. Coolidge's poems, as we have seen, typically create the illusion that we are witnessing an act of writing developing itself before our eyes, letters and pieces of words leading to more and more complex structures. He comments on this process often in his work, particularly in *The Crystal Text*:

> I didn't think of myself. I said to myself
> I will make something up in a moment. Then
> I will look at it, perhaps I will dispose of it
> by writing something further.
>
> I still don't easily think of myself as a writer.
> I still don't think of myself. I look at the writing
> and sometimes see the self in there, out there, and wonder
> how I was somehow that self being written, writing
> itself out as if unwinding a spool of . . .
> I only see certain strands.
>
> There are great lakes, but not in the Casbah.
> The foot often slips, off what?, and I pay
> out more lengths, I follow with an unrecorded eye.
> The ear has no problem following. I often wonder if

it is in fact leading. It will always be the
mystery, that self ends up out there as those words,
a mirror impossibly deep. Never enough words
to the bottom of the distance. Sometimes voices
that echo from nothing ever visible. If I am
asked what I am doing I look and make up
for that person.

I quote the passage at length not merely because its explicit subject is "the process of writing," but because the text employs many of Coolidge's most characteristic techniques for enacting that process. Here the writing and the writing's subject (and I use the latter term in its double sense of "topic" and "agent") are one.

But the political and scriptural references in the phrase "The Developed World" are thrown into their most problematic relationship by the filmic process (still and "movie" images alike) called out through the word "Developed." Coolidge's work is obsessed with optical processes—his long work *Polaroid* (1975) involves no merely passing interest. Once again the connection to Blake is interesting. The latter imagines the exposure or development of an "immense world of delight" through the process of relief engraving, which Blake so memorably described in *The Marriage of Heaven and Hell* as "melting apparent surfaces away, and displaying the infinite which was hid." Coolidge similarly imagines writing as a "developing process" (in both senses) through which images are generated figures rising up on the surface of what first appear as white and empty sheets of paper.

In the phrase "The Developed World," however, an ominous overtone emerges when the optical process crosses over to connect with the political significance of the phrase. The suggestion arises, like one of the work's own "developing" images, that such writing has found us (and itself) in a "World" (whether subjective or political) that is fundamentally a network of Baudrillard's simulacra.[6] "The Developed World" is a carefully constructed artifice, a product of certain engineering processes "developed" by, and historically connected to, modern capitalist industrialization.

3

Like Ron Silliman, Coolidge produces a great deal of writing, much of it in long works. Even the collection of short pieces, *Solution Passage,* is an enormous book of verse: 389 pages of work (and this from only a three-year period, 1978–1981!) This scriptural abundance, however—and here Coolidge is quite unlike Silliman—is characteristically located in narrow and closed circumstances. Coolidge's interest in geology and spelunking helps fund that constellation of enclosures so fundamental to his work (cave/brain or skull/poem/house/room). "Jerome in His Study" (from *Solution Passage*) and the twice-printed *Melencolia* (in 1979 and 1987) both call attention to Coolidge's characteristic space; and *The Crystal Text,* which emerges through an extended act of crystal gazing, reinforces our sense that Coolidge's writing is immured. It is a poetry of great wealth and abundance, yet it is the poetry of an imaginative shut-in, the immense product of a deep privacy.

But isolation is what Coolidge covets, all the more so because he is aware of the political threat to poetry:

> The worst danger for an artist's work:
> assimilation. And this is a country of
> highly refined assimilating mechanisms.
> To make like (how I hate that trait),
> to leaven, make digestible, democratize,
> ultimately strip of individuation.
> Art is isolate. Its obduration is
> unacceptable.
>
> —from *Notebooks*

This fear of assimilation, of the loss of what Blake called "the bounding line," is closely related to what Coolidge names "the plethora, / proliferation of all forms, making a muck / unforeseen previously" (*Notebooks*). In the same work he quotes with approval Beckett's statement (1961): / "To find a form that accommodates the mess, that / is the task of the artist now" and adds that this remark "seems pointed / exactly at our condition." Coolidge's own version of such a project is what he calls "the impulse to make a work of as many and varied elements as possible and still all the more wondrous because somehow unified" (*Notebooks*).

Coolidge's "obdurate" and hungry word-generations struggle against what Bernstein has recently called "Artifice of Absorption."[7] Taking a cue term from the tradition of objectivism, Coolidge distinguishes between poetic "movement" (which "has that arrow edge nerve to it") and poetic "motion" (the "plethora" that "sounds like a washing machine") (*Notebooks*). Yet the distinction is purely imagistic and ultimately fetishistic: an "arrow" has no more inherent virtue or grace than a "washing machine," though Coolidge here argues such a view because of his fear of America's consumer society.

The distinction is nonetheless important to Coolidge and hence illuminating of his work. "Movement" is preferred to "motion" because the one seems an absorptive mechanism and the other a strategy of multiplying particulars. Toward the conclusion of *The Crystal Text*, Coolidge says of the poem that "I have made up a procedure here to which / there never can be an end." The "procedure" is what he also calls "my beloved / momentum," the "movement" that Coolidge typically sees and characterizes in geometrical terms:

> The object of scrutiny. A phrase is also a wave.
> Carved to see better. Looking at angles not designed by men.
> For that matter the race leaves no direction but
> follows them all. That nothing may be left to stand.
> I let it go in all directions here.
> ....
> No story. I can't discipline myself to follow the
> single thread. There is no single road
> leading off. A road does not just start
> but it does lead. How it leads, all over,
> never finished. And I strictly see
> all the sides, what the tangents are pursuing me,
> consuming me, with. With as a halt on
> progress? We are battered by chromaticism.

This being the case, Coolidge adds: "Open the mind to everything, and then follow the ink." The "beloved / momentum," whose "natural" forms and laws Coolidge sees fixed and coagulated in the structure of crystal, rhymes with the act of writing in the structures of a language.

The project of *The Crystal Text* therefore becomes the effort to clarify what in nature, history, and personal experience might otherwise appear only as "mess" and "motion":

> To grasp the relation of words to matter,
> mind, process, may be the greatest task.
> The batter. The worst of the winter.

What I discover in writing comes out of the
mess, the mix.

But Coolidge, presumably thinking of Dante, says that his "imagination is not pure enough to present / a single beatific image," which
would produce the desired understanding. Instead he postulates what
he calls "the spread beatitude of image, / the hose to the slaughter."
This is an initial (impure and single-image) formulation of "let[ting]
it go in all directions." Ultimately the writing itself will "spread" its "be-
atitudes" and reveal thereby its own movement to be "the spread beatitude of image" itself.

That is the general project of *The Crystal Text*, but to evaluate its significance we have to try to put ourselves in a critical relation to the
work. This is difficult to do with poetry, in our day at any rate, because its study and use now commonly arrive at completion through
acts of professional interpretation. Coolidge's poem itself calls attention to this problematic situation because it has so clearly presented
the homology between (Coolidge's) crystal gazing and (anyone's, "the
reader's") act of reading poetry. In each case a presumptively "deep"
or revelatory object becomes the focus of an extended series of meditations and queries, as if it were the repository of secret and essential
knowledge that it could, under proper circumstances, be made to deliver up.

In this view one goes to the crystal (Nature, the poem) for messages
and lessons—for instance: "All that remains here is enclosed loss" or
"you must see, use own / eye ears original mind, This is the lesson of /
the crystal: I was there and I saw, my proof." That "lesson" is a variation on the lesson that Demogorgon gave to Asia when she interro-
gated him about the meaning of history: "Each to itself must be the
oracle" (*Prometheus Unbound* II.iv.123). The poem, the oracle, the crystal: like Ahab's doubloon (and Melville is the appropriate precursor
for Coolidge),[8] each of these reflects back nothing more than the subject's original inquiring spirit, the answers that are concealed in the
questions. The knowledge they offer is in fact a restoration of the subject's own original, if occluded, faith:

I can finally write the word "belief" here.
I believe that the crystal is where I left it,
the exact point at which I last saw it.

In that sense it can be said to *depend on* me.
My knowledge of it, however slight so far, has
become its life.

Thus the poem comes to circle back to a self-conscious confirmation
of the work done in *Space* and *The Maintains,* a statement of the "meaning" of earlier work that now preserves its spirit in a more extended
and inclusive form:

Soon I will stand up from this page and wonder about.
Words allow things that don't much exist beyond them.
Like: the edges of a cloud touch. Pieces of the poem
are all you'll get.
    The edges of a cloud touch.
    Snow ash?
    Lazy blap. Roilercoats.
    And the bars open
    and the stems float out,
Now. Pieces of the poem are all you'll get.

4

That last quotation represents one of the culminating "statements" of
The Crystal Text, a gesture of completion that—typically for the modernist text—seeks to secure a triumph through its own enforced incompletion. The passage is especially interesting because it uses a
word, "like," which we know Coolidge associates with "assimilation"
and "leavening." Or consider this passage, where "the stillness of knowledge" is connected to "the crystal":

He imagined it standing
on a sandy plain like a fire in the fire.
There seemed beauty in this but no knowledge.
Nor any motion.
Will the motion contained in these words continue?
To insure that, he put them away.

Here the hateful "motion" stands in for what Coolidge customarily
terms "momentum" or "movement."

The appearance of "like" and "motion" in these two passages represents scriptural deviations from Coolidge's conceptual understandings. Paradoxically, the words help to justify the entire project, for they tell us that the work cannot censor itself, that the writing will utter what its own self-consciousness does not wish to imagine. Indeed, the two texts show how words transcend (inevitably?) the conceptual environments that writers, or readers for that matter, imagine for them. As a consequence, "impossible" conceptual formations are always emerging in spaces where they "should not" be appearing. In the case of the "motion" text above, therefore, we register critical lines of thought growing as simultaneous counterstatements within the text's manifest content. We cannot read that text without thinking, against linguistic appearances, that knowledge emerges where there at first seemed only beauty.

This textural event may be shown to occur repeatedly in *The Crystal Text,* and it corresponds to what Coolidge, in *Solution Passage,* named "A Fear":

> Sometimes the words will not mean
> what they must mean to others to me.
> Have I changed them so their
> meaning only I will know
> and yet do not?

Coolidge's fear that he will not understand his own writing has two aspects: he will not understand because the words will be interpreted along independent lines by "others," and he will lose their meaning because he will have driven them to such an arcane and secret perfection (the "beatitude of image") that they will have passed entirely beyond human ken. And yet both of these conditions have been cherished as his own most desired poetic goals. The former is the situation whereby the "meaning" of the crystal (text) comes to be situated in the "reader"; the latter is the linguistic state where word and thing become identified, where no space intervenes between an "object" and its "name."

Both aspects of "The Fear" erupt in the context of the symbolism of a brief poetic narrative called "The End," in *Solution Passage:*

And that whole sun afternoon I drove through
vast rockpile room of Wyoming worrying
I'd never see another signboard never mind
a single human again and just keep on steering
off the edge into further and more wild rooms of
same stone and sun. Everybody else slept
throughout, dreamlessly aback. It was a
stroke of The Fear come on me, all in
what I now know was normal blue sky
sunshine somehow making it all worse
and lone and racing loss of finitude until
the light lowered to sundown and with it
came a town. Sometimes you just sheer get lost
in bright time of day. But those rocks
on the floor of that sizeless room. . . .

The penultimate statement involves a jocular and defensive irony based on a playful representation of western American dialect ("Sometimes you just sheer get lost"). The effect is particularly striking because Coolidge's verse everywhere proclaims its "eastern" orbit. But here the playfulness comes as a "sunshine somehow making it all worse," and the last trailing sentence fragment enters the poem's rhetorical structure only to immortalize The Fear.

One has to see that such a poem figures terror for Coolidge because it has glimpsed the terror in Coolidge's most "beloved" forms. Most dramatic, I suppose, are the terrorist valuations that arise here in relation to the words "stone," "rocks," and "room." In all of Coolidge's poetry these are promoted as key words in his lexicon of white magic. But if Coolidge (or Coolidge's writing) is serious in declaring "The world is not enough. I want something / else to appear," the work is bound to dismantle itself. "Something else" that is not "the world" may still be human, but whatever it is it will be, must be, wholly Other; and if the wholly Other is not truly fearful, then we are only in the presence of fictions, of "literature."

But "the world," including the world of Coolidge's verse, is not enough for his writing. "Something else" repeatedly appears in the interstices of his work. Coolidge seeks for this result, but like all of us his desires are limited by his imagination and his will. "The Fear" represents that barrier we *will not* cross. On this side of the barrier stands the idea of "something else," an idea we can imagine and even grasp. On the far side awaits the unimaginable, and it is only a desirous writing—a determined act of consciousness that cannot *in its act* turn its consciousness upon itself—by which one may be carried across.

Poetry is transport, an effect as evident in Pope's cool numbers as in Shelley's passion. The effect is secured only through writing that is utterly determined in every sense of that word. So far as the writer is concerned, determination appears as a commitment to the mastery of technical resources and an unflagging pursuit of certain specific intellectual goals. These are the means by which a particular human life and way of life get transported into language, and through language into the larger human world. Once transported, that specific set of ideas and desires (call it "Clark Coolidge") defines and exteriorizes its own limits, and in so doing causes "something else" to appear, some more or less extensive range of the larger world.

Coolidge's work comes out of the American transcendentalist tradition. Because of this, he often writes about "beyondness" in ways that suggest he has known or comprehended what it entails. Thus, confidence may reign even when his work insists upon its incomprehension ("Pieces of the poem are all you'll get"). But such confidence—Coolidge's word is "solace"—is nothing more than the illusive face of his transcendentalist ideology, and the writing repeatedly turns upon itself to discover the crucifixion that such confidence is, and that it brings.

That pattern reveals itself most clearly in Coolidge's negations, rather than his affirmations. *The Crystal Text* opens by committing itself to the particular, the concrete, the personal. To Coolidge this involves certain correspondent anathemas:

> I hate history because it has never entered the
> world as a life. It has no direction
> but back into the fold. No touchingness
> very following to its black boxes.

Coolidge's poem shows something that has "entered the / world as a life": the writing itself as the continuous recording of "a life" stretching between the determinate dates "25 VIII 89–9 VI 83" (these the last words of the poem). Coolidge hates history because he has never known it in the form of his desire, has never known it to enter the world as human life. But this failure, we must surely see, is "Coolidge's" and not "history's"; and Coolidge's own text transports us to that revelation, for *The Crystal Text* could scarcely be a more "representative" example of late twentieth-century American writing.

Furthermore, History enters the world as the life of this poem, and part of that life is its determinate introversion, its determined effort to establish its "life" beyond or apart from "the world." The "touchingness" of *The Crystal Text* is partly the physique of its own social vacancy, a condition dominated and created by the transcendental subject and its transparent eyeball. Thus, one of the meanings of the text's denunciation of "History" is a denunciation of "the closed voice" of *The Crystal Text* itself, where "all that remains . . . is an enclosed loss." The "loss" revealed in this text is by no means "enclosed," and the "History" hated by the text is a history in which the text itself participates and shares.

That history is one in which human meaning is conceived and imagined in the intensity of the eye and its speculative brain. Agency therefore assumes the form of acute receptivity, and "meaning" is imagined to emerge as the revelation of a "real" that is "given":

> You should not fiddle with things as they are.
> No matter that at once they may all arc in the air.
> We are, said everything. And we have not really
> noticed, said the others. Those whose breasts
> primped to be noticed, and those who were not
> noticing them.

But Coolidge's imaginative agent *notices* and strives "to hear only what that thing allows." Stationed before "the beneficent limit" of "infinity," he peers intensely to "see where and what that horizon may lift." But "what the thing allows" may be "everything" or it may be "nothing" (these are recurrent terms—in both senses—of the text), and if the horizon at one point signifies a visionary breakthrough, at another the text simply declares, "I approach catatonia looking into the horizon." The geographical metaphor pressurizes the term "catatonia" to emerge in our minds as both a psychic state and some (now first named) geographical and political entity.

The history this poem unfolds takes place in a particular land, and one of its names is Catatonia (it has others). It is a land whose people might say:

The point of it all is that everything
is important, not just

The passage appears this way in the poem (no punctuation after "just," and the pair of lines set out as an independent unit) because Coolidge wants to wrest a double meaning from the word "just." We may take it either as an adverb (signifying "merely"), which would suggest that things are important in themselves and not because of some additional (substantive) reason; and we can take it as an adjective, which would argue along the same lines by going even further—by going on to suggest that in this world people measure value by a criterion of "importance" rather than a criterion of "justice."

But perhaps the ultimate "point of it all" is that the poem's own world takes the measure of itself. "Clark Coolidge" presumably means it when he says he hates history for its abstraction, but when "his" words appear in "his" poem, the scripture breaks the text open to its antithetical and unimagined meanings. One of the most impressive aspects of *The Crystal Text* is the way it has managed to ground its authority in a critique of its own efforts to achieve authority. In this way the work has successfully negotiated the passage to that form of poetry solicited by Adorno in his *Aesthetic Theory*[9]—a form in which the goal of truth, by clearly assuming the (philosophic) form of ideology, once again emerges as an achievable result.

When Coolidge says that "the world is not enough," that he wants "something else" to appear through his work, he expresses not merely art's fundamental will to truth, but his modernist sense of the difficulty of achieving that end. Adorno expresses a similar view when he says, unequivocally, that "Truth is the antithesis of existing society" and that art's function is "the determinate negation of the status quo." Coolidge's understanding of "the world" appears less critical than Adorno's. His "world" has already expelled most of "existing society," because his "world" begins from that common American ideology, the resort to "nature." Thus Coolidge's work lacks the conceptual clarity of Adorno's. But it operates with forms of desire that have already committed themselves to the deep truth of suffering and illusory beliefs, and therein lies its great strength—its *truth*—as poetry: that it exposes the (mutual) incoherences of the world it flees and the "something else" it desires. Blake, at the dawn of modernism, deliberately chose the same path. He called it "giving a body to Falshood that it may be cast off for ever" (*Jerusalem* plate 12, line 13).

3
The Alphabet, Spelt from Silliman's Leaves

At the limits of reflection, the value of knowledge, it seems, depends upon its ability to make any conclusive image of the universe impossible. Knowledge destroys fixed notions and this continuing destruction is its greatness, or more precisely, its truth. . . .

Truth starts with conversations, shared laughter, friendship and sex, and it only happens *going from one person to another.*

—Georges Bataille, *Le Coupable*

Footnote (FN): But when someone says that poetry is best taken as a certain kind of writing process (rather than a certain kind of writing product), we have to be very clear about what is meant by the term "process." Ron Silliman's importance as a poet of "the American longpoem" is closely connected to his extended meditations on the history of poetry, especially poetry in English, and on the theory of language and the (possible) structures of communication.[1]

Printer's Devil (PD): Is he thinking of Bakhtin when he says that "literature [is] a total social process"?[2] His word "process" indicates a dialectic by which a scene of writing undergoes various "reading" transformations. "What can be communicated through any literary production depends on which codes are shared with its audience. The potential contents of the text are only actualized according to their reception."[3] By such an account, language is rhetorical, and writing is reading.

FN: Yes, which means that every text is potentially open to an indefinite number of "readings." So Silliman writes, in *Oz:* "Meanings diverge / for different readers, as well / they should."[4] And: "Perhaps poetry is an activity and not a form at all." The latter remark, from a poem called "The Chinese Notebook," enacts his thought in the text itself—I mean, by its gesture of self-questioning and its implicit invitation to the reader to think about the question.[5]

PD: And about Silliman's own views on the question.

FN: Necessarily. Here the poem is the focus of thoughtful inter-change in a highly concrete and materially defined situation. Two other poetical notations in "The Chinese Notebook" underscore the situation.

21. Poem in a notebook, manuscript, magazine, book, re-printed in an anthology. Scripts and contexts differ. How could it be the same poem?
27. Your existence is not a condition of this work. Yet let me, for a moment, posit it. As you read, other things oc-cur to you. You hear the drip of a faucet, or there's music on, or your companion gives a sigh that represents a poor night's sleep. As you read, old conversations reel slowly through your mind, you sense your buttocks and spine in contact with the chair. All of these must certainly be a part of the meaning of this work.

It is a nice touch, that request to the reader for permission to "posit" the reader's presence: the gesture illustrates the social character of the text Silliman is producing. If I understand his poetical project, then, it involves word constructions that display, via enactments that are contextualized in highly particular ways, the presence of this "total social process."
PD: Which reminds me of Silliman's protest, in *What*, against reading that work "as neo-romantic" and of his more comprehen-sive demurral: "Rodefer / has referred to me / as a romantic / which I'd deny."[6] Process in Silliman isn't to be understood ac-cording to the structure of a Romantic *Bildung*, for example. He implies as much in his critical review of Barry Ahearn's book on Zukofsky. Silliman points out that Ahearn organizes his study of Zukofsky's "A" as "a history of the poem's growth . . . following the chronology of its composition rather than the numbering of its 24 sections."[7] This procedure "carr[ies] the reader's atten-tion away from what was actually right there on the page, toward some (always deferred) moment of 'total unification.'" Accord-ing to Silliman, however, the "process" of "A" is very different. In Zukofsky's work, the "primary function of a given statement is not its contribution toward a thematic association or image . . . so much as in its contextualization within the present language of a particular usage."[8]

FN: Presumably, however, various *Bildung* structures permit various ways of *reading* Zukofsky's longpoem. (After all, "One writes / not to draw conclusions," as Silliman says in *What*.[9])

PD: Of course, and the quotation from *What* is very much to the point. The critique of Ahearn is even more interesting for what it implies about Silliman's ongoing longpoem, *The Alphabet*. Zukofsky's longpoem is patently the work that has had the greatest single influence on Silliman's own longpoem project. But suppose for the moment that all twenty-six sections of *The Alphabet* were complete and even published; and suppose Silliman, or someone else, or various persons collectively (including or not including Silliman) decided to publish *The Alphabet* entire. Silliman's own ideas about the longpoem, which are even now being carried out in the writing of that work, throw into the sharpest relief the problem of organization that the editor(s) would have to face.

FN: Meaning?

PD: Meaning—what is the proper "shape" of *The Alphabet*? The obvious editorial procedure, of course, would be to publish the completed work with the various sections arranged from *A* at the start to *Z* at the close. But this arrangement would not at all reflect either the order of the work's composition or the order of its initial publication(s). By order of composition, the section titled "Force" (published in *Hills 9*) was being drafted at a very early period, and among the earliest completed sections of the work were "Skies," *ABC,* and "Manifest." By order of publication, these are not the first three sections to appear in print. Furthermore, although *ABC* was published as a (chapbook) unit in the Tuumba series in 1983, each of its three sections were also published separately, and the "A" section as separately published appeared under a different title ("Procedures").

That initial scene of heterogeneity is replicated in the random composition and appearance of later parts of the work. "Ink" is a late section and appeared in magazine form (in *Temblor*), whereas *What* and *Toner,* more recent, appeared as small books.

In the past, only scholarly readers would foreground for themselves these kinds of textual differentials. Tennyson's *Idylls of the King* was neither composed nor published in the order in which its sections were finally arranged by Tennyson, and the same is true of Zukofsky's "A." The general reader of such works, however, cannot know about those differentials from the editions commonly available to her. One has to resort to a book like Barry Ahearn's for the information about Zukofsky or to an edition like John Pfordresher's *A Variorum Edition of Tennyson's Idylls of the King* in the case of the laureate.

In Silliman's case, the question of the ordering of *The Alphabet* goes to the very heart of the project he has proposed for himself. *The Alphabet* is "an attempt to reconceive what I take to be the archetypal American poetic genre, something that has come to be known (for want of a better term) as the 'American longpoem.'"[10]

FN: But you talk as if *The Alphabet* were some integral thing when in fact it is, according to Silliman, "a stage" in a larger, continuous process of writing. He once told me that *The Alphabet* was one portion of an even longer, ongoing project that he began to produce in 1974 when he was working on the longpoem *Ketjak*. The latter would become the first part of another "work" that was to include the three poems eventually published as a unit in the book *The Age of Huts*: "Sunset Debris," "The Chinese Notebook," and "2197." Silliman then imagined those four works as "the first stage of a larger structure; *Tjanting* [1981] is the second stage, and, to my mind, *The Alphabet* stands as counterpart to those two stages to make up a larger stage, or station of the cycle. So, in one very real sense, I was starting to figure out, to strategize, what to do next all the while composing *Tjanting*, just as I am now wondering what comes after *The Alphabet*, circa 1992 or '3, whenever this is done."[11]

PD: The fact that *The Alphabet* can be imagined as part of a larger project only reinforces the point I am trying to make. According to a "Statement for the Guggenheim" that he prepared, Silliman offered *The Alphabet* as a model for a way of succeeding in the genre of the longpoem where previous American efforts had—according to Silliman—"failed":

Olson's, Duncan's, and Dorn's masterworks simply dissolve; Williams never finished book six of *Paterson;* Zukofsky gave up on closure and tacked on a work of his wife's. From Pound's *Cantos* to the untitled and abandoned 1,000 page work of Clark Coolidge in the 1970s, it has been as if the longpoem inherently must be a poem manqué.

My thesis is that such poems have failed because, for reasons that are historical and in fact specific to the history of the U.S., they typically have been constructed upon organicist assumptions about poetry and form in general.

The history of the longpoem's failures signals a history of writing (and writers) committed to, and seduced by, the illusion of "inherent form" in its various manifestations (the "false unity [imagined] in an analogy to music, as [in] Pound and Zukofsky . . . or to conventional narrative, or to architectural form . . . or even to a process like Olson's parody of archival research"). Silliman, by contrast, argues that form "is not inherent, but is profoundly social, a contract with the reader that is deeply conflictual, inevitably partial and tending always toward contradiction and overdetermination." *The Alphabet* is therefore a work constructed "on other grounds" entirely. "[The] unity in *The Alphabet* is phenomenological, the way unity (which I prefer to think of as 'the unity effect') is experienced in the world, as something immediate, apprehended and rendered problematic by investigation. The reader is kept aware of their [*sic*] presence as an active producer of meaning during the consumption of the text." "The unity effect," the experience of wholeness, shifts as the text is "investigated" and transacted by the reader, by various readers at various times of reading. This concept of poetry as a scene of "investigation" is explicit throughout *The Alphabet*. Thus, for example, in *What:*

> End lines precisely
> where it makes least sense, until
> a new order emerges—then examine
> that.

But the thought appears throughout the work in various forms— for instance, on the first page of its "first" (its "A") section, "Albany": "This form is the study group."[12]

As far as the "unity effect" is concerned, then, one of the principal objects of the writing seems to lie in casting forward, into consciousness, the many ways that a unity effect can come into being: that the reader should become aware of those effects and of the limits of the effects. So in *What,* when Silliman takes (for the moment) the concept "narrative" as a sign for unity and totality, he unfolds an image of his idea of poetic form as it would/ might operate in a completable (which is not to say a "unified") longpoem:

It is not that
there is no narrative
here (each sentence
is a narrative,
each line moves)
but that there is
no hierarchy
of narratives (not even
the story of the
poem), no sentence
to which the others
(all the others) defer
and are ranked
(the map is not
built about the city).

FN: Was Shelley attempting to convey the same experience in "The Cloud" when he imagined that ideal atmospheric creature explaining why, though he must "change," he "cannot die"?

For after the rain, when with never a stain
      The pavilion of Heaven is bare,
And the winds and sunbeams, with their convex gleams,
      Build up the blue dome of Air—
I silently laugh at my own cenotaph,
      And out of the caverns of rain,
Like a child from the womb, like a ghost from the tomb,
      I arise, and unbuild it again.

PD: The imagination of a ceaselessly transformational world seems to me very similar. But I also see an important difference. Like all the Romantics (with the partial exception of Byron),

Shelley wrote on the assumption that poetry, like the "Power" celebrated in "Mont Blanc," "dwells apart in its tranquillity," that poetry is not subject to those fundamental illusions and dissolutions which are its subjects. Silliman, by contrast, thinks (with Adorno) that "[t]he whole . . . is false,"[13] and (with Foucault) that "Power's sole value lies in the sharing."[14] Therefore he will write things like: "The tyranny / of the whole submits all / to instrumentalization"; or, "This sentence points not / to the 'work as a whole' / (no such thing) but to your, / the reader's, life." In Silliman's poetry there is a "social contract / between writer and reader [that] demands trust: / distance, not absorption, is the intended effect."[15] This paradoxical situation—trust grounded in distance rather than (Romantic) absorption—means that Silliman's texts are there to be used and interacted with.[16] The prize being sought is knowledge, clarity of vision, understanding:

> The despair
> of a supermarket far from home
> or of any airport terminal
> is simply the clarity: one's own place
> with a sense of proportion.

This excellent textual scene from *What* is an emblem of Silliman's writing, where no term, event, or point of view is bruised to pleasure another. It is a scene that draws everything and everyone concerned into relationships where "power," for good and ill alike, has to be shared. It is a scene, finally, of writing and reading, with those activities imagined as the basic tools for dealing with our textualized and spectacular world:

> The system here
> is there is no system, tho one might discover
> the cumulative pattern, and from this
> propose a structure, a set
> of procedures to be methodically employed
> in yet another composition, utterly different.

More than what this text explicitly declares, *The Alphabet* asks every reader to "propose" her own readings at every point: for

The Alphabet is a work so composed as to necessitate, via its encounters with the reader, "yet another composition, utterly different."

FN: But you seem to read Silliman's texts as if they were repositories of abstract and abstractable ideas. That seems to me an extremely misleading approach. Instead of talking about the "social contracts" between readers and writers, one would do better simply to illustrate the ways that this writing works, the opportunities it offers to the experience of reading. I think once again of the "process" that his writing involves. Silliman's work has been strongly influenced by information theory, and he has made a point to lace his writing—particularly the texts of *The Alphabet*—with the vocabulary and insignia of the word-processing computer. One is not surprised to find, therefore, in "The Chinese Notebook," the following pair of texts:

111. . . . A poem, like any language, is a vocabulary and a
    set of rules by which it is processed.
190. It was Ed van Aelstyn who, in his linguistics course,
    planted the idea (1968) that the definition of a language
    was also the definition of any poem: a vocabulary plus a
    set of rules through which to process it.

That (operational) formula appears most graphically, I suppose, in Silliman's various a priori organizational schemes for his works. He has a special fascination for the Fibonacci number sequence, which he uses in various ways to generate his texts. But all of the poems are produced in analogous ways: "Skies" is a composition whose generative rule was "one sentence a day for the period of a year"; "2197" is the number 13 cubed, and the text is generated through a complex series of repetitions of 13 basic sentence forms; "The Chinese Notebook," a parody of Wittgenstein's *Philosophical Investigations,* is a sequence of 223 sections; "Toner" plays certain variations on a five-line stanza; and so forth.

What interests me is the significance of such procedures for Silliman's writing: How do they work as poetic devices, and what kinds of meaning do they propose? But such questions also connect with Silliman's strong claim that the project of *The Alphabet* "solves" the "problem" of the American longpoem. This seems to me a most unfortunate way of formulating what *The Alphabet* is doing. It suggests, for one thing, that a "solution" is achievable, even a "final solution"—as if American writers might henceforth turn to Silliman for the answers to their writing problems with the longpoem, as if Silliman himself might now settle back and let the good times roll.

PD: But that representation of Silliman's work is close to travesty. Silliman's whole effort has been to oppose the imagination of transcendental orders. I thought that point was clear. His project means to substitute a poetic "activity" for a poetic "form": poem as "study group" instead of poem as "thing of beauty."

FN: But your point only highlights the contradiction in his thinking about "solutions" to the "problem" of the American longpoem. Those are themselves transcendentalist problems, and to my mind Silliman's work—its importance—lies in its having sidestepped them altogether. If *The Alphabet* "solves" the "problem" of the American longpoem, it does so by refusing to enter the contest of trying to write one. To read *The Alphabet,* or any part of it, is to realize that it is not an "American longpoem" at all. We are not to see it as a poem; we are to engage with it as a textual and communicative process. To recall an important distinction once made by Coleridge, I would rather say: *The Alphabet* is not a poem, it is poetry.

Besides, if *The Alphabet* is one part of a continuous writing project, and if it is, itself, at war with "the tyranny of the whole," Silliman should not be speaking of it as having solved the problem of the longpoem. The problem cannot be "solved"; it can only be tackled again and again, according to those changing historical circumstances which he himself has called attention to.

PD: But there is an important sense in which we want to think of *The Alphabet* in terms of a concept of totalization. The fact that the completed work will have exactly twenty-six sections is an unevadable sign of its commitment to totalization. Indeed, there is a sense in which one ought to see the work as already completed, even though it's not finished, and hence as already having "solved" the problem of the American longpoem. Were Silliman to die tomorrow, without the final sections having been produced, what remains of the work (the remains of the work) would remain "complete." This is so for two reasons: first, *The Alphabet* is already conceptually finished and needs only the presentation of the as yet unwritten parts; second, and more important, the conceptual scheme is such that, once it has been sufficiently (even if not fully) materialized, the whole of it has gained its implicit presence.

FN: Meaning?

PD: Your own insistence on the word-processing model points to what I mean. For Silliman, the very existence of an alphabet (any alphabet) declares the existence of a specific language, and it says in addition that that language has both a vocabulary and a set of processing rules. (It does not necessarily tell us whether the language is "dead" or dynamic—we learn such things definitively only in the actual practice of a language, in its "usage.") As a scriptural event in the historical development of language, an alphabet is therefore both the sign and the limit of everything that particular language can do (phonetically, lexically, syntactically, socially). The existence of an alphabet tells one that a specific language has achieved conceptual completion.

When all its parts are written and gathered together, *The Alphabet* will carry an epigraph from Lyn Hejinian's poetical sequence *Writing Is an Aid to Memory* (1978): "the sentences of the alphabet." The epigraph functions in the same self-referential (even tautological) way that the final line of Blake's *Jerusalem* functions: to tell us that the "meaning" of the poem is the act of the poem (or, more properly, the acts of the poem). One must not imagine, however, that *The Alphabet* is therefore a solipsistic text, closed off from "the world." On the contrary, the acts held out through the poem require interactions with others, for it is, as we have already seen, an engine of communication, a "total social process."

Silliman has discussed some of these theoretical issues in two important essays, "The New Sentence" and "Towards Prose."[17] In "The New Sentence" he refers specifically to what is for him a crucial alphabetical conception: the idea of the twenty-seventh letter. This "letter" has no name, being rather "the blank space, between words or sentences."[18] Within that space is gathered the entire manifold of a language's possibilities of meaning and communication—is gathered, in short, "the sentences of the alphabet." The twenty-seventh letter is the emblem of differentiation ("distance, not absorption"), the hidden sign of all the relationships that a particular language (and so a particular world with its characteristic "forms of life") is capable of.

In a sense, Silliman's poetry never deals with any other subject— though of course *this* subject is potentially so rich that he would need no other. The following passage from *What* renders Silliman's preoccupation with particular brilliance:

> If the
> function of writing is to X-
> press the word, world
> (alphabet is no name), what
> is the name of my poem?

I will concentrate on only two of this text's acute moments: the "expressing" of both words and worlds, and the question of the "name" of "my poem." To put it as simply as possible: this passage illustrates how the "identity" of something (anything—whether word, fact, thing, or event) is a function of a "nonidentity." "Word" and "world" are both equated and differentiated, as is the activity of "expressing" something (an event framed here in the form of a negative—an X press[ion]—as if to print or script a word were to visibilize and obliterate at the same time).

The text, furthermore, comes to us as a figure of itself, as a kind of tautology, and that characteristic of the writing is underscored in its presentation of the question of its name. This passage tells us, correctly, that "What / is the name of my poem," but the assertion is simultaneously put forward in the form of a question—and correctly so, because *What is* the "name" of the text's "poem" only if the text is read from a particular vantage. An alternative name is suggested but immediately withdrawn ("alphabet is no name")—and once again we are impressed with the dance of the rhetoric, with its "correctness": for if we read on the dedication page of the book *What* "Being a part of *The Alphabet*," "alphabet" is not the "name" of the book *What*. Furthermore, "alphabet" is, in Silliman's understanding, "no name" in any case— at least so far as the project known as *The Alphabet is* concerned. The "alphabet" in *The Alphabet* is not imagined as a name by Silliman; it is imagined as a vocabulary plus a set of processing rules. So if *The Alphabet* is, in one sense, the "name" of the work of which

What is one section, it is not the name for some thing, or product, but for a particular "process" of writing: "the sentences of the alphabet."

Though this brief passage plays wittily with all these ideas, the issues are far from trivial. For one thing, the question of the possibility of a successful American longpoem is being addressed in a passage like this. For Silliman, it is important to see the alphabet as the minimal form and index of a language, and to understand further that this language (and its world), if always unfinished, is also always complete. A project like *The Alphabet* is *not*, therefore, an effort to "complete" the world (or its poetical sign, the longpoem). The effort is to build a structure of words where the endless transformational potential of the language (and the world) may be displayed.

The Alphabet is, to adapt a phrase of Roy Wagner's, a symbol that stands for itself. It does not seek a (deferred or absent) vehicle of completion, for two (correlative) reasons: first, it has not grounded itself in the experience of a transcendent I/eye; and second, the Other of the text, the world, is an assumed presence in the writing from the start. We observe Silliman's determination to write beyond the limits of the I/eye most clearly, I suppose, in his insistence on the purely phonetic aspects of language. Ultimately he assigns a philosophic and political importance to melopoeia: "The value of sound is that it's outside the rational."[19] As for the Other of the text, this appears in two of Silliman's great preoccupations: with what he calls the "purpose of particulars" and with the "social contract between reader and writer." Silliman's dense networks of particulars are closely related to his concern with phonetics—"the flood of details itself thwarts reason," as he puts it in *Oz*—and if his writing represents a "social contract" this is because, in Silliman's view: "That which is merely personal / is controlled by the state."[20] Or, in the strong (and impersonal) dialect of *Oz:* "The idea that the poem could be experienced by individuals was that culture's biggest myth." *The Alphabet* is a symbol that stands for itself because it is, in the fullest sense, a social text. As an illustration of itself, it means to be a revelation of the entire human world, the "total social process," including the (human) "thingness" and physique of that process.

FN: I am not sure I understand what you mean, but listening to you reminds me of two alphabetical passages—one from *Oz* and the other from the section "Toner":

> The symbolist is unable to see the forest for his parents.
>   Oh tree
> of life so full of strife, this knife is to carve initials. Slabs of
>   sheet-
> rock by a pink roll of insulation (we are building the
>   alphabet,
> a pyramid in the desert, a campsite for the caravan,
>   feeding the
> ostriches, the tiger, bonfires on dry night).
>
>   * * *
>
> Alphabet seen
>   not as a line
> but a cycle,
>   or torso and spine
> merely as where limbs run together,
> skulls in infinite variety,
> this a melon, that a flower,
> And this something stepped upon.
> Let us go then
>   you and I
> through fluorocarbons in the sky
> whose particles will get you ghi
> until your prose
>   becomes unstable
>   Imitating modes of speech
> each to each.

Both texts are engines for extending their systems of signification. The critique of the "symbolist" in the passage from *Oz* is a particularly interesting example of the way Silliman multiplies meaning by overlapping texts. Putting "parents" for the proverbial "trees" allows Silliman to call up Baudelaire's proto-symbolist "Correspondances," and the resulting palimpsest of texts becomes an illustration of Silliman's preferred, post-symbolist writing technique. The argument against the "symbolist" is that the personal/

psychological orientation of symbolist procedures attenuates one's ability to experience the world, that symbolism may lead one into a forest of lost distinctions, including certain fundamental social distinctions. The passage then goes on to illustrate a nonsymbolist process of textual enrichment. Without explicating each particular of these texts, one can nonetheless see, and say, that the textual units are generated through a randomly shifting series of associational developments. For example, the (present) "forest" and (absent) ["trees"] of the first sentence move to the "tree of life" of the second sentence, which is itself in two parts. The "knife" that carves initials is a transformation of the "strife" we associate with certain primal events recorded in Genesis; and both of those images generate another scene of "building," which is then turned into its most literal form (the word "building," whose "initials" are now carved into the text of this poem); and so forth.

A similar process of explication could be produced for the rest of the passage and for the passage in "Toner" as well. Whether or not *The Alphabet* solves the problem of the American longpoem— whether or not there is such a problem in the first place—Silliman's work remains important, for me, because of its unusual imaginative resources.

Nor am I suggesting that we should ignore Silliman's theoretical and programmatic interests and simply "read" the writing. Silliman is not merely a strong poet; he is an important writer who has significantly extended our technical and theoretical understanding of poetry. The immense textual richness of his work, for example, seems to me a direct consequence of his insight into the hidden resources of language:

> Even the one syllable word,
> the simple morpheme (the letter "A")
> contains a caesura.

Even at a language's minimal levels, where "things" appear at last to possess a final identity and noncomplex integrity, Silliman discovers distinctions and dynamisms. To imagine the letter "A" containing a caesura is to imagine it as a complex identity. This passage from *What*, which is in part an interpretation of what is at stake in Zukofsky's "A," grounds itself in an unusual insight, which might be framed in the following (non-Euclidean) form: "A equals A if and only if A does not equal A." For Silliman, every *thing* is riddled (in both senses) with distinctions because the "total social process" is at all points marked by various kinds of tensions, incommensurates, and antithetical relations. "One writes to display / not words but the spaces between them" because those are the spaces you have called *The Alphabet's* twenty-seventh letter: that is, "the total social process" of the human world.

A work like *The Alphabet* consequently moves along a series of revisionist processes. These range from the most elementary to the most complex (*The Alphabet* being itself the sign of an ultimate complexity). The section "Demo," for instance:

> The logic of morning (is no logic) is complete.
>
>   Insertions, against the false silence of the City,
> voiced comma: the cat just stares at the fearless hen,
> hissing.[21]

The parenthetical phrase in the first passage is an example of what the second passage calls a "voiced comma." Indeed, throughout "Demo" marks of punctuation are highlighted as key devices for breaking the "false silence" that can pervade a managed and instrumentalized language. Both (fearless) hen and (hissing) cat are figures of these necessary dynamic insertions. Or consider the following pair of texts, also from "Demo":

> Her breasts formed a narrative.
> Rounded—rounded first and held up as the cutoff man
> took the throw from left field.
>
> Temporary as morning, these words like shadows fall
> across the page, the value is the inversion, an old woman in
> the park recalling her childhood in Taiwan.
>
> You're telling me something urgent, but I'm only
> counting the syllables as you speak.

In each of these two cases the "voiced comma" appears as the spacing between (and within) the paired units of text, and it works to multiply meanings. The first passage involves a triple play (as it were) on the word "rounded." The metaphoric statement "her breasts formed a narrative" is explicated across the word "rounded," which refers at once to the shape of "her breasts" and to a commonplace idea about "narrative form" (that it should be "well-rounded"). In this context, "her breasts formed a narrative" *is* "a narrative" on (the subject of) "her breasts." It is "rounded" off as an integral line by the space following the line. But that space functions as well as a temporal pause so that "rounded" comes into the text as a punch line comes into a joke. In this case, the wordplay is multiplied across yet another space, where the dash delivers us to the baseball term "rounded." At this point an entire new set of "narrative" possibilities is opened up (for example, we may imagine that the passage as a whole is "narrating" a scene that took place at Candlestick Park).

The second (paired) text offers more complex relational possibilities to be elaborated between and among the different units defined by the various "voiced commas." This "couplet" of texts plays variations on the theme of the content of poetry—whether we read it as "word" or as "world": the form and physique of the language ("counting syllables" and other linguistic units), or an engagement with reality ("telling . . . something urgent").

PD: Of course those "relational possibilities" you mention are partly being defined by actions which do not seem to be a part of Silliman's "text" as such. Two nonauthorial agencies are clearly at work here. The first, and most obvious, is you yourself—a reader who has arbitrarily set certain frames around certain parts of the text. You thus reveal yourself as a necessary part of the demos of "Demo" when you give your particular demonstrations of how to read the writing.

The second agency is perhaps even more interesting because it represents a form of random intervention, a writing agency whose effect on the work—whose precise form of intervention—cannot be anticipated except in the most general way. Because "Demo" is written in prose units, the right margins of the different parts are not preset by Silliman: those margins will vary, depending on the actual page layout, and the variances will have a distinct effect on the character of the text. This result is especially clear in the case of the unit that begins "rounded—rounded first and held up." Typed on a standard word processor or typewriter, and working from a standard left-hand margin, this unit of text will break at the right-hand margin after the words "took the." Typed in the same way, but this time by a "reader" (for example, a critic writing about "Demo"), the text would begin indented slightly from the left margin, and it would therefore break differently, perhaps after "cutoff man." As "Demo" was in fact first printed, in *Temblor,* the text broke still more differently, after "as the"; and of course when and if it is printed again, we will probably confront another variant of the line break. As it turns out, of the three variants I have mentioned, the *Temblor* variant would probably have to be regarded as the most dramatic of the texts since it does not clearly deliver the alternative meaning of "rounded" until the eye moves to the next line, to the "cutoff man."

FN: I am reminded of "The Chinese Notebook," where Silliman has several times called attention to this aspect of writing—for example in section 21: "Poem in a notebook, manuscript, magazine, book, reprinted in an anthology. Scripts and contexts differ. How could it be the same poem?"

PD: The "poem" clearly does shift and change under those kinds of changing circumstances. But what interests me is the way Silliman's texts consciously anticipate and solicit—even though they cannot control—such interventions and changes. His texts can easily overwhelm a reader with their sheer volume—recorded "life" details and ingenious linguistic inventions pouring across the voluminous pages of his works. "The social contract of writer and reader" in Silliman, however, means that *The Alphabet's* "flood of details" is not the possession of "Ron Silliman." The text is thickened by other readers and users, for whom "the same" words, phrases, and lines will never be "the same"—for themselves, for "Ron Silliman," for anyone else.

FN: Yes, of course—but I think one would get closer to the "meaning" of *The Alphabet* if we forgot about its "meanings" and paid more attention to its procedures. A crucial feature of the work is the way it has released the hypertextual powers of the writing. *The Alphabet's* chief distinction, I believe, lies in its having found a way to escape the control of a governing and a priori principle of order. Most apparent here is the text's refusal to allow "Ron Silliman" the customary (lyrical and Romantic) privilege of authorial control. "Ron Silliman" is no more than one part of *The Alphabet's* "flood of details": an important part, to be sure, but only an incorporated element which can be and is displayed in many different and shifting vantages. The "particularizing" of "Ron Silliman" is most apparent, I suppose, in passages like the following:

> In the dream
> I meet a blonde in Woolworth's
> who gives me a blowjob on the spot
> amid the bright and crowded shelves
> —Not so much, she gasps, gulping
> to swallow it all (this is not about sex
> but the lack of power).[22]

The text involves (and demands) a critical examination of itself and in particular of its (male, and politically grounded) fantasy and of the politics of sexual relations in American culture ("Woolworth's"). Cast in a dream form, the scene emphasizes that "Ron Silliman" is a divided being, subject to his own (suppressed) fantasies of domination and power. Of course, the passage explicates the dream as a political anecdote and a self-critique. "Ron Silliman" understands the meaning of the scene. But the final turn of the text lies in its revelation that this "knowledge" does not result in a final deliverance—that the truth does not set one free. The truth, according to this view, always appears as a structure of contradictions. It therefore cannot be gained, but only regenerated, represented, and reexplored. *The Alphabet* does not give Ron Silliman (or "Ron Silliman") mastery of knowledge or truth. On the contrary, it puts him in subjection to these ideals—by including him within the "subjects" taken up in the poem. In the present instance, the reader is not permitted to decide for certain whether the "I" of the text reports a dream experienced by the Romantic subject ("Ron Silliman") or by someone else entirely.

"Ron Silliman" as writer, as reader, and as subject of *The Alphabet:* the text frames "him" in each of these situations and then multiplies the points of view and the scales by which "he" can be observed or known. And the same is true of each of the text's linguistic and referential particulars. This is why the "voiced comma," the "spaces between" words, are so fundamental to the operation of the poem. Silliman's writing is highly paratactical, but its great power comes ultimately from its *discretions,* its carefully managed spacings, its power in drawing distinctions. *Oz* states that "We want a new / line break, more visible, more irrational / than anything" because the line break, like the "voiced comma," is the sign that a distinction is being drawn—and hence is itself a declaration that the distinction is arbitrary and can be redrawn. *The Alphabet* seems as rich as it does not so much because it is so long and so full of words, but because it is so full of the spaces between words, because it is so full of silences and (perhaps in the Buddhist sense) "emptiness."[23] The gaps and distinctions and voiced commas are the work's devices for placing one in a position to treat the writing (to "read") within constantly shifting scales and viewpoints.

The "processing rules" are themselves types of spacings. "Albany" is composed (arbitrarily) of 100 sentences; *Paradise* is a sequence of paragraphs each of which was written at one sitting, with these paragraphs arranged in "monthly" groupings and with the whole comprising "a year's diary." *Skies* is a text containing one sentence written each day for a year, and the whole is divided into four parts (corresponding to the seasons).[24] In each of these cases a gap necessarily opens up between each of the sentences because the processing rule has intervened into the (highly narrativized) inertias of the scene of writing. The procedure introduces a type of "new line break" that forces the text to develop rich orders of unexpected relationships, "more visible, more irrational / than anything" one has become accustomed to. Set free of the relationships that we are accustomed to make according to the processing rules of narrative, logic, and syntax (the dominant forms of rational textual orders), each sentence— each letter, word, and phrase—is instantly placed in a condition of extreme openness. Connections of various kinds (melopoeic, phanopoeic, logopoeic) become more accessible, more *thinkable,* and they appear in an endless variety of scalar possibilities. The text becomes "chaotic" in the technical, mathematical sense: it streams with varieties of order, some swirling in different local "basins," some appearing and disappearing at long intervals.

PD: And yet, paradoxically, this "chaos" is a display of poetic form all the more effective for not having appeared as some transcendental idea of order. It comes as the practice of a writing designed to release the full resources of a language and to let the reader in on that activity (in both senses of "let the reader in on"). So, at the outset of *The Alphabet*, Silliman is careful to inform the reader—to put her in the poem, as being obligated to know what is at stake and in store: "if it demonstrates form some people won't read it."

FN: Well, the work is difficult, but perhaps most because it exposes so well the limited demands we make upon our capacities for communication and social intercourse. As readers (and writers) we are too often too easily satisfied. The section titled *Lit* is especially concerned with precisely these issues—with "literature" and the light that it has (or has not) lit. "The light at the end of the pencil" is by this text once again lit:

> Hand-held, the image through the pen's lens wobbles as
>   it pans,
> sweep to right margin, pins sound to paper but the mind
>   adrift
> hobbles after, gathering few vague echoes of intent, so
>   tend the
> senses wisely or they tangle, angles frame the object
>   hued by
> light, hard edged, wedged into an imagined sight but
>   lost, the
> page turned, the cost of dreaming as you stare at words,
>   birds
> migrating toward a punctuation, partial truths are all
>   we get,
> letters home, honed, the bone of thought rings in the
>   head, hurt,
> herds these small black beasts of graphics forth. I sit
>   and you
> set the table, used it and able to do so again (you sit
>   and I set

the table, used it and able to do so again): which of us
reads,
which writes, or writing reads, seeds of a process which
binds,
not blind to the separateness of different lives, always
we find
strangers on the bus, but print is a bond we learned by
rote, in
rows, years ago. Each step taken jars the old porch, beams
crack-
ing along the grain, white spots of bird drops speckle the
brown
paint, the horizontals bowed and perpendiculars slanting,
a few
nails painted over when they should have been hammered
back
down.[25]

Lit is obviously about itself, and about *The Alphabet* as another
structure in the enormous room of letters. The "I" and the "you"
sit partly at an allegorical table of reader and writer, exchanging
roles, in a house (introduced to us in the next sentence) whose
marks of ancient use (and abuse and disuse) are well known to
anyone who has studied Western culture and its literary depos-
its. It is a beautiful, celebratory passage, appropriately placed at
a climactic moment in the section called *Lit*. But of course "L" is
only the twelfth letter of the alphabet, so that—read by another
scale, in the context of *The Alphabet* as a whole—this great passage
drops away from its climactic position, recedes into the work's
massive textual world, one more passing moment. Nonetheless it
remains an instance (an instant) of the "light at the end of the
pencil" ("Keep hope alive!"), one of the work's endless opportunities to defeat the "abstractions of history" according to the explicit "credo" of this writing: "Form gathers force (my credo) for
what purpose but use, source for an assault upon habit."[26]
PD: A credo laid down not as a truth but in the (positive) form
of a question to the reader.

4
The Apparatus of Loss
Bruce Andrews Writing

> I don't give anybody hell. I just tell them the truth, and they think
> it's hell.
>
> —Harry S. Truman

> Late in my poetic professionalism I renounced the satisfaction
> of poetic success in words. *The Telling* is descended from that
> renunciation. I speak in it at the common risks of language,
> where failure stalks in every word.
>
> —Laura (Riding) Jackson, *The Telling*

> Audisne haec Amphiarae, sub terram abdite?
>
> —Shelley's motto for *Prometheus
> Unbound,* from Aeschylus' *Epigoni*

Nothing is more obdurate than the writing of Bruce Andrews—in the
current scene of writing.[1] He is hard, and all the more difficult because
of his outspoken didactic aims. For a poet who continues to make
much of the politics of poetic form, the texts can appear anarchic,
indifferent, even meaningless. Who are they addressing? What is their
language?

Like Blake's Urizen exploring his dens, Andrews wanders the streets
of a strange world—for Andrews, an estranged world. That world is the
origin of the difficulty of his work. Though it can appear, like its discourse, ordered and transparent to itself, it is in fact a debased world,
dominated by the illusions that are captured, with perfect irony, in recent marketing labels like New World Order, Axis of Evil, and Culture
of Life.

Resistance to administered propaganda has typically assumed various Romantic forms that assume a self-identical subject who wills to resist. Andrews's work is difficult because while he is a resisting writer,
part of his resistance is raised against Romantic form itself. Andrews
approaches Romantic forms as historically quixotic—from a present
vantage, part of the solution to the problems his work addresses only

because they have so clearly emerged as a central part of the problem of estrangement in an administered world. In political terms, Andrews would say that social injustice has come to be romantically organized. Consequently, his intransigence, reflecting that organization, holds out against conventional literary expectations, pleas, or invitations to write in ways he is unable, given his project, to follow. Images and forms of ruin dominate the landscape of his texts. Such forms are, as we know, historically Romantic. But in a Romantic imagination ruins focus nostalgia, and they typically symbolize an order of invisible blessedness. In Andrews, by contrast, fragments and ruins are not blessings but *blessures*—the manifest signs of a violated (social) body in pain.

What then rules here—in the poetry, in the horizon of the discourse: order or chaos, truth or its disastrous consequences? That is the question perpetually raised by Andrews's texts, and it locates a second level of difficulty in his work. We find the question difficult (as we should) because, in Andrews's view, it is a question that can only be properly answered with an act. To approach it as a conceptual problem—for readers of poetry, as a problem of "interpretation"—is to insure only further depths of confusion and difficulty.

So Andrews's poems are rich, unstable, disorienting. They appear this way by design—really, by a double design: the design of their discourse, which the texts inherit, and the design of their counter-discourse, which they deploy. To read Andrews's texts is therefore like entering some volatile urban landscape. Portentous with obscure and perhaps catastrophic significances, the texts (like the city) seem poised for a final reckoning. We move through the texts, but the reckoning does not arrive. Instead we encounter a thick distribution of random appearances swirling into brief basins of local order. These ambiguous conflicts and energies are Andrews's signs of life:

> everybody wants to have their piece, piece of pie, world
> peace, motherfucker, let's carve it up right now!
>
> —"Confidence Trick"

A little peace of order, this text, in the savagery of its metaphors and linguistic usages. Such energy and evanescence can take your breath away, the way Byron—longing hopelessly for the liberation of Greece (with everything implied by such a longing for the Euro-American mind)—argued the taking and giving of breath at a time when, as in our time, "The worm, the canker, and the grief / Are mine alone":

If thou regret'st thy Youth, why live?
    The land of honourable Death
Is here: —up to the Field and give
    Away thy Breath!
              —"On This Day I Complete
              My Thirty-Sixth Year"[2]

The Byron analogy, far-fetched, is for that very reason most apt. In a culture where language is so vastly thanatized—the Culture of the Living Dead—the speech of the truly dead brings clarity from its perfect alienation.

Byron and Andrews are both poets who view their worlds with mordant eyes. Not born without illusions, they acquired their disillusions—in a wholly inverted Arnoldian sense, perverted now toward something else entirely—by "seeing life steadily and seeing it whole." The steady sight of the hole in reality reappears, for both, in their pitiless and often cruel ways of writing—their disconsolations—and with all the emergent sense of a beauty that appears to inhabit "the real" (at its worst) and not some imagination of the real.

In this respect Andrews's work may be usefully seen to carry forward the program of objectivism. One recalls the definition of objectivism that Oppen gave to Serge Fauchereau: "a realist art in that the poem is concerned with a fact which it did not create".[3] Oppen's comment has to be placed beside Lyn Hejinian's recent characterization of Andrews's work: "The words are neither ciphers nor pointers; they absolutely are the poem."[4] The formulation is exact but could be misconstrued. It does not mean at all that Andrews's writing constructs an autonomous world of language, a *Gesamtkunstwerk* in the Romantic tradition. For Andrews, the "totality" of the real is not compassable in the reproductive processes of poetry or imaginative writing. Andrews's texts are certainly arbitrary constructions, but the totality they invoke—in utter contrast to every Romantic project—is no symbol or index of what is longed for but unseen. The language in Andrews's texts does not (want to) transport us to the beyondworld of a fulfilled desire, does not want to continue in that way in any way.

The text's desire is not to create but to reveal, to analyze, to know.

Given "the way we live now," the orders of our spiritual indigence, the knowledge in Andrews's texts is a way of knowing, at once disconsolate and energetic. (Were his work to lack either such cynicism or such determination, we would not be able to believe in what he is doing.) It is the language of a comprehensive struggle:

> Define comprehension as something other than consumption. (*Other then.*) So it's politicizing: a radical reading embodied in writing . . . "We've been misread!" The job is to go beyond these norms and limits, to read them *backwards,* to offer up a different refraction of the circumstances. Let's let the status quo read itself being quarantined, scolded, frag'd, and interrupted.
>
> —"Poetry as Explanation,
> Poetry as Praxis," 28

The last sentence here points toward that characteristic estrangement one experiences on entering an Andrews poem. Though his texts are what we are ("the status quo"), they are not what we want. Reading ourselves, we are repelled. And perhaps we think, "So where's the poetry?"—as if we were expecting Andrews to minister to the diseased mind his work represents? But Andrews does not come as a ministering angel. Like Jacob, we have to wrestle with this visitor. Called upon to "define comprehension as something other than consumption," we may come to follow the backwardness of the text. So we study the only signs that are available—negative and dark signs ("motherfucker, let's carve it up right now!"), signs of misreading and rewriting ("other than," "[*Other then.*]") that lead toward startling changes of attention and awareness.

As the title of Andrews's 1987 collection suggests, the writing "means" to give its readers enough rope to hang themselves. (Blake called the same process "piercing Apollyon with his own bow.") Andrews's work consequently holds out few resorts. It comes as a challenge—and with a revelation of very bad odds. The project is for writer and reader

> to grasp what the animating pressures (or constructions & arrangements) of intention & desire are given, are up against, are faced with.
>
> —"Poetry as Explanation,
> Poetry as Praxis," 29

This is what Andrews calls "the whole that needs altering, a total which is close to the false" (ibid.). Poetical writing is therefore an attempt to see and to know, even as one also knows that the truth of the writing will not—in a social or political sense—set one free. There is only the struggle toward that goal.

> Test the horizons—to make an agitated totality, not a rested one. Context needs a Contest: & so writing contextualizes as it contests the limits. . . . "Incomprehensible"—beyond bounds.
>
> —ibid.

The "totality" for Andrews is only "close to the false" because—one thinks of *The Matrix*—"the system outside isn't all structure, with no room for praxis. It's criss-crossed by struggle, by matters that can't be systematized. It's unstable" (ibid., 30). For Andrews, the great locus of such instability is the objective and intransigent gap that both separates and joins the writer and the reader. As Leonard Cohen sang in "Anthem": "There is a crack in everything. / That's how the light gets in."

Displaced Palestinian and Likud Israeli; Belfast Protestant and Belfast Catholic; antiabortion militant and pro-choice activist, Evangelical Christian and secular humanist: if we imagine a language drawn between poles like these, we will have entered the kind of chaos postulated in Andrews's writing: "where the distances writing creates appear as hospitality." This is a poetry of "new relationships by crazed collision" (ibid., 31), of dangerous liaisons that appear to have turned wholly away from the civilized conversations of Plato's dialogues or Heidegger's "discourse on language." Or rather, liaisons (disrupted syntax, discordant metaphors) that establish "questions and doubt" and "readers 'talking back'" (ibid.) as the measure of what human intercourse might imagine for itself. By such a measure we may begin to reopen a dialogue with even our most ancient and monumental texts—those dead resources whose deaths we need so badly. So we may glimpse in the Platonic conversations the trial and death of Socrates, or—perhaps worse still—the debacle of Athens at Syracuse, and the part of Alcibiades (and Socrates himself) in those events; so we may read the barbaric document running just beneath the civilized palimpsest of Heidegger's "project of Being."

To Andrews, all such moves—these new poetical mensurations—

involve neither debunking nor deconstruction: "here, an open horizon gets defined by failures of immediate sense." What Andrews calls
"syntax as demolition derby" (ibid., 31) is a new metaphor for imaginative writing—a metaphor for metaphor that invokes one of America's
greatest comic (and ritual) displays of society as self-consuming ar-
tifact.

> flourish
> where it sounds with speech
> as two lines
> specially erected
> kindly feeling
> by playing the coward
> me
> yourself included
> which proved irresistible
> straying
> note the rhyme
> i.e. simple truth
> supposed to be
> now lost
> I've had about enough—want more
> characteristic bathos
> breaks
> bravest
> wad
> appropriating
>
> —"Praxis," 49–50

The text is an arbitrary construction of playful and self-attentive differences. Its "purpose" is partly to survive—to keep going on, despite
the constant threat of its own wreckage—and partly to make a splen-
dor of its slapstick continuity and "simple truth." What grounds the
excellence of such verse, however, is finally its acceptance of the terms
within which the "simple truth," in this here and now, must be pursued. The last two lines, with their absurd and quixotic turn and turn
again, epitomize the antithetical determinations of the writing. The
desires of this text have not been stayed, it will go on, like a character
in Beckett. Nonetheless, in going on it resolutely avoids a romantic clo-

sure, including the Byronic temptation to take a measure of rest in a comic glance at the text's own "characteristic bathos."

A dominant influence on Andrews's work has been, clearly, Bertolt Brecht. Both argue for an activist/constructivist approach to artistic work, both emphasize the need for (what Byron called) "a mental theatre," both look toward the possibilities of social freedom through "alienation effects." Andrews's critical reflections on his own work, moreover, underscore his Brechtian heritage by making constant resort to theatrical tropes and analogies. A recent essay, "Paradise and Method," is typical:

> The auratic has not dispelled distance, but merely given an image of its irrelevance, its violation, or its status as a prop. An implicit theatricality (even in the most seemingly transcendentalizing guises) is recognizable. But that theatricality, that endistancing at the heart of intimacy, can itself be theatricalized. Distance, if it really is to serve as a stage, can itself be staged. An address of mutuality, & a mutuality of address, can be performed to emphasize its staginess . . . The hope: to see how we might recast Reading/ Subject/Dialog within different contextual horizons. These stagings & restagings make up a body—of meanings. This body, like all bodies, is social. (13)

Andrews aims for a double reflection, as it were, upon the original Brechtian project. Brecht's mental theater is now to be restaged—the way one would have to rethink entirely a production of the *Threepenny Opera* in the context of our postmodern Age of Bronze. The consequence is a final debasement of the aesthetic scene, the staging of the stage. When the ultimate "distance" is imagined as distanced, we are pitched into a kind of primal immediacy. So not without reason does another important ancestor of Andrews's work—Gertrude Stein— constantly make an appearance in the writing, especially the recent writing. "Poetry as Explanation, Poetry as Praxis" ties Stein to Andrews to the politics of poetry. The opening (long) poem in *Getting Ready to Have Been Frightened*, "Vowels," recalls Stein's *Stanzas in Meditation*:

> ghosts a glacier.   while some actions are
> better at times are there exceptions
> this does not need to happen at first

at once, but later. if you advance
into the sensation.   twice-blessed
as error-like, you can still be near it
even if you feel someone else also can.
explain it would mean describing
it.   that way we all can.

This might be a pastiche of Stein's writing, with its characteristic nervous turnings and returnings—its arrivals at meanings and statements and its immediate departures toward other meanings and statements, or immediate recoveries of the moments that have been departed. In a text like this we have rediscovered Keats's famous desire for a life of sensations rather than a life of thoughts: or rather, we enter a text that desires nothing more than to heal the ancient division between mind and body by making that division an immediate and full apparition; i.e., by staging the division—"endistancing" it, according to Andrews's telling (and quite Keatsian) wordplay. ("Not to the sensual ear, but more endeared, / Pipe to the spirit ditties of no tone.")

The procedure is equally apparent in the next two sections of "Vowels" (each numbered section, by the way, is set on its own page):

16
this did not really happen
17
this does not really happen

We turn a page to move from section number 16 to number 17, and it makes a difference that we do. We are not dealing with either explanations or descriptions but with acts—acts of writing and acts of reading. Both of these texts, different as they are, tell a whole truth about the writing—at the particular moment and place from which a truth may be told. The truth involves both the temporality we are to understand for the text and the reality it represents. The wonderful play of the words hinges on that ultimate grammatical shifter, "this." The text demonstrates that "happening" is something that is always done, is a function of a deliberate act (whether conscious or not). Writing/poetry is an eventuality, something that takes place (and hence is akin to Oppen's pursuit of knowledge as knowing). But the double reflection of Andrews's work debases "poetry" as a model for liberated action, for an ultimate freedom. Poetry becomes not so much a touchstone as an example: a model of a behavior choosing to undergo a continual emergency and need. It thus may fitly be compared to what Raymond Williams called "the long revolution"—because such writing carries only this promise: that its existence must be struggled for.

It seems little enough, such a program. Writing whose goal is simply to keep the act of writing alive. Where is the "content," where the splendid ideas that might summon to action the noble living and the noble dead? Well, as Stevens would say, they are there as they are there, a universe of conceptual possibilities suspended in the magnetic field of the writing:

> Equality demands no less: history begins with old man crying, logic you know, airplay your fingertips is not freedom—The disintegrating slop situation on outlaw: read it in the voodoo prospectus, keep trying death squads paid for by our *Christianity* radiation taxes so that human rights clone improves because there are so few rebels left to kill, like iron filings—Polkadot mentality you capsulize it with a commemorative stamp, slunk down in the heroic mode for comfort. Belfast, Capetown, compose loonee tunes that could be written in the mind by institutional simpletons
> —"Confidence Trick," 152

Passages like this conjure the torn world we know, along with the looney tunes it dances to. Despite its dreadful vision, however, the writing executes a decision to get on with the (matter of the) living: to accept the given terms (in both senses) and the bad odds, but not to accept the "institutional" representations of coherence and order. The text therefore literally recomposes the imperial (Disneyworld) comedies of mindless and illusory happiness.

The passage has its humanities as well, of course: noble riders echoing in the sound of its words ("Equality demands . . . history begins"), living thoughts maintained (impossibly) alongside, even within, unthinkable (yet actual) evil ("keep trying death squads"). Such a text would not dream of concluding in those humanities, however. Its own most humane phrases, after all, lie open to any sort of appropriation, wicked as well as benevolent. The text understands—indeed, it deploys—the equivocalness of words and their meanings. The humanities of the text are nonetheless preserved, even cherished—a part of the composition no matter what the perspective.

But we are not finally to be inspired by the thoughts of this writing,

by its knowledge or wisdom or insights. It means to pursue what Andrews typically calls (punning, as a poet should) a radical level of discourse. "The words are neither ciphers nor pointers," the words "absolutely are the poem"—as they comprise a linguistic event whose object
is the maintenance of its own critical action. As in Swinburne, the poetic action depends upon the self-conscious re-action of the reader,
which the texts solicit. The dark double of Andrews's work, therefore,
is the managed language of institutional deceit and self-deception—
presidential, commercial, whatever. All of Andrews's texts deliver us
over to the vulgate of the world:

> I'm too proud to think
> you want to be liberated but basically you're just a d
> ental supply fixture, shoot them in the head to
> anaesthetize them; hype anchors the argument like Mary
> Poppins under the thumb of a filthy vein body just
> another android fun machine. Quadriculus circuli
> sweethearts maneuver their sanitary napkins into
> impenetrable cabinetry; startled starlets squared by
> squids, alla-y'all sucker sucker muhfuhs—punk
> beliefs can be bought. 6 trolls out of 7 news be sweat
> holiday
> prophylactic fishhead bloodclot—meanwhile back at
> the political
> Who wears the blonde wig in that family? Dollies hurt
> leg: I feel whoops shame; friends look for quick
> profits in communist misfortune. I AM SOMEBODY It's a
> Fun World friends you to buy their own money Because
> Politics Stinks, act insecure & put other people at
> ease. I went from Hegel to Mighty Atom comix
> Afro-cubist that mass equals crass dim men pop
> a sauce that monsters fault.
>
> —from "Isolate Your Fuse"

Andrews's poetry inherits and inhabits the discourse—the textual
condition—we recognize all too well, but it has a different (antithetical) object in view: the revelation of its mazed and debased orders. The
poetry does no small thing, then, simply to hold itself open to its own
defeat and to find ways to keep itself going under that rule. As such it
comprises an inspiration not by its truth but by its example.

"The words absolutely are the poem." What this means, however, is that "the words" are absolute in the immediacy of the poetic action. Once Andrews has written (or printed) "the words," they absolutely are the poem for whatever process of interaction and exchange they are immediately involved with. "The words absolutely are the poem," then, only because the words are indefinitely (re)usable. One of Andrews's works in progress—parts of it have appeared in various journals— is a long poem called *I Don't Have Any Paper So Shut Up (or, Social Romanticism)*. That is its title, however, only at certain moments—for instance, in the excerpt printed in *Washington Review of the Arts* (1983). In excerpts printed in *Temblor* (no. 4, 1986) the title is *I Dont Have Any Paper So Shut Up (or, Social Realism)*!

In historical fact, this textual difference represents a printer's error in the *Temblor* text: Andrews meant the title to be stabilized in the word "Romanticism" But the textual transformation is difficult to resist given the dynamic writtenness (as it were) of the work. Besides, the historical relation of the terms "realism" and "romanticism" is not an antinomy; the two stylistic movements are historically congruent, symbiotic forms of bourgeois artistic strategies that have reached a kind of grotesque apogee in our current "Reality TV" and *American Idol*. Thus the typo represents a kind of Freudian slip in the text, a drift of meaning from a writer's to a reader's orbit of attention. The immediacy and writtenness of Andrews's work appears in all of its textual conditions. For example, one of this work's sections appears as follows in its *Temblor* printing: "A socialism based on mildew after debunking with mental turncoats I'm sure the decapitationists would agree. Post-modernist just means lets forget about the social barriers & political economy that kept modernism from becoming socially possible—*& not carry it through*. Any institution makes mistakes—who's wearing the panty hose?" But in the text printed in *Washington Review of the Arts* we read the following: "Don't you just think speech is too populist? I spit every time I use the word 'expository.' Modernity versus populism. Sorry, wrong culture. Post-modernism just means let's forget about the social barriers (or political economy) that kept modernism from becoming: socially (collectively) possible, *and not carry it through*. Heart stays in code. Grammar auditions generalities. Words we cannot revise: sentences we cannot swallow. Rules have more bile. Despise yourself for conforming. Duty fritters away desire." This passage is from a text here titled "Equals What?" And of course the question of that title is exactly to the point. "The words absolutely are the poem" because the words are perpetually open for review and reuse. Because Andrews returns to them again and again, the reader understands that the writing is being executed under a set of dynamic signs.

The notorious instability of Andrews's texts functions then as invitation and opportunity. "More light," as Goethe cried on his deathbed. The same words, those "breeding flowers, will never breed the same." Andrews's essay "Constitution/ Writing, Politics, Language, the Body" weaves—textualizes—a newly composed critical commentary through a series of passages drawn "from books and poems of mine." The genre of the text is explication, but the point of all the self-citation is exactly not to settle the question of what the (original) writing means. Rather, it is to put the issue of meaning into question, to solicit thought about the issue (including the issue of what is "original" writing). Andrews cites his earlier work and runs it through a critical commentary. The effect is to theatricalize "the medium of writing": "And once we characterize the nature of writing's medium in a certain way, we can read out of it (corrigibly) an epistemology and a political practice. Different ways of characterizing the medium allow the medium itself to be evaluated—as a vehicle for revealing or directing acting upon domains of existence." In this case, the "domain" chiefly under review is "literary criticism" itself, as well as the "poetry" that it explicates. Crucially, it is the criticism and poetry of Andrews himself. By taking his own work for his critical text, Andrews becomes, as it were, a double agent. His own writing (critical and poetical alike) is brought under close surveillance. Andrews's procedure calls to mind (by contrast) the work of Paul de Man, who spent a lifetime pursuing this kind of "criticism of criticism." He neglected to take the kind of bold step that Andrews insists upon: he neglected to make himself, his own writing, a central subject of his attention. The postmortem that overtook de Man's work supplied the perspective he could not bring himself to take—and of course the work has been the better for the coming of that postmortem.

One of the poems featured in Andrews's critical commentary (of 1983) is "Getting Ready to Have Been Frightened," which did not appear in its full textuality until 1988. Parts of it had appeared in various little magazines, however. This procedure of publishing excerpts from long works in journals prior to full book presentation is now such a commonplace practice among writers that we scarcely give it any critical (or political) attention. The practice, however, is an important "medium of writing" that lays down a textual trail full of import (as Andrews says in his "Open Letter" essay, "an epistemology and a political practice"). It makes a difference what texts Andrews chose to put in circulation just as it makes a difference where he chose to circulate. Most writers today operate within this circulation system ("medium of writing"); very few call the medium into critical review. That Andrews does so indicates the depth of his investment in writing as social practice and in his critical effort to illuminate the presence of such practices.

The illumination calls attention to the limits of writing. It is as if Andrews had defaced poetry's monument of unaging intellect in graffiti from Shelley's "Ozymandias": "Look on my works, ye mighty, and despair." The despair of the mighty is part of the pleasure—the carnival of Andrews's texts. "Getting Ready to Have Been Frightened" is spatially structured as (what scholars call) "a critical text" (sometimes—wrongly—called "a variorum edition"). Each page of the work consists of a triad of "superior texts" standing (in the form of free verse poems) above an "apparatus" of "variant readings" strung out, according to convention, at the foot of the page. The work appears, in other words, as if each page printed three "versions" of some specific work (or the fragmentary remains of such a work in three "authoritative" state[s]), along with a set of alternate readings (or are they to be read as textual glosses?) organized in a textual apparatus.

we both know it
we both hate it
....
lost & found
....
self that acts
self that judges
I lose
that evacuates
....
Splice or ground purpose to the things in order to a longer
view   Each skirt higher toward vanishing point than
next   My Aristotelian in a bathing suit in the age-
grading system   Demoter Widened idealism

Those who have attractive relatives, those who are
getting clearer reception

As we read in another of this work's "apparatus texts," "Only structure
& rough approximations of the 'privileged reading.'" Each page of
"Getting Ready to Have Been Frightened" is a machine designed to invite rereading and textual investigation—more particularly, designed
to promote the habit, as it were, of intense textual scrutiny and manipulation. The final page of the work has only two superior texts:

mustard womb

....

little knots
applied asleep

....

Mud in storm   Patriots quake   Failure, that radical
    demotion

While there could be no "privileged reading" for such a text, its general import is clear. Begun under the birth sign of "mustard womb"
(which is "(k)not" a "mustard bomb"), the passage performs a kind
of descent to earth where a transvaluation of values may be imagined
to begin. The "little knots" of the text locate moments of resistance
and upheaval as the upper world (the "superior text") turns over, and
downward, for its dialectical completion. "Demotion"—wittily, the
text's last word—recalls the earlier "Demoter Widened idealism," and
through that intratextual echo calls up the figure of Demeter. The poem's final statement—"failure, that radical demotion"—thus reveals
itself as Andrews's equivalent of the famous conclusion to Shelley's
"Ode to the West Wind": "If Winter comes, can Spring be far behind."
Persephone's descent into hell is glimpsed as a model of "radical demotion," the "failure" that alone makes possible, in the order of what
Shelley called "Intellectual Beauty," an "awakened Earth":

Drive my dead thoughts over the universe
Like withered leaves to quicken a new birth!
And, by the incantation of this verse,

Scatter, as from an unextinguished hearth
Ashes and sparks, my words among mankind!
Be through my lips to unawakened Earth

The trumpet of a prophecy! o Wind,
If Winter comes, can Spring be far behind?
—"Ode to the West Wind"[5]

Andrews would never allow himself that kind of Shelleyan rhetoric. The severity and diminuendo of his poem, with its extreme obliquities, give a firm refusal to Shelley's romantic dream. In fact, gestures of refusal—Andrews's resistant "little knots"—comprise the bleak activism for which his work is always "Getting Ready." Here again Byron—Shelley's dark friend and a figure confessedly (for good and ill alike) "born for opposition" (*Don Juan,* canto 15, st. 22)—seems the more apt comparison.

II
It Must Change

5
Art and Error
With Special Thanks to the Poetry of Robert Duncan

> "Sadie, you can't sing."
> "You wish!"
>
> —*Georgia*

Error, evil, failure: each word names a problem that emerged with the aesthetics of Romanticism and flowered in the twentieth century. A common route into this complex matter has been through the work of a writer like Ezra Pound, where a set of interlocking moral concerns centers in his fascism. Important as that approach must be, I set it aside here. It is an approach that has in any case lost much of its clarifying potential because it can leave us too confident about the ethical issues. Instead of Pound, let us begin with one of his inheritors, Robert Duncan, whose cultural credentials present hardly any difficulties at all.

Duncan is peculiarly apt for this discussion because he had a theory, perhaps even a myth, that covered the problem in at least one of its important aspects. The fullest statement of his views comes in his "Essay in Essential Autobiography," *The Truth and Life of Myth*.[1] In the second section Duncan sets out to demonstrate how "a poetry of history itself was created." This poetry climaxes, for Duncan, in his treatment of the lives of certain "men who lived in the Christian myth"—specifically, St. Francis, St. John of the Cross, and St. Ignatius Loyola, "the Saints who were also Poets," as Duncan says (64). The lives and works of these men expose a prevenient underlying meaning, or "myth," that pervades all of reality. "Self-made men and self-made poems take pride in their rise," Duncan observes (60), but those prideful selvings are caught up in a more "momentous design in which men in their acts participate." So the example of these poet-saints is a key "passage"— to appropriate a useful term from Duncan's repertory—to the general conclusion Duncan is aiming for at the end of the essay's second section: the idea that "the grace of the poem, the voice, comes from a will that strives to waken us from our own personal will," the idea that the poet "strives to waken to the will of the poem, even as the poem strives to waken that will" (63–64). The whole complex of thought is at once deeply Pauline and deeply Freudian.

At this point Duncan opens the essay's third and final section with an extraordinary paragraph:

> Recalling the Saints who were the Poets—Francis, John of the Cross and Ignatius Loyola, in whose lives a poetry of history itself was created, men who lived in the Christian myth, I had the sense too of how in time in each order an antithesis or antipoetry had appeared in their names, and I set about craftily to sketch out this part of the plot. Just here, the delite in cunning fashioning carried me into the false illustration of the Franciscan antitype in the invitingly monumental *Summa* of Aquinas, and such was my satisfaction in the juxtaposition of these two, Francis and Saint Thomas, that he *had* to be a Franciscan. Only the baffled look of a friend as I read the passage brought me to check myself. But, the false note was to remain. In the demonstration of how myth operates in the life and truth of the poet's work contained in this paper as our immediate example of that work, I saw the good of the error. For a time it must jar in the reader's appreciations, and I must incur the being-seen-through, caught in the act of a would-be clever effect. (64)

Duncan is recalling a crucial moment nine pages earlier (55) in his argument. There he was working to describe the mythic dimension playing itself out in certain religious events of the sixteenth century. But in trying to sketch "the reality of a divine history within what men call history" (58), it seems that Duncan got his *facts* wrong. Trying to emphasize the mythic symmetry in certain events, Duncan had made St. Thomas Aquinas a Franciscan!

But Duncan is undaunted by his misprision—indeed, he makes his "error" the (unforeseen) *felix culpa* that will culminate his essay's argument. So he declares that "I must force myself to remain responsible to the error that sticks in pride's craw; not to erase it," which would be the customary editorial move of the essay writer, "but to bring it forward, to work with it, even if this flaw mar a hoped-for success" (64). This move is the sign that he intends his writing to be carried out under the sign of a Confucian "Sincerity." The latter term he takes to mean "to perfect" or "to bring to focus." Fully translated it becomes:

"Focussing in on the process itself as the field of the poem, the jarring discord must enter the composition" (64–65).

From this idea, born equally of Duncan's desire to show poetry as a discourse of the Truth and his awareness that the desire must inevitably be enmeshed in error, comes—what?! Why, "the opening of the field," the well-known and now fully elaborated Duncan program of aesthetic redemption. Section 3 of his essay thus marches to its splendid conclusion by showing that, of all the "wisdom-professions" (as Laura Riding ironically called them), only poetry survives as a reliable discourse of truth because only poetry incorporates its own errors into its self-representations. Philosophy, religion, science: these are discourses committed to normative truth. Poetry, by contrast, is committed to truth as a continual process of knowing and unknowing.

I will come back to Duncan and the problem he represents in a moment. But first, to complicate how we think about Duncan's imagination of poetical error, I want to glance at a few other poets whose work exemplifies the presence of error or failure. These examples vary from deliberateness to carelessness to ignorance. Certain writers appear to think it important to correct errors, others are indifferent, a few even solicit error, many imagine and work for error's redemption. Most troubling of all, these cases raise the issues in embarrassingly elementary ways.[2]

I begin with Blake, the opening text page of his masterwork *Jerusalem,* the prose address "To the Public" (plate 3). The problem here is that the text comes to us badly and deliberately defaced. The poet himself went back over the copper plate and gouged the text at various points so that its linguistic coherence would be ruined. All copies of the poem he finished and sold bear the signs of that dreadful visitation.

Analogous to such textual errancy is what happens, inadvertently, in Keats's sonnet "On First Looking Into Chapman's Homer," when he writes his ignorance about American history—the infamous "stout Cortez"—into the text. Although Keatsians like to assure us that the error doesn't matter, one can hardly agree. The error is flagrant and embarrassing because of the poem's declared subject. Indeed, in a certain way of reading, the error enriches the text: a ludic note enters the poem exactly at the moment of its high rhetorical climax. That kind of move is a staple of Byron's style, of course, but it forms no part of the "intentional structure" of Keats's sonnet.

My third example is Byron, first of all the famous passage toward the beginning of *The Giaour,* where Greece is described through an extended comparison with a corpse (lines 68ff.) Byron draws out the comparison for so long, however, that he neglects to complete the grammar of his construction and ultimately leaves undefined the idea he asks his readers to consider. Matthew Arnold attempted to mitigate the offense by giving the text a fancy name ("trailing anacoluthon"), and Ethyl Mayne spoke elegantly of "the strange, slipshod loveliness where He never fulfills his destiny as the subject of the opening phrase. Bent o'er the dead he remains immoveable to the end of time." But in fact the verse is slipshod, and it reminds us why Byron's work has been aptly called (the phrase is Byron's own) "the spoiler's art."[3] His work exhibits many errors of this kind—for example, the infamous solecism in the "Address to the Ocean" at the end of Canto IV of *Childe Harold* (st. 180).

> His steps are not upon thy paths,—thy fields
> Are not a spoil for him,—thou dost arise
> And shake him from thee; the vile strength he wields
> For earth's destruction thou dost all despise . . .
> And dashest him again to earth:—there let him lay.

In this case, when the error was called to his attention, he simply let it *lay* and gave as his reason "the *post* and *indolence* and *illness.*" So much for artistic conscience.[4]

Finally there is Wordsworth, whom I take up last because the structure of his aesthetic thought has so much in common with Duncan's. My example is *The Prelude,* which is Wordsworth's story of the Imagination: "what it is, and what it would become," how it was "Impaired" and how it was "Restored." The problem is that this uplifting story regularly, and I think inevitably, belies itself. Inevitably, because Wordsworth's aesthetic is committed to a dialectical "counter-spirit." So at the end of Book XII, when the tale of the restored Imagination is being completed and the benevolent theory of the Spots of Time fully set forth, Wordsworth's vision turns dark. The restored Imagination foresees its own death:

> The days gone by
> Return upon me almost from the dawn

Of life: the hiding-places of man's power
Open; I would approach them, but they close.
I see by glimpses now; when age comes on
May scarcely see at all. . . . (XII. 276–81)

We are moved by such undefended sincerity and would perhaps rather
that the poem had ended (like Pound's *Cantos*) with a revelation of
its failure.

It does not. The concluding Books, and in particular Book XIV,
turn to dispel the darknesses raised by Wordsworth's narrative and finally propose the work as an exemplary moral tale. The consequence
is a series of dismal recapitulating texts that we may register as either
deliberate acts of bad faith or as moments of lapsed awareness induced
perhaps by the "more habitual sway" of a certain kind of writing and
thinking that Wordsworth has programmatically cultivated. So, for example, when Wordsworth assures us that his autobiography has not left
out anything of consequence—that it has "told what best merits mention" (370) and regularly determined

> to stand up
> Amid conflicting interests, and the shock
> Of various tempers; to endure and note
> What was not understood, though known to be;
> Among the mysteries of love and hate,
> Honour and shame, looking to right and left,
> Unchecked by innocence too delicate,
> And moral notions too intolerant,
> Sympathies too contracted. . . . (333–41)

We are only too aware that Wordsworth knew very well how much of
importance he deliberately left out, how many of those "conflicting interests" of "love and hate, / Honour and shame" in particular. We now
name them, generically, Annette Vallon.[5] So a passage like this decon-
structs itself, as does Wordsworth's declaration that finally

> the discipline
> And consummation of a Poet's mind,
> In everything that stood most prominent
> Have faithfully been pictured. (303–6)

The Wordsworthian program of sincerity is here exposed, by the law of its own dialectic, into a program of bad faith. Has he simply forgotten, this disciple of memory? It is hard to believe. The structures of memory that Wordsworth himself so cherished will return upon these passages—it will take some one hundred years—and force them to deliver up their larger ranges of meaning. Those meanings infect and trouble the poetic surface.

Different as they are, all these cases of poetic error share an important feature: an arbitrary intervention occurs (ignorantly, carelessly, thoughtlessly, deliberately). The intervention opens the field of the poem to an awareness of an aesthetic dysfunction, as if the writing were divided against itself.

2

With these examples in mind let us return to Duncan and his idea about the poem-as-a-process-of-writing. As we know, Duncan uses the theory to justify a certain kind of poetic error. He begins his work under the assumption that all writing must involve errant and arbitrary elements. Poetical imitation is thereby directed not toward the golden world postulated in (for instance) Sidney's *Defence*—it does not try to render an idealized order of things. On the contrary, the imitation aims at a perceived order of things. In the process poem, the entire field of the text, including its unconscious and even unwanted elements, is called to the attention and judgment of the reader.

Duncan is the child of the benevolent Wordsworth (rather than of the spoiler Byron) because he wants to say, after Wordsworth, that all this process "is cooperant to a mighty end" (*The Prelude* XIV). But he wants to follow Wordsworth by correcting his errors, as Blake sought to correct Milton's. The correction comes, in Duncan's post-Poundian view, when poets begin by acknowledging that "their errors and wrecks lay about" them, that they are "not . . . demigod[s],"[6] and that their work should seek not to obscure but to discover and illuminate the fields of error as of truth. Out of this vision comes a new idea of poetic realms of gold and a redemptive imagination like Duncan's: "Sodom is blessd / in the Lord's eyes."[7]

The countercultural move made by Laura Riding offers a clarifying differential to Duncan's aesthetic.[8] When she abandoned poetry, she explained that her decision came from an awareness that poetry in her age was obscuring the truth about language—about language in an absolute sense (and irrespective of different national languages, each of which has its own quasi-absolute character) and about the English language circa 1930 in particular. As she studied (and practiced) poetry, she judged that in her epoch it had grown to a master of deceit, perhaps the chief of the many masters of deceit populating the world. Poetry deceives, she argued, by setting itself up as a sign of the possibility of true and even perfect expression: indeed, as *the* sign of that ideal. Poets offered their work under that sign for two reasons: because they perceived a historical process of linguistic debasement descending into the twentieth century; and because they saw the need for establishing standards of linguistic performance that could arrest or even reverse the process of debasement. We define modernism as a complex engagement with those two perceptions.

Riding's modernism is antithetical, a critical turn against the movement's good-intentioned hopes for art. To her, poetry is a special subdiscourse of language, and the snow is general all over the Ireland of language, as well as the society transacted by the language. Poetry is a master deceit because it pretends to a special freedom from the corruption that, it agrees, has infected its own groundwater. How then does one write poetry in such a historical situation? Riding decides that one shouldn't. Rather, one should construct a "Telling," in the plainest prose, of the truth of the situation.[9] That truth-telling may, in her view, provide the basis for a hope that a language—our English language—might be restored to health.

From Riding's point of view, Duncan's project is a pathetic romantic dream, as if Matthew Arnold turned up saying, in his most magisterial tones, "Evil, be thou my good." This is the Wordsworthian legacy that Arnold passes down to us: from loss, "abundant recompense." In the present context, Riding's critique can serve as the basis for two hypotheses, one having to do with poetic interpretation, the other with poetic tradition. First hypothesis: if Riding's position shuts down the possibility of poetical discourse, it may have opened (however unintentionally) a new way to think about works of high cultural seriousness. I will explore this hypothesis shortly in Duncan's "This Place Rumord to Have Been Sodom."

Second hypothesis: that poetry and art need not offer themselves as "wisdom-professions" in order to justify their cultural authority. Indeed, there is a counter-tradition of poetry flowing from the Romantic period itself that repudiates all high offices. Burns is the great progenitor of this tradition, although many women writers—Ann Yearsley, for example, or Ann Batten Cristall—cultivate other versions of his de- or ec-centricity. In Burns the mode comes through an appropriation of the same resources that fed Villon's work in the fifteenth century. "Love and Liberty: A Cantata" is in every sense a lawless performance, a celebration of life and letters that are out-of-bounds:

> I never drank the Muses' STANK,
>   Castalia's burn, and a' that,
> But there it streams and richly reams,
>   My HELICON I ca' that.[10]

Liquor, that is, and a language that explodes through outrageous wordplay. In this kind of text, bard and poet and Burns himself all sink into an encompassing language—a polyglot tongue flaunting its rich impurities. It is a language aspiring to no "marble" or "gilded monuments," nor even to the "powerful rhyme" of Shakespeare's alternative desire. The aspiration is at once more common and more elemental—the choral breath of the singers themselves:

> See the smoking bowl before us,
> Mark our jovial, ragged ring!
> Round and round take up the Chorus,
>   And in raptures let us sing—
>   CHORUS
> A fig for those by law protected,
>   LIBERTY'S a glorious feast
> Courts for cowards were erected,
>   Churches built to please the PRIEST.

Descending from texts like these is a living tradition of the highest and lowest kinds of poetic forms. It includes Byron, Poe, Lautréamont, and in our day Patchen, Helen Adam, even Kathy Acker. Only the crude outrages and absurdities that accumulate as *Blood and Guts in High School* create the possibility of the book's astonishing conclusion, that brief and unforgettable poem:

Blood and guts in high school
This is all I know
Parents teachers boyfriends
All have got to go.

Some folks like trains,
Some folks like ships,
I like the way you move your hips
All I want is a taste of your lips,

$\qquad\qquad$ boy,

All I want is a taste of your lips.[11]

As with Burns, the idiom here is popular song, and no camp aesthetes are allowed. There's nothing cool or hip in those lines, no trace of a New York School style that would cultivate, in every sense, these kinds of low forms. The verse enacts an experience of nearly total loss. That is to say, it's alive.

This kind of writing encourages us to think more freely when we engage with poetry that imagines itself in high cultural terms: for instance, with Duncan's work and a poem like "This Place Rumord to Have Been Sodom." That it is a work of high art makes it neither a better nor a worse thing than Burns's or Acker's works—just a different thing. Formally it engages much the same place, one that is cursed, devalued, condemned. But the manifest content (as it were) of the poem is to return to the cursed place and discover its redemption.

The poem develops from a set of elemental tensions of both morality and language. The central issue is love, more particularly the love that (once) dared not speak its name. Structurally it builds on a traditional (Christian) separation of the biblical inheritance into an old and a new dispensation, with a god of judgment being superseded by a god of love, the despised and rejected Jesus. When Duncan's poem has finished, the reader is to understand that the doctrinal core of Christianity has been redeemed and renewed in the experience of yet another despised and rejected generation, whose type was prefigured in the city of Sodom.

The argument of the poem reworks certain biblical phrases and ideas to reimagine their customary meanings: phrases like "the Lord" and "the hand of the Lord that moves" and "measured by the Lord and found wanting." In each of these cases the biblical texts yield to immediate pressures, and "the Lord" emerges as that figure Duncan liked to call "the poet," whose hand moves over this very text, remeasuring its measures. Wordplays at the poem's opening define the redemptive action:

> THIS PLACE RUMORD TO HAVE BEEN SODOM
>   Might have been
> Certainly these ashes might have been pleasures.
> Pilgrims on their way to the Holy Places remark
> this place. Isn't it plain to all
> that these mounds were palaces? This was once
> a city among men, a gathering together of spirit.
> It was measured by the Lord and found wanting.

Throughout the poem, words and phrases appear to lift themselves randomly into pertinent suggestiveness: here we double-take "plain" and "city among men," and if we know the entire poem we do the same with "remark" and "this place." These textual events are signs of the poem's textual unconscious, manifest forms of a latent content. They are of course devices of style, poetic conventions—perhaps the most common and programmatic in Duncan's repertoire.

In more elaborated forms they also invade the poem's syntax. For instance, here at the opening Duncan works the syntax so that "might have been" will mean both "might have come into being" as well as its more literal idea ("this place might actually have been the infamous city of Sodom"). The latter meaning is drawn out of an ethnohistorical discourse, the former out of a language of visionary-affective desire. The two discourses, intersecting across the entire poem, here culminate in the line that ends the first strophe and begins the second: "It was measured by the Lord and found wanting." This line is double-faced not simply in its linguistic significance but also in its dramatic placement on the page. In each form it comes to us as the figure of a cursed end that conceals a new beginning grounded in love and desire.

As the poem moves along we discover a city of Sodom being rediscovered by a Lord "whom the friends have named at last Love." The rediscovery works a transvaluation of values. Sodom, we are told, was destroyed once by "angels that inhabit longing," the messengers of the Lord of judgment. But the text here remeasures the words "wanting" and "longing," which now, in this poem, reflect (and reflect upon) each other as equivalent signs of a failed eros. As the hand of the Lord moves again through Duncan's poem, the children of the promise return:

> The devout have laid out gardens in the desert,
> drawn water from springs where the light was blighted.
> How tenderly they must attend these friendships
> or all is lost.

The angels of longing reappear as the "new friends" who "gather here" to re-found the great city of Sodom, the city of love. And the city is "THIS PLACE" where the "images and loves" of the poem move through a process of re-writing and re-creation.

At the heart of the action is a deep appreciation of impermanence and a reciprocal understanding that green places must be *held green* by a perpetual and devout faithfulness. A city of love is re-erected in Duncan's poem through gestures that are as fragile as they are immediate. Without them

> all is lost. All *is* lost.
> Only the faithful hold this place green.

The lines celebrate a band of angels who cultivate secret gardens. These are the lost souls driven out of their Israel/Sodom into a land of bondage, where (however) they sing the psalms of their lost home of love. Duncan's poem is the green place of its own "longing" imagination.

> In the Lord Whom the friends have named at last Love
> the images and loves of the friends never die.
> This place rumord to have been Sodom is blessd
> in the Lord's eyes.

Wordsworth called this enginery of salvation "the ministry of fear," and I suspect that Duncan may be explicitly recalling Wordsworth's thought. Certainly the sequence of ideas that "the world like great Sodom lies under" both "fear" and "Love" is pure Wordsworth. The idea is that love (as both faithfulness and longing) is sustained and developed through disciplines of loss. A perfection of loss can thereby

turn to a vision of perfect love. It is a vision or idea as old as the
story of Abraham, which Christians take as a type of the story of Jesus.
Here Duncan, after Wordsworth, recuperates the whole sequence—
he would call it the myth—through a contemporary figure of forbid-
den love.

But in all this lurks a contradiction that I will frame as a simple question: if, as the poem finally declares, "Sodom is blessd / in the Lord's
eyes," then in what sense are we to understand (as the poem declares
earlier) that "all *is* lost"? Friends tenderly attend their friends, and a
green place of love is faithfully maintained by the devotees of love. Indeed, a great city is raised up again, and if it appears only (as we say) in
imagination, that event clearly comes to re-found the place at a more
fundamental level. The truth seems to be that all is not lost, though
the idea that all is lost appears important to preserve.

Indeed, the phrase "all *is* lost," if pressed closely, will yield up not
merely its contradiction but its radical untruth. A cliché of romantic
hopelessness, the words get reimagined in Duncan's text until they
come to mean their opposite, come to mean that "the images and loves
of the friends never die." A process of (total) loss emerges as a perpetual system of love and desire. Particular factive losses are redeemed
in the process and gathered up through its ceaseless and devotional energies. It is entirely to the point that the love celebrated in the poem is
figured in the highest of cultural forms: as a great city, as a cultivated
garden, ultimately as a work of art—this very poem (which joins itself
to that vast process of imaginative writing celebrated by the captains
of culture and the sailors who serve them).

The simple truth is that all is NOT lost, and Duncan's poem is "not
lost" to show that simple truth. It is a truth that conceals far more than
Duncan's poem has been able to imagine in its benevolent work. To
say, for example, that "all is not lost" need not by any means bring comfort or satisfaction; it is not necessarily a text of hope or redemption,
anymore than to say "all *is* lost" need be a text of hopelessness. Duncan's own verse works hard to transform itself into a text of hope and
pleasure and blessing. But there are other phrases that may come to
mind when we are drawn into Duncan's dialectic of romantic loss. Even
using Duncan's generalized language we can see that: some things are
lost, some are not. Some of the lost things are cherished but will never
be recovered. Not all will cherish these lost things; some indeed will

long for their destruction. Some things that remain and persist seem horrid, perhaps evil—to some, but not to others.

"All is lost" vs. "the images and loves of the friends never die." Duncan's encompassing Romantic dialectic manages the contradictory and reciprocal truth of these assertions. In doing so, however, the poem begins to leak at random, as chaotic moments of order and disorder make themselves apparent. What shall we make of all those arbitrary internal rhymes? Or the idiosyncratic spellings? Each to himself may be an oracle, as Shelley's Demogorgon said to Asia. Or what of those "cries" that

> ring in our ears, where such fears that were once
> desires walk, almost spectacular,
> stalking the desolate circles, red-eyed.

Words call to each other here—for what reason? (They don't call in other lines.) And the ambiguous syntax that gives us "red-eyed" fears walking in ears? The verse in this case hovers at the ridiculous, and for many it will have passed over. Is this a splendid surrealist passage? Is it deliberated (or nondeliberated) trash? The matter is absolutely undecidable.

I very much like that undecidability in Duncan's verse, which is riddled (in all senses) with its own contradictions. I especially like to realize how appalling this kind of work appears to other readers; and perhaps even more, how what appears appalling to one strikes another as grand, even mystical. If poets sing amid their uncertainty, why shouldn't critics enjoy the same privilege in their prosings?

So I propose error and failure, unredeemed, as measures of aesthetic appreciation; and I close by recalling Byron's imagination of creation in both Art and Nature as "at the worst a glorious blunder" (*Don Juan*, canto 11, st. 3). "At the worst," he wrote?! Didn't he actually mean "at the best"? Perhaps, perhaps not. You pays your money and you takes your choice. Like Duncan, Byron fashioned a program of bad and evil writing. It is signaled in Lucifer's comment to Cain about a certain class of "Souls who dare look the Omnipotent tyrant in his Everlasting Face and tell him that his evil is not good" (*Cain* scene 1, 139–40). That pronunciamento, as splendid as it is ridiculous, defines "the spoiler's art" that is Byronic writing, where lines may or may not go on spavined feet. What is most astonishing about such work is its deliberateness, as if Byron's greatest care were to ensure that his writing's trash would be carefully preserved as such. When he said that he wrote his famous tales "standing on one foot," after a night of debauchery, the joke is at once sophomoric and (for poets) professional.

Such a program culminates in the great catastrophe of Ezra Pound's *Cantos,* whose "groundwork," as Duncan might have said, is a network of beauty and horror. Nor am I talking here simply of the infamous "moral" derelictions of Pound's work. It is grounded as well in passage after passage of derelict writing. One recalls, reading it, Byron's many descriptions of the Byronic Hero—for instance, Napoleon as such a hero, fallen at the great victory/defeat named Waterloo: "There sunk the greatest, nor the worst of men," a "spirit antithetically mixt" (*Childe Harold's Pilgrimage,* canto 3, st. 36). Though a world famous man and poet, Byron knew very well, better than most, that his work was a network of illusions and deceits, not least of all linguistic illusions and deceits. Cultural prophets would soon grow confident enough to argue that it was a bad poem, full of bad writing. But these readers, correct in one respect, simply misunderstood the issues that Byron's work was (consciously) raising. Baudelaire would later name them the hypocrite readers. Collectively their name in England is Matthew Arnold.

When I have argued this way of seeing our recent poetic history with friends and scholars, I am often asked: what are you saying here, that there might or should be a poetry which is badly written? And I say, yes, indeed, of course. But then such a possibility is not easily entertained by culture industries or by artists and poets who function in their orbit. In that world, art is a museum waiting to receive the best that has been known and thought in the world. How or why could one imagine an art committed either to moral error or tactical and procedural dysfunction?

Because poets must be committed to go to the limit and beyond: "beyond the fitting medium of desire" (*Childe Harold's Pilgrimage,* canto 3, st. 42). Desire, the special province of art's knowledge, will have little truck with what is either fitting or mediocre. And so, thank Somebody, they have. Eliot and others deplored the wasteland of nineteenth-century sentimental writing, but *The Waste Land* is a monument to that tradition, a poem made of its lovely trash. There are souls nauseated by the fine writing of W. B. Yeats and more nauseated yet by his numerous offspring, say Seamus Heaney. What a tradition of verse we have there, worthy of its nineteenth-century parallel tradition stretching from Wordsworth to Tennyson.

Yet it all may be made to make sense, the nonsense of those whited cultural sepulchers, even when someone comes along to threaten their illusions with a "spoiler's art": in the nineteenth century, let us say Byron or Laetitia Elizabeth Landon; in the twentieth, Jack Spicer or our horrifying contemporary Kathy Acker. For there is, finally, only one sure aesthetic rule. It comes to us as a proverb about art as Faustian play:

> In play, there are two pleasures for your choosing,
> The one is winning, and the other losing.
> —*Don Juan*

6

Private Enigmas and Critical Functions
With Special Thanks to the Poetry of Charles Bernstein
Interlocutors: Anne Mack, J. J. Rome, Georg Mannejc

> He imagines a vast science, into the utterance of which the knower
> would finally include himself—this would be a science of the ef-
> fects of language.
>
> —Roland Barthes *par lui-même* (1975)

GM: Doesn't it *bother* you sometimes, this kind of writing? As if
you had to be someone special to read it—as if it were meant for
a coterie of initiates or a literary intelligentsia. Look at this:

Verdi and Postmodernism

She walks in beauty like the swans
that on a summer day do swarm
& crawls as deftly as a spoon
& spills & sprawls & booms.

These moments make a monument
then fall upon a broken calm
they fly into more quenchless rages
than Louis Quatorze or Napoleon.

If I could make one wish I might
overturn a state, destroy a kite
but with no wishes still I gripe
complaint's a Godly-given right.[1]

What is one to say of such nonsense? I observe that each stanza
is dominated by (introduced by) a distinct "literary" allusion:
Byron is echoed in the first line, D. G. Rossetti in line five, and
some nursery doggerel in line nine.[2] But the absence of an in-
tegrating element among these three simple allusions is an in-

dex of the text's chaos (as is the poem's title, for that matter). The work is a travesty of "meaning"; it flaunts its own deliberate wreckage of meaning. It's an arbitrary construction of elements yoked by violence together.

JJR: Bernstein would regard your phrase "arbitrary construction" as what he was after. He's fond of Humpty Dumpty's retort to Alice about words, their users, and their meanings.[3]

AM: And why do you expect a "comprehensible" meaning from a poem anyway? Russian futurist poetry, which has clearly influenced Bernstein, moves "beyonsense"—a modernist reprise on "nonsense" traditions of verse: the riddle poem, the enigma, sound poems, and all the rhetorical/ornamental forms which call our attention away from the "content" and toward the physique of the text, or what Bernstein has called the "extralexical / strata of the poem."[4] The semantic strata are not alone those elements to which a relatively fixed connotative or denotative meaning can be ascribed. We can't restrict meaning that way; it would make real meaning impossible. "After all, meaning occurs only in a context of conscious & nonconscious, recuperable & unrecoverable, dynamics" (AA 8). "Verdi and Postmodernism" is not *zaum* poetry, but it is evidently "meaningless" within a similar functional horizon. Its outrageous music comes partly from its having invoked that most traditional of forms, the quatrain, and then scattered its songs and their customary expectations.

GM: So you agree it *is* meaningless.

AM: No—but I agree it's a work that disrupts certain traditional forms of meaning. Part of its meaning lies in its having exposed . . .

GM: Travestied!

AM: Alright, *travestied* the fact that we expect poems to "mean" in certain ways. We expect from them a Coleridgean balance and reconciliation of opposite and discordant qualities, so that when a text (like this text) works to *un*reconcile its materials, our reading codes are upset. I suppose I don't have to detail the devices Bernstein uses to unbalance normal reading procedures. They're clear enough.

GM: Clear enough, yes, but to what point?

AM: Well, partly to demonstrate the presence and character of the reading codes. Reading this text *as outrageous*—at what Kant would call its "moment" of travesty—we realize some of the forms of poetry we have internalized and shaped to our desires. To register this text as "meaningless" says that we expect poems to "tell" us something: that a poem possesses some definable content, that it walks in a beauty or a truth that it's trying (however indirectly) to communicate. The reader's part in such a theater of meaning is to recuperate the content—to produce an interpretation. The more generally acceptable the interpretation, the more true (or beautiful) it's taken to be.

That set of meaning-expectations is invoked by this text as part of the meaning of the text. The reader's part in the poem is thereby shown to be included in the work, subsumed in a quest for "meaning." The poem's dysfunctions are partly devices for exposing these readerly aspects of the work's "meaning" and partly maps (or invitations) to other kinds of meanings.

Bernstein has described this imaginative textual dynamic in the following way: "Out of fear of being opaque to one another, we play the charade of comprehensibility. . . . To be comprehensible to all—the telos of the language of what is called science— is to censor (a collective repression) all that is antagonistic, anarchic, odd, antipathetic, anachronistic, other. . . . So poetry can be the *censer* of these spirits from the unknown, untried, unconsidered—really just *unacknowledged*—that now, as if they always had, bloom in vividness."[5] The blessing "censer," in Bernstein's work, emerges through the summoning of the demonic "censors." His texts "censer" the "censors" by refusing to offer themselves as tabernacles of the Truth. As Bernstein goes on to say: "For after all it is only after a work is completed—a journey that begins at the point a *text* becomes a *work*—that others may enter into it, trace its figures, ride its trails along tracks that are called lines. . . . It is only an *other* that, *in the final instance*, constitutes the work, makes it more than a text (test), resurrects it from the purgatory of its production, which is to say its production of self-sameness" (127).

GM: All of that describes the kind of writing professors have wet dreams about and classrooms were made for. The simple fact is that "Verdi and Postmodernism" is a classic instance—I've been to school too!—of a meta-poem. Who would read it except as a school exercise or assignment? No one, any more than they would read *Finnegans Wake*.

JJR [to GM]: You wield "Verdi and Postmodernism" like a weapon, as if you *wanted* to defend yourself against Bernstein's writing. And for the life of me I can't imagine why you [addressing AM] are agreeing to discuss Bernstein's work in such a restricted horizon.

AM: Well, I like the poem's minor key—or I like its implicit suggestion that we stay in touch with matters—like nonsense—that are too easily taken as trivial and inconsequent.

JJR: But to start reading Bernstein from such a text can be so misleading—as if he were a writer to be safely passed by, the way we pass by Edward Lear as a minor Victorian children's writer. Why not begin from evidently "major" works? Even a hostile reader (are you a hostile reader [GM]?) will register the strength of poems like "Dysraphism" or "Ambliopia." The dislocations in those works—the "mis-seamings" and mis-seeings[6]—evidently function as opportunities to reimagine the world:

> Such is the space that, called
> into being, or given,
> transforms everything from what we
> know it to be, mishandled by
> the world, to what it never was, blessed.[7]

Bernstein defines this "space" of blessedness for nine more lines and then appears to launch his text from it (or toward it):

> So begins the long march to the
> next world. Custom is abandoned
> outright as a criterion of moral
> conduct. Everything must be justified
> before the courts of the New Criteria, which
> spring out of the old with the resourcefulness
> and tenacity of the truly ingrained. The theory
> of primary colors is rejected as elitist
> empiricism and the wavelengths of the spectrum
> take their proper and equal place in

the constitution of perception. Garrulousness
is taken for honesty.
(116)

The verse is another of Bernstein's travesties, this time a serious
joke on programmatic imaginations of revolutionary events. The
joke is grounded in the vocabularies and languages of the demo-
cratic and utopian left.

AM: There's such a thing as being too serious. Besides, you talk
about "misleading" but completely sidestep GM's misrepresen-
tation of Bernstein as an "academic" writer. Bernstein's work
began and grew outside the academic arena. His poetry wasn't
published by academic presses, and insofar as it penetrated the
academy at all, it was avoided. Like the modernists trying to break
into the early twentieth-century writing scene, he and others had
to create new journals, new (small) publishing houses, even new
distribution outlets.

GM: But now the internal exile is over, and their avant-garde positions are being taken up, happily it would seem, among the peda-
gogues. Superacademic journals—*Critical Inquiry, boundary 2*—
publish essays about them. Bernstein and others like him speak
at the MLA; they even take academic teaching positions. Surprising? Not at all. It is the blight they were born for.

AM: What are you saying: that in the end Dave Smith and Robert
Pinsky are no more or less academic than Bernstein and Hejinian, that the differences between their work are superficial? Or is
this some kind of weird polemic for Edgar Guest? *Lyrical Ballads*
makes a virtue of rustic places and common men, but the book
was written for the London intelligentsia, was written specifically
to alter the way England's cultural center thought about poetry.
All interesting poetry is directed at specialized readerships—"fit
audience, though few."

JJR: So you see Bernstein's poetry the way we now see the *Lyrical
Ballads*? As part of a critique of certain traditional ideas about poetry, writing, and reading. Like "The Idiot Boy" and "The Rime
of the Ancient Mariner," "Verdi and Postmodernism" is an "academic" poem because it revises the writing and reading that
dominate our received (academic) thinking.

AM: Precisely. And therefore our entire poetical inheritance as well.

JJR: Well then, let's try to clarify the specific shape of Bernstein's program. We can do this in fairly traditional ways because Bernstein, like Silliman, has written a great deal of critical and theoretical prose (and poetry!) on the subjects of poetry, writing, and reading. Not since Pound, Stein, Riding, and Eliot have we seen poets like Bernstein (or Silliman, Barrett Watten, Susan Howe, Lyn Hejinian, etc.) who set out to investigate and polemicize these topics with the same kind of range and critical intensity.[8]

Let's start with some remarks Bernstein made in a 1982 interview.[9] He describes his poetic interests as not "so much in disconnected bits . . . [as in] how these bits form an overall weave." He calls this a "critical, analytic" goal by which "the poem itself becomes a machine that spells and dispels illusion upon illusion, so that illusion's engendering can be witnessed" (CD 392). Thus, "Mine is an interest . . . towards focusing attention on the constitutive nature of conventions" in reading and writing, toward "the relentless theme of how language socializes us, but so often without a trace of this socialization that would illuminate, like the phosphorescence of an all-permeating world-soul made manifest as world-body" (CD 391–92).

So here are three of his basic ideas. The first—that is, the constructivist premise about writing and poetry—we've already touched on. In the second, he makes himself an inheritor of the Saussurean legacy that sees "reality" as a function of the language(s) by which we speak of it.

AM: It goes back a lot further than Saussure. Think of Blake, of Wilde.

JJR: Fair enough. Whatever, the corollary of this idea (that "language socializes us") is a correspondent imagination of "reality" being cast in human rather than abstract or technical terms. The "reality" that Bernstein talks about is irreducibly "social," and from the human point of view, there is no such thing as a non-human world. Scientific and theological imaginations of sub- and super-human worlds are themselves, in this view, human imaginings. When Bernstein opposes Terry Eagleton's statement that "literature does not exist in the sense that insects do," his argument proceeds from the latter perspective: "Of course, all Eagleton intends to say is that there is no objective, value-free sense of literature. . . . But this is also true of *insects, fiction,* and *ideology*" (CD 375). Bernstein's italics here are eloquent: they declare his (Blakean) belief that for human beings the world—including the natural world—is human, that is, is the precious responsibility of human beings.

The third key idea in the passage deals with the function of poetry. For Bernstein, poetry is the paradigm form of a language (a "socialization") that "illuminates." Bernstein recurs to this topic frequently:

> Alphabets . . . remain perhaps the most formidable technologies human culture has produced. Readers can usefully be regarded as operating highly sophisticated technologies. The technology of writing has many more dimensions than are "read" by most users: the technology is not fully "accessed." Poetry has an important, if often vacated, role in supplementing minimal reading values and in this sense can be understood as among the most useful tools for making alphabet technology available. *Literature* is the best word we now have for a writing that critiques itself not only at the level of represented ideas but prosodically, acoustically, syntactically, visibly: which is to say gives these dimensions equal methodological weight as it gives to more traditional notions of semantic content. (CD 370–71)

Bernstein repeatedly asks his readers to "imagine a literature that proposes its own interpretations," a literature that makes its own "production of ideas audible—in measuring and placing, sounding and breaking; and visible—in page scoring and design" (CD 368–69). The thought is toward a kind of naked poetry where the limits of the writing—its own ideologies—are made an explicit desire of the work. So the reader comes to see that poetry is (what Bernstein, punning, calls) "Thought's measure" (see CD 61–86), the measure of the ideology of language. "Style and form are as ideological as content and interpretation" (CD 368) because all aspects of language operate socializing mechanisms. Poetry's special function, in Bernstein's view, is to foreground these matters.

So "the question persists: How do we read writing that unmasks its own discontinuities, flaunts its core ideas as candy coating, and insists not on its deferred meaning but its enacted meaning? Not that such work transcends its historical/ideological situation. It is the conscious contemporary of its readers/critics, anticipating their habits of reading. It discounts the privileged status that may be lorded over works 'regressive' of their interpretive horizon" (CD 380). So the question is exactly the question raised by a work like "Verdi and Postmodernism." The poem is not "a travesty" of itself or of poetry in general. If it appears an outrageous work—a travesty—it has merely lifted into view the "regressiveness" of certain "interpretive horizons" that poetry and the readers of poetry (too) often agree to accept.

GM: What is "regressive" about expecting a poem to make sense? Bernstein himself seems to hold out that requirement for writing at least some of the time. *Artifice of Absorption* is organized in lines of verse, but it generally reads like prose. And what of the superb opening of "The Klupzy Girl," with its excellent pun on "senses": "Poetry is like a swoon, with this difference: / it brings you to your senses." Of course the descent into the maelstrom comes quickly:

> Yet his
> parables are not singular. The smoke from
> the boat causes the men to joke. Not
> gymnastic: pyrotechnic. The continuousness
> of a smile—wry, perfume scented. No this
> would go fruity with all these changes
> around. Sense of variety: panic.[10]

I suppose many would subscribe to this kind of writing for its bold flaunting of convention.

JJR: Perhaps, but they wouldn't include Bernstein: "Certainly . . . agit-prop has its own commendable values. But it's not as much as poetry can do. . . . Richard Kostelanetz has generally put forward this kind of reactive 'experimentalist' line, actually calling Stein in his introduction to the otherwise wonderful new Yale

Gertrude Stein 'nonsyntactical'—an appalling remark to make of someone who wrote 'I am a grammarian,' meaning that she wasn't being antigrammatical she was discovering what the grammars of our language are by making them" (CD 395–96). Bernstein desires a poetry "which is not essentially reactive but generative" (CD 395). It would work "by diminishing diversions from a constructed representation" (CD 36) and operate a "structure that can't be separated from the decisions made within it" (CD 38).

Why not *try*, at any rate, to read Bernstein in the same spirit that the author writ? Why not try to read "The Klupzy Girl" on such terms? It doesn't commit you to anything except "understanding poetry" (as a particular poem or way of proceeding in verse). You don't have to like it, and you may even learn something you didn't know.

Here is Bernstein speaking explicitly about his writing practice:

> Let me give an example of what "generative" might mean. I think of some of my poems as a series of remarks, either in the aphoristic sense or in the sense of observations, constructed items, etc., occurring at the level of phrases or sentences. These can be interpreted in multiple ways: they are each, perhaps to say, polyentendres (that is, any given remark can be taken as true, ironic, false, didactic, satiric, fantastical, inscrutable, sad, funny, my view, someone else's view, and so on . . .). Polyvalences and polyrhythms occurring overall throughout the poem create a music of the text . . . creating *chords* of the simultaneous vectors of the several interpretations of each polyentendre, and with the combination of these chords with other chords, durationally, in the sequence of the writing, and simultaneously, in the overall structure. (CD 396–97)

Using this as a kind of elementary instruction manual, we see what "The Klupzy Girl" is asking from its readers. The "grammar" of the passage is a set of discontinuous sentences and phrases. It is dominated by its special "sense of variety," which swings between a swooning *voluptas* and nervous "panic." Everything in the passage hangs on the management of the differentials: the line endings, obviously, and the stops between phrases and sentences. We're asked to come to a kind of "hyperattentiveness" in a text evolving polyvalent parables—and parables whose "meanings" are not primarily cognitive in any case.

>   the power of
>   making aware, which necessarily involves a
>   disruption of a single plane of attention or
>   belief, results in a hyperattentiveness
>   that has its own economy of engagement.
>   (AA 61)

"The Klupzy Girl" constructs ("generates") its differentials in order to multiply its possible engagements. We see the effect with special clarity when Bernstein rings his "changes" in the "sentence" that begins "No this"—a text only to be *read* if its parts are "changed around" (KG 47).

In general one could say of this poem that it works to *sensitize* meaning, to free meaning from the narrow cognitive frameworks of "singular" (in the "sense" of one-to-one) parables and release them to new "singularities" (in the "sense" of concrete particulars). From a purely rhetorical vantage we may take "yet his / parables are not singular" as an approving or disapproving remark, and we may imagine it to be spoken by anyone. Is the poem's opening statement an aphorism being quoted by Bernstein, so that the second statement might be Bernstein's own response to that ("his") aphorism? We don't know, the text won't tell us. What it *will* do is order itself to multiply these kinds of generative "polyentendres."

One paradox of all these apparent discontinuities is that the verse acquires an incredible degree of seamlessness. To borrow one of Bernstein's own images, it has "the continuousness / of a smile wry, perfume scented" (KG 47). That's an image of a complex particular whose many "parts" we register *as* many but which we are reluctant to separate or disentangle. Likewise in Bernstein's verse, we don't find it easy to isolate or define passages for quotation (or commentary) because they're always being pressed toward transformations, like Swinburne's verse.

The writing calls attention to Bernstein's belief that poetry isn't doing "as much as poetry can do" if it merely serves to carry some (parabolic/referenced) "meaning." Its chief function is to illustrate its own resources for creating meaning and the possibilities of meaning. So the poem's poetry is rarely reducible to fixed units. Though his writing is riddled with gaps and disjunctions, they function as little deaths of verse, eroticizing and re-energizing the language: "The music in my heart I bore / Long after it was heard no more."

GM: Doesn't this reading simply cave in to Bernstein's own writing contradictions?

JJR: But the point is that contradictions prevail everywhere. Artifices of enlightenment, of noncontradiction, get called out for exposure in this writing. We know these artifices in the engineering programs of theology and science. But another order of artifice is available: poetry. In *Artifice of Absorption* Bernstein argues for the differential play of a poetry's "absorptive" and "antiabsorptive" elements: music and cognition, "dream" and "content."

> In my poems, I
> frequently use opaque & nonabsorbable
> elements, digressions &
> interruptions, as part of a technological
> arsenal to create a more powerful
> ("souped up")
> absorption. . . .
> This is a
> precarious road because insofar
> as the poem seems
> overtly self-conscious, as opposed to internally
> incantatory or psychically
> actual, it may produce
> self-consciousness in the reader in such a way as to
> destroy his or her absorption by theatricalizing
> or conceptualizing the text. . . . This is, then, the subject
>   of much of my
> work.
>   (AA 38)

Even in this expository moment Bernstein flaunts the candied character of his ideas ("his or her absorption"). That witty use of contemporary jargon unfolds the "selfconsciousness in the reader" that the text is discussing. It "enacts" Bernstein's special form of a literature of knowledge. Ultimately he represents it as a contradiction of the word made flesh:

> The *intersection*
> of absorption & impermeability is precisely *flesh*. . . .
>   This
> is the philosophical interior
> of my inquiry. . . .
> The *thickness*
> of words ensures that whatever
> of their physicality is erased, or engulfed, in
> the process of semantic projection,
> a residue
> tenaciously in—
> heres that will not be sublimated
> away. Writing is not a thin film
> of expendable substitutions that, when reading, falls
> away
> like scales
> to reveal a meaning. The tenacity of
> writing's thickness, like the body's flesh, is
> ineradicable, yet mortal.
>   (AA 63–64)

The contradiction partly proceeds from the "inversion" of Christian incarnational ideas that Bernstein executes. What "will not be sublimated / away" comes as the physical turns of the verse, which become "on the contrary the sole" of the desublimated soul. "Meaning" does not consist in a "fall" away from "the tenacity of / writing's thickness" to achieve a mere revelation of things not seen. It's rather a Shelleyan revelation, an injunction to imagine what we know. The "scales" are not to fall away but to appear in a more generous, positive condition: "scales" of the many possible "meanings" (and grammars and rhetorics of meaning) that the word has known and that it can be remade—as here—to know again.

This effort to produce *through poetry* a cognitive transformation of a central Christian conception connects to Bernstein's long-standing critique of the science-based model of knowledge. In part 5 of "Three or Four Things I Know About Him," headed "Comic Interlude" (wordplay, as usual, intended), Bernstein writes: "It is, then, *our thesis* that political writing becomes disoriented when it views itself as description and not discourse: as not being *in* the world but *about* the world. The hermeneutic indicts the scientistic that it has once again subverted the dialogic nature of human understanding" (CD 20). Like the Lady of Shalott, poetry as "discourse" comes into the whole world, abandoning its exclusive residential areas—what the interpreters call beauty, truth, and disinterestedness. This move makes a descent into the comic interludes that poetry defines by taking its part in them. So far as Bernstein is concerned, "writing" is a "dialogic" event of "production / exchange that must be entered into, not observed" (CD 376).

So *Artifice of Absorption* ends by playing out its theatrical approach to knowledge and poetry:

Absorption & its many con-
verses, re-
verses, is at heart a measure
of the relationship between
a reader &
a work: any attempt to isolate
this dynamic in terms exclusively of
reading
or composition
will fail on this account.
As writers—
& everyone inscribes
in the sense
I mean here—
we can
try to intensify
our relationships by considering

how they work: are we putting
each other to sleep
or waking each other up;
& what do we wake to?
    (AA 64–65)

That third phase of Bernstein's last dialectical question splinters the text's latent drive toward conceptual synthesis. The "verse" of this text thus appears not simply as "con" and "re," but as "in" and "per" and "ob" and "trans" and whatever else we might choose to imagine. Here we can see that "everyone inscribes / in the sense / I mean" a poetical passage that—like the rest of this text—may be read in a variety of different ways.

AM: Indeed, the "understanding" of the passage, the "knowledge" it's committed to, *is* the transformation(s) that the reader/composer carries out through it. The opening section of Bernstein's essay "Thought's Measure" is headed "Writing (as) (and) Thinking."

JJR: Yes, Bernstein's is a philosophical poetry not because it's a "poetry of ideas" but because it's a "poetry of thought and thinking." One might abstract from the work an "idea" about knowledge as a process of knowing—as opposed to a set of knowns, whether factual or ideological. But the writing would mean to make it clear that such a view is itself another way of knowing the writing.

AM: And the poetry "unmasks" itself by its Brechtian theatricalities, by flaunting its artifices of absorption. Everyone is caught in these networks of illusion because everyone is moved by them to produce their meanings.

JJR: "A literature that proposes its own interpretations, enfolding these in sequence with interpretations of these interpretations" (CD 369).

AM: And thereby an imitation of the human world, since that world is defined as a world of signs, a signifying world, a world precisely made up of meanings.

GM: And a world with an impressive unanimity of academic thinking—"precisely" like your own! Not that I'm unimpressed or even uninstructed. But I don't believe either of you have really thought through what must be involved in this kind of writing. Bernstein's own "question persists" more emphatically than ever, about the appropriate "interpretive stance" toward a writing which "unmasks its own discontinuities" and "flaunts its core ideas as candy coating."

This is a poetry without a center, like Los Angeles, abandoned to its own flux. By refusing objective norms of order, by making "Thought's Measure" the musical arrangements that are discovered and laid down in the writing of writing, the verse loses the common reader. *The Sophist* is an impressive book of poetry, perhaps, but its title is suspicious and not a little disturbing.

AM: Perhaps Bernstein is working a poetics of suspicion and means to disturb the public order of language.

GM: Surely he is—and that's my point. Take the opening poem, or the opening lines of the opening poem:

The Simply

Nothing can contain the empty stare that ricochets
haphazardly against any purpose. My hands[11]

(Addressing AM) I recur to your earlier "instruction manual" on how to read this text. To take that direction is to put oneself in a "sophistic" situation where anything can mean virtually anything. The first sentence, for instance, may be taken to mean that "the empty stare" is uncontainable by anything—or, that "Nothing" is able to contain it (with or without the implication that containment is possible by other means). "The [sentence/poem] Simply" means/does not mean what it says—by which I do *not* mean to imply that that reading of the title is what it means. Rather, it's what it may be taken to mean.

This way of reading may take "the empty stare" as a figure of itself, where "Nothing" may be taken as the text (in an imagination of "Nothing" that follows upon the imagination of Wallace Stevens). Or perhaps the figure of the text is "any purpose," so that "ricochets / haphazardly" is the writing's figure of free interpretive possibility. On the other hand, "the empty stare" might just as easily be taken as a figure of the writing, with all the other terms shifting their significances accordingly.

Nothing (or "Nothing"??) here *insists* that we read the verse within the horizon of "literature": the terms might be read in another discourse framework altogether. So we're stymied again. The style signals Bernstein's deliberateness—but what else? Nothing. What does it *mean*?

Didn't you compare this writing to Swinburne's? All I can say is: indeed!

AM: It "means" that you have to answer your own question—like Asia in Shelley's *Prometheus Unbound*. Bernstein and Shelley—and Swinburne, since you bring him up again—argue that meaning does not preexist the language, or the specific acts of language, that make meaning. These poets use their own work to figure the activities of the social body of the world: as Swinburne once memorably put it, "being now no more a singer, but a song" ("Thalassius"). The opening poem of *Rough Trades* sets these ideas down as virtual (in both senses of that word) *propositions:*

The Kiwi Bird in the Kiwi Tree

I want no paradise only to be
drenched in the downpour of words, fecund
with tropicality. Fundament be-
yond relation, less "real" than made, as arms
surround a baby's gurgling: encir-
cling mesh pronounces its promise (not bars
that pinion, notes that ply). The tailor tells
of other tolls, the seam that binds, the trim,
the waste. & having spelled these names, move on
to toys or talcoms, skates & scores. Only
the imaginary is real—not trumps
beclouding the mind's acrobatic versions. The first fact is the social body,
one from another, nor needs no other.

Like *Artifice of Absorption,* the verse follows an observable expository line. Does it help to know that the work is a "generational" text not simply in an aesthetic but in a social sense: that Bernstein's father was a manufacturer of "ladies' dresses" and that the poem was written around the time of the birth of his first child? Perhaps, for "the first fact is the social body," and poems are, as JJR says, imitations of life.

Nevertheless, the poem's "argument" is inseparable from its

textual generations. In face of passages like "Only / the imaginary is real," the title may recall Marianne Moore's famous observation about poetry, imaginary gardens, and real toads. For whereas there are—in New Zealand—"real" kiwi trees and kiwi birds, their appearance "in" this poem, as much as the textual bird "in" the tree, is purely imaginary. The very oddness of the title argues this.[12] The poem's "social body" grows from its various real/imaginary correspondences.

GM: Sometimes you do make me laugh—I mean when you use phrases like "textual generations" and respond to ideas about the "social body" of poems. You ought to resist your tendency to think so abstractly about these matters. You ought to take the poems you like *into the streets.* Here, for instance, is some important information about this poem's real "social body" and "textual generations." "The Kiwi Bird and the Kiwi Tree" was first printed in *Jimmy and Lucy's House of "K".*[13] A bit later it appeared with three other poems by Bernstein in an issue of *Rethinking* MARXISM.[14] Now there you have some "social body"! I suppose I don't have to add that the poem is inclined to "mean" in very different ways when it's encountered in one or another of its three (current) textual contexts.

AM: Why so smug? What you say is interesting, I see that, I even think about it sometimes on my own. But a poem's "social body" isn't defined by its bibliographical codes. The "social body" of poetry is dispersed across all aspects of the work and not least at its ordinary language levels. It's a crude materialism that imagines the physique of writing gets exhausted in the bibliography and sociology of texts.

Take this poem's "real/imaginary correspondences"—so crucial to the work, in my view. They don't show themselves off very well at the text's bibliographical levels. But they do at the semantic and grammatological levels—most dramatically, perhaps, in the text's extreme playfulness. Bernstein's style means to rhyme with the "substantive" presence of the child and its world of toys and games: for example, through the wordplays in "tropicality" and "trumps," the latter making witty allusions to Christian days of judgment, on one hand, and to those very worldly Donald Trumps on the other, the contemporary incarnations of Mammon who are the princes of this world, the masters of its cities. Or think about the exceedingly suggestive connection of ion clouds and "acrobatic vers[e]."

The text enables these and a host of other "connections." Its insistent and (reasonably) organized thematic lines may encourage a fairly traditional reading—following on, for example, "The first fact is the social body" and (or) "Only / the imaginary is real." But even so the verse illustrates what Alan Davies has named the "Private Enigma in the Opened Text."[15] The poem's personal ("private") allusions cut this enigmatic figure in a traditional way, but the enigmatic appears throughout the work in even more *literal* forms. Our traditional thematizing will have no difficulty making sense of "be-" and "cling" and perhaps "vers-" and "ions" as well. But while the text opens itself to these "meaningful" fragments, it leaves behind certain troublesome residues (perhaps "the waste" spoken of in the poem). What, for instance, are we to make of "yond" and "encir-"? While these are the text's most manifest "private enigmas," they resist interpretive absorption, emerging as touchstones of what is most rich and meaningful in the poem. Because "yond" and "encir-" make (no) sense, they go begging for meaning.

So I conclude by repeating myself: Bernstein's poetry, even at its most statemental, operates a "production/exchange" that makes demands on the reader. Bernstein's "signification" put into play a system of autopoietic feedback loops, a generative intercourse. Paradoxically, it functions most clearly through its resistances, particularities, and "impermeable" features. His ideology of language—that everything signifies—reveals its inherent contradictions: minimally, that the ground of significance is the tension between the private, the enigmatic, the (non)sensical, on one hand, and the public, the plain, and the (in)sensible on the other. "Privacy [is] a central aspect of writing," he writes. "Poetry is a private act in a public space" (*CD* 77).

GM: If your reading of Bernstein's work is accurate, why doesn't it come under his own critique of "ideological mimesis" as he develops that concept in his essay "Living Tissue/Dead Ideas" (*CD* 363–82)? I realize that he's careful to distinguish a "literature" that works with "ideas [as] representations of concepts" (364) from a "literature"—Swinburne again!—that works with "ideas . . . as sound . . . *Thought* as mediating among these, superideational" (*CD* 368). And I also see that his own writing, especially the poems, tries to avoid the first and embrace the second. But if, as he says, all of poetry's "core ideas" are "candy coating," if no work "transcends its historical/ideological situation," then its living tissue will always be full of dead ideas. That metaphor embodies an objective and more than literal truth.

AM: "The Lives of the Toll Takers" is a good illustration of the symbiosis of living tissue and dead ideas—for example, through its simultaneous critique and reimagination of poetry in the slick idioms of contemporary linguistic junk.

> Our new
> service orientation
> mea
>
> nt
> not only changing the way we wrote poems but also
> diversifying
> into new poetry services. Poetic
> opportunities
> however, do not fall into your lap, at least not
> very often. . . .
>
>
> Keeping up with the new aesthetic environment is
> an ongoing process: you can't stand still. Besides . . .
> (studies show higher levels of resistance to double-bind
> political programming among those who read 7.7 poems
> or more
> each week
>).
> Poets deserve compensation
> for such services.
> For readers unwilling to pay the price
> we need to refuse to provide such
> service as alliteration
> internal rhymes,
> exogamic structure, and
> unusual vocabulary.
> Sharp edges which become shady groves,
> mosaic walkways, emphatic asymptotes (asthmatic
> microtolls).[16]

The text is a parodic recovery of certain key Shelleyan ideas. Not least significant is the understanding that poetry always speaks in a contemporary idiom—that its dialect(s), like everything else about it, are time and place specific.

Poetry must live and/or die in those idioms and particulars. This means that it must participate in their contradictions. The whimsical brilliance of "The Lives of the Toll Takers" calls to mind Shelley's "The Witch of Atlas," but the (t)issues are the same as those raised up, more famously, in the "Ode to the West Wind."

GM: But your argument, and Bernstein's poem, only re-situates the problem I'm seeing. Suppose I accept your Shelleyan analogue. It makes me want to ask: what part do "dead thoughts" play in the poetry of a "new birth"; why deliberately drive (those presumably dead) thoughts through (a presumably living) language into the world? Shelley imagines a poetry that comprises both "ashes and sparks"—like Bernstein's living tissues and dead ideas. But in your representation of Bernstein's work—and often in Bernstein's own self-representations—the best poetry is all spark ("superideational"), whereas the worst is ashes ("ideational mimesis"). This view struggles against the (contradictory) thought that poetry doesn't escape ideology (read here: Shelley's contemporary idiom). My difficulty is that Bernstein never resolves the contradiction. Nor do you.

AM: Why do you want it resolved? Who says it ought to be resolved? The poems *are* ashes and sparks—it's just that, in their living tissues, one cannot decide once and for all what is ash and what is spark. These distinctions are forged (are defined and imagined) when the poems are "read," in the writer's own initial reading of the text as well as in the many subsequent rereadings that rewrite the original work. "The Lives of the Toll Takers" reimagines some of the most corpsed language and thought of our day, including the language of promoters, of advertisers, and of poets (left and liberal alike).

GM: Is this just deconstructive and theoretical play you're involved with, or are you actually prepared to take your program to its limit?

JJR: Defenders of "traditional values" repeatedly issue dire warnings that if critical "free play" is licensed and approved, civilization will unravel. But there's no need to invoke the specter of wholesale cultural collapse to argue against a consumerist poetics.

I recall that Ron Silliman once criticized Bernstein's arguments (in the essay "Thought's Measure") for privacy and idleness in poetry: "Poetry is not produced in the personal sphere by those who publish—this is a major distinction between those who consume what they produce & those who exchange, as we do, their productions."[17] Like Bernstein in his response to Silliman, I would agree that poetry should be seen as a system of textual exchange rather than a system of production and consumption.

AM: On that argument, *anything* can be poetical.

GM: And Bernstein's poems plainly want to include as much diverse material as possible, from garbage to computers, from Verdi to postmodernism.

> David Melnick's
> *Men in Aida* may one day seem no more strange
> than Verdi's *Aida*—both composed in a foreign
> language, but once we know the score,
> it's pure song (AA 62–63)

But not everybody *wants* to know that score.

JJM: So? Frank O'Hara's "Manifesto" goes to *that* matter. Let a thousand flowers bloom. And there is such a thing as taking one's self too seriously.

Appendix to Chapter 6

Reading "The Simply"

> being less interested in representing than enacting.
> —Charles Bernstein,
> "State of the Art/1990"

For Bernstein, poetic "meaning" is never a product and hence cannot be coded or decoded. It's a process of writing through which "the before unapprehended relations of things" have to be attended to (in both senses of that phrase).[18]

Among the most important of those unapprehended relations are the ideological formations—the constellated sets of different social

opinions and understandings—that define (sometimes even dominate) "the way we live now." The poet's office, for Bernstein, is to put
those constellations at the reader's disposal.

Like Shelley, Bernstein pursues this revelation not for its own sake,
but to break the spell of ideology by dislocating its forms of representation. To read Bernstein is to take part in a (comic) play wherein "meaning" is dismembered. The difficulty arises from a process by which we
are alienated from the meanings of things that we thought we knew,
that in fact we did know. As Brecht might have said, "the fourth wall"
between poet and reader is taken away.

To do this means dramatizing the linguistic and semiological forms
by which social relations are constructed and managed. Bernstein's poetry often reads like a catalog of current clichés (drawn from various
social groups and institutional contexts), advertising slogans, nonce
expressions, and the like:

> *Something like* after
> a while I'm reading my book, go to store to get
> more stuff. "You're about as patient as the flame
> on a match." After the ceremony lunch was served
> by Mrs. Anne MacIssac, Mrs. Betty MacDonald, and Mrs. Catherine
> MacLeod, and consisted of tea, bannock, homemade cheese
> oatcakes and molasses cookies. We thank the ladies. Waste
> not, want not; but there's such a thing as being shabby.
> Which seems finally to move the matter, but in despair
> seeing "lived experience" as only possible under
> the hegemony of an ideology, an "imaginary." Started
> to do this, I corrected, he (they) demurred, I
> moved aside. Don't look up but she goes off. "Pleasant Bay news
> really hasn't dropped out, it was just on holiday."
> —"The Simply"[19]

This passage is a collage (or mobile) of social texts whose arbitrary
juxtaposition forces a clearer awareness of the specialized character
of each one and of the local world from which each draws its peculiar
life. The collaged structure may be taken as a minimally representational image of a modern or postmodern field of experience. Unlike a
modernist mobile, however, this ordering of randomness—the "meaning" of collage—is not the object of our attention. The text preserves

its nervousness and incompletion, as one would see even more clearly if the quotation were allowed to continue.

This passage does not have, that's to say, an order of finality. In terms of meaning, collage itself is a recognizable convention of meaning in a postmodern scene of writing (whereas in a modernist scene it appears as an innovation, an original meaning). In the present case the convention serves, on one hand, as another problem of meaning (e.g., "fret which is whirled / out of some sort of information"), and, on the other, as a *selva oscura* where one may find one's way, but only with difficulty (e.g., "guided by irritation"). I quote here from the opening section of the poem, and I signal both quotations by "e.g." because neither are precisely what my commentary might be taken to have said. Rather, the parts of this poem work by suggestion and are always dissolving away from the meanings we're tempted to bring to them. The heart of this poetry lies in those temptations toward meaning.

The text is not so much a secret communication as "a vocabulary and a set of rules by which it is processed."[20] What comes of such a text depends upon how the reader reconstructs the linguistic relationships: because choices will and indeed must be made if even the simplest act of reading is to proceed. But even that simplest act of reading emerges as a difficult operation to perform, in this sense: that readers can only go on if and as they are paying attention to their (chosen) act of reading. To read this text is to be forced, as Thoreau would have said (had his subject been texts rather than nature), to read deliberately. The ultimate subject of a text like this is the reader. It is a linguistic/ideological field, with textual units mirroring (or quoting from) a wildly various group of subject positions: from New Left discourse to society column news.

To read the text one must construct relations and relationships. As soon as one does so, however, the text responds by (as it were) reading the reader. For "the poem itself" does not "have a meaning" that the reader is expected to discover and articulate. The poem's difficulty arises exactly from its having refused to proceed according to those conventions of language use. The text assembles units of (various) conventional meaning-forms, but as a poem—as a field in which those units are ordered and encountered—their relations are left to the reader's devices. As soon as the reader acts within the textual field—as soon as he chooses certain options of reading—he is immediately drawn into the poetic space and reflected back to himself.

In these last comments I deliberately used the pronouns "he" and "himself" in order to emphasize the highly particular forms that every reading decision always involves. (Had I used the pronouns "her" and "herself" this fact would have been patent.) Those pronouns are a sign that the reader's subject-position is always gendered—masculine, feminine, neuter—whatever the sex of the reader. It makes a difference, according to the poetic logic of this kind of poem, how (and of course by whom) the reading is gendered. This is part of the subject of the poetry, just as "the reader" is always a specific individual.

The passage above is preceded by the following, which is the opening of the poem:

The Simply

Nothing can contain the empty stare that ricochets
haphazardly against any purpose. My hands
are cold but I see nonetheless with an' infrared
charm. Beyond these calms is a coast, handy but
worse for abuse. Frankly, hiding an adumbration of collectible
cathexis, catherized weekly, burred and bumptious;
actually, continually new groups being brought forward for
drowning. We get back, I forget to call, we're
very tired eating. They think they'll get salvation, but
this is fraudulent. Proud as punches—something like
Innsbruck, saddles, sashed case; fret which is whirled
out of some sort of information; since you ask. We're
very, simply to say, smoked by fear, guided by
irritation. Rows of desks. Something like after. . . .

The title itself "enacts," as Bernstein might say, a problem of reading and thereby puts the reader in an acute state of attention. As one moves through this text one searches out relations and (inevitably) discovers various kinds: the odd sequence of adverbs, for example; the repetitions with variations ("something like" and "Something like"; "we're / very tired eating" and "we're / very, simply to say . . ."; "The Simply" and "simply to say"; etc.); and possible thematic rhymes among different parts of the sequence. For the latter, one cues to several phrases and images that suggest boredom, irritation, and a general condition of quandariness. The text as a whole seems to take no particular attitude toward its various units, but in that very appearance of indifference, certain possibilities of meaning emerge. One wonders, for example, if the first sentence might not be taken for the poem's "topic sentence," a statement about the rich (uncontainable) value of the poem's flat and "empty stare" back at us. In this reading the "purpose" would be an equivalent of the reader's search for meaning, and the "empty stare" would be the poem's device of indifference, which might only increase the reader's imperative toward meaning.

Other readings are of course possible. Indeed, the way the units of this poem "ricochet" off each other may be taken as a sign that it is enacting its own stimulus toward reading and meaning.

Bernstein's poetry turns out, as a result, a kind of comedy of errors, with the reader (we are many) playing the principal role(s). American traditions of screwball comedy—the Marx Brothers, Laurel and Hardy—have had a deep influence on his work. There is a wonderfully comic moment about half-way through "The Simply" when the text turns to satirize "the reader of poetry." The passage appears as a random quotation from (evidently) some missionary's journal or letter to a friend or superior.

> "For all that
> we have not up to the present noticed any more
> Religion among these poor savages than among *brutes;*
> this is what wrings our hearts with compassion, if
> they could know themselves what they themselves are
> worth, and what they cost him *who has loved us all*
> *so much.* Now what consoles us in the midst
> of this ignorance and barbarism, and what makes us hope
> to see the Faith widely implanted, is partly the *docility*
> they have shown in wishing to be instructed, and partly
> the honesty and decency we observe in them; for
> they listen to us so diligently concerning the mysteries
> of our Faith, and repeat after us, whether *they understand*
> *it or not,* all that we declare to them."

Part of the joke here is plainly the double take that such a passage encourages. This text's "we" will be read to mean something like "the sentences of the present poem" or (more generally) "poets"; and "these poor savages," with their "honesty and decency," are . . . ourselves? Yes, of course. The joke is especially wonderful and outrageous because the passage is so elaborate, and yet every one of its details may be translated to an immediate application for "the reader." Once again, not a representation but an enactment of meaning, with the reader as a key player in the events. And the passage allows its further implications to wind out—for example, that reading is as much a social act as practical behavior in the world is a way of reading; or, that acts of appropriation break open the world in ways that power cannot contain and control; or even that anything can (and does, or does not) mean anything.

As the poem proceeds, its subject—the enactment rather than the representation of meaning—becomes, I think, more strongly thematized at the level of the enactments. The missionary passage is blatantly thematic, and so is the following, toward the poem's conclusion:

> Don't you find it chilly
> sitting with your Silly? Yet things
> beguile us with their beauty
> their sudden irascibility: the hay of the
> imagination is the solace of a dry soul; which
> is to say, keep yourselves handy since
> you may be called on at any hour.
> One wants almost to shudder (yawn, laugh . . .) in disbelief
> at the hierarchization of consciousness in such a dictum
> as "first thought, best thought," as if recovery
> were to be prohibited from the kingdom;
> for anyway "first thought" is no thinking
> at all. There is no 'actual space of.' So
> quiet you can hear the clouds gather. Weep
> not, want not; but there's such a thing as being
> numb.

"First thought, best thought" is a reference to Allen Ginsberg, who liked to take this "dictum" as an essential truth about poetry. Bernstein's text moves against such a thought—rethinks it—by situating us in a text that foregrounds the process of reflection. At all points Bernstein's text seduces us with imaginative options—"shudder (yawn, laugh . . .)." Its religious faith is the "disbelief" that Brecht said would move mountains, and its "kingdom" is of *this* world rather than an imaginary other, this world of imaginative reflection and recreation.

One tracks the movement of such poetry at its many odd transitional points, where readers are forced to swerve out into unexpected directions. These may be simple moments of syntactic conjugation— the "yet" of the second quoted line; the colon and the semicolon of the fourth and fifth—or semantic dislocations ("beauty"/"irascibility")— or unexpected connections to other moments in the poem (e.g., the arbitrary rhyme that the last sentence of this quotation makes with the seventh and eighth lines of the first passage I quoted).

The closing lines of the poem are, in all these respects, typical of the work:

> "You have such a horrible sense of equity which
> is inequitable because there's no such
> things as equity." *The text, the beloved?*
> Can I stop living when the pain gets too
> great? Nothing interrupts this moment.
> False.

The joke of that final word is that it also, simultaneously, means its opposite. But not only its opposite. The movement away from fixed meanings is not always, or even principally, a binary recoil. It takes place rather at tangents and Dickinsonian slants, at what Tennyson called the "strange diagonal" of poetry. In the last two sentences, for instance, the reader may observe that the "nothing" that does or doesn't "interrupt this moment" recalls the "nothing" from which the poem originally set forth:

> Nothing can contain the empty stare that ricochets
> haphazardly against any purpose.

Not for nothing is "The Simply" placed as the opening poem of a book Bernstein titled *The Sophist*.

7
From Sight to Shenandoah

A few years ago the editor of the *Bellingham Review* proposed the following two works—a passage from Scalapino and Hejinian's *Sight*, the text of Bernstein's "Shenandoah"—as representative examples of contemporary experimental writing.[1] What kind of commentary, she asked, "might help a general audience understand these poets' tactics a little better"?

The academic commentaries in the earlier chapters of this book address the editor's question. But that kind of writing isn't what the editor wanted. Why? So that a professor with academic credentials might come to the rescue of some estranged readers? Perhaps. I've never known. But the assignment made me think that such a question is always in play, even for our traditional poetic inheritance. Has it used itself up? Was Byron talking about more than himself when he observed:

> I have spent my life, both interest and principal,
> And deem not, what I deemed, my soul invincible.
> —*Don Juan*, canto 1, st. 213

And yet how inspiriting that expression of bankruptcy! Several years earlier, when he was shoring up his ruins with a bolder front, he put the same point very differently, imagining himself as a Promethean figure,

> Triumphant where it dares defy,
> And making Death a Victory.
> —"Prometheus," 58–59

Not only is there a time for every purpose under heaven, there is a style
as well. Even among enlightened and professional critics, we who are
trained and "presumed to know." *Nous sont une autre.*[2] Then what of "we
who love to be astonished"?[3] How do we express ourselves when our astonishment tells us that "an adequate mode of expression is senseless"?[4]

There are ways, as we know from the writings of Lewis Carroll, Swinburne, Wilde, and any number of twentieth-century writers, not least
Gertrude Stein. Sometimes these astonished styles come seriously engaged, as in the commentary on Goethe that culminates H. D.'s *Trib-
ute to Freud* or as in Susan Howe's *My Emily Dickinson*. Sometimes it is
playful and even outrageous, as in many of Bernstein's critical works.
In any case, the style requires that nonnormative procedures be made
a regular feature of the critical method.

Here then are the two pieces of "experimental writing" chosen by
the *Bellingham Review* editor. They took me by surprise because I had
no hand in their selection. That surprise, I would later see, invited a
less enlightened style of commentary.

I begin in full astonishment mode, this time on your behalf, by getting out of the way of both yourselves and the poetry

from *Sight*
by Leslie Scalapino and Lyn Hejinian

I find myself listening to music as if struggling against
inevitability—it and I are (as) one, at the limit, and I'm about to
make one of those ludicrous false steps that fell one. That's fate:
I can't go on (with remorse and regret). Like the philosopher I
must say, I'm no one's guilty conscience, and certainly not my
own
        —rain freezing on slick asphalt, people falling,
perhaps I'm feverish, I want to see—I seem to be the only one
who isn't cold—but then a suicidal riderless horse dragging its
reins appears, eyes wide, neck broken, head bent to the right,
chest straining, it moves against orders—every struggle for
thought pits the ponderous against the fast—yes, well, so as to
hide but also so as to see, they eat into each other's lips, that's
what it's like to say inevitability can't be unemployed—
        in a struggle.

The successful struggler must constantly add positions.
She jumps graciously out of the field with her skirt up and into

an interval. This event has its own duration—it doesn't "unfold over time," it remains in its fold, employed—
her great neck wet with sweat from pulling.

(LH)

The suicidal riderless horse wide-eyed, neck broken already, is the emanation of one to oneself in exhaustion but appearing to others "inevitably"—who are unemployed in the sense of happening by chance to be seen there also, not "for a purpose."

The struggler in the state of exhaustion is the observer within that one—"within" is what unfolds though not appearing to, not caused by exhaustion, separately transpiring to a clear aim (not in apprehension). (Is the exhaustion the same as the illness?—sense of it not being)

The viscous wet neck after it is dawn—one having missed seeing dawn/separation—has its own duration, apart from that observer
                    the eyes are not of the neck
                    wide-eyed the neck being a "mere" appendage
                        flapping

(LS)

The neck of a sibling being is visible in the shadow under the chin of the leaning rider who keeps his consciousness of choices (the rider feels the weariness of false choices)
    Faltering
                visibility *makes* the being
                    lean over
    "marking out form"
Coupled to visibility's trembling form
Eyed by inevitability
    But, really, inevitability is what accumulates ahead of false continuities

(LH)

Visibility makes what is seen—?—Empty careening head that is in angry circular rushes, where there isn't substance for these it occurs anyway—as its physiological habit.

           ghosts are only during life.

    Accumulation ahead of continuities: a woman who was going to be married had been murdered by a prowler, leaving her boyfriend wrecked by this event.

    Two days after her death as if a wind she entered and passed through the house at dawn to the bedroom of the couple who had been going to perform the ceremony. The woman of the couple shot up in bed in fear, the man saying to be calm the dead one would pass on. The intense presence was restless and in disturbance. She passed through the wall and left the house.

    So they're making the life going on past occurrence.

Which could be then pleasurable.

    The wild motions in one are seen and their former substance or origination is a "visibility" itself—which may be hardly remembered or remembered with utter clarity—but the

        tortured

wild motions in one would occur anyway.

    Without what bothers one. (Yet one is tortured.)

    The Romantics either European or Japanese were perhaps the discoverers that one is living-ghosts as being present activity—not being of dying—dying seems utterly separate.

           fear is expanded—

                  (LS)

    A ghost comes of its own volition "to work on the wall."

This would be very expressive activity for the living previous person, the one existing before it cast its ghost, but the ghost is, as it were, working on the wrong side (the outside—*beyond the limit*) of the wall.

    The sound it makes is too loud, but this work is a past occurrence—carried out by someone very beautiful (in "wild motions") and thus too much looked at (shown up).

    But one cannot offer the ghost a smile of recognition.

    Jalal Toufic says the great problem for the dead is that of continuation (unfinished business). (The ghost) it has the problem of not being there where it hasn't been—a problem of regret, yes, but also of self-replication: (the ghost) any self is constantly remaking the person from which it was cast to no end.

The sudden (shown up) death of a youth (unfinished) is separated from him by a narrator: a preliminary comment: a great number of stories are based on errors: the lover is mistaken for a thief: the (plucked) necklace turns out to have been the simplest form of plot construction: handsome and innocent, your head will forever sleep on your hands.

(LH)

We're on the level here of winter light only—no one out—yet in it trees enflamed in a red leaves sea.
   the one dead isn't fatigued

Whereas work in jobs for living—generates more and more of itself only. There is a sole consciousness existing in winter light, so that is apart from one too.
   The sole consciousness, of ones, that begins to exist in red leaves sea aflame only—outside—isn't part of a dead person or one
   self-replication—a double which is also sole, empty
   fear that in living ones working on the wrong side of the wall with those others (dead) being on that side, the same side of the wall—and can't be to be there
   a double membrane—who may be one—though can't be with them
   people clamor as in a bureaucracy—for more and more events—the one without a soul isn't drunk—In loneliness and beached—the wild motions do not meet up
   yet—Occur—as them—attentiveness to oneself, who is not existing
   faculties aren't dulled in winter light separating—there's a sole consciousness at one time or another

(LS)

Shenandoah (for Ben Yarmolinski)
by Charles Bernstein

Oh Shenandoah, I long to near you
Through fogged and fumbling shallows
Oh Shenandoah, why don't you hear me?

Astray, I'm bound to sway
Midst these stifling borders

Oh Shenandoah, why must I trample
All that I behold before me?
Oh Shenandoah, I wish no other
No other than to sway
Near your wobbling borders

Oh Shenandoah, I'm only moisture
Only fog and fumbling shadows
Oh Shenandoah, I'm all deception
Astray, I'm bound to go
Midst these heaving waters

Oh Shenandoah, why don't you take me?
Engulf me in your weaving?
Oh Shenandoah, why must I lose you?
To lose, to lose myself
Near, so near, your borders

Oh Shenandoah, I long to near you
Past the wobbling endurings
Away—beyond the steaming shadows
Away—I'm bound away
Bound to these stifling borders

Oh Shenandoah, I hear you coming
Come and go and never touch me
Oh Shenandoah, I'm more than moisture
Swept away swept away
I'm more than moisture swept away
From your enduring

Oh Shenandoah, I've traveled far to hold you
Don't deny my desperate pleadings
Oh Shenandoah, I wish no other
Other than to sway
Other than to sway
Other than to sway
Within your rolling borders

Oh Shenandoah, let me forget you
I want no image of your teeming valleys
Oh Shenandoah, let me forget you
Forget the promise, forget the promise
Of your hollow heaving

What makes this writing difficult? Is it that the poetry seems to lack a clear subject or theme, like Yeats's "The Second Coming" or Lowell's "Skunk Hour"? Not all poetry proposes to be about something. Are Edward Lear's best poems about anything beyond the pleasures of their texts? Or what *about* Stevens's "The Emperor of Ice Cream" or Ashbery's "Farm Elements and Rutabagas in a Landscape"? T. S. Eliot urged people who had no Italian to read Dante in Italian. Dante, that most intellectual of poets! Eliot thought such a regimen would help train one to read poetry better.

Some poetry, it's true, emphasizes ideas or other referential content—known or rememberable conditions or persons. It needn't do so, it might deal in nonsense or pure fantasy, it might play games with images or sounds. And then there are poems that plainly deal in content—*Sight* is an excellent example—but they mean to hold their content in pure prospect. *Sight* is a poem that doesn't face backward, as it were, but forward. It begins in a discovery ("I find myself") that passes immediately into a figure of desire, a figure "listening to music as if struggling against inevitability." These are words that strain forward precisely because of the "limit" they experience. They are their own limit, these words, and so the heard melody of desire transforms itself through its desire and becomes—another sense, "sight": "I want to see." Desire being the law of this text, desire gets fulfilled in the revelation of the "suicidal riderless horse." And so it goes, careening through its transformations. As the text passes on its words, it discovers (we discover) that the passage produces further ranges of "meaning." ("The successful struggler must constantly add positions.") And so "content" accumulates along the way as the messages are carried out (carried forward). *Sight* is a text going through that kind of discovery of meaning.

"Sight," seeing—what is it? You fix your eyes on something and then, you think, there it is. A definite thing, defined? Yes, but only for a brief moment. If you keep looking you will keep seeing it change, you will see it differently. It changes because the act of seeing alters what is seen just by imagining a defined site of seeing. In that act of definition we are forced into a dialogue with what we have imagined to be the case.

Sight is a site of dialogue, an exchange. It keeps going on, and as one goes with it, one sees and sees again. The metamorphoses of the riderless horse, visible forms that come back as ghosts, "wild" words and their associates. And what we see turns obscure even as it grows defined. Words seem to slip away from themselves in their intercourse with each other. Shapes change as well as the negative spaces of the shapes. And through this process a world you hadn't imagined continues to reappear, you see it unfolding, emerging from what you saw and from what you didn't see, from what was said and from what was left unsaid, from what was called attention to and from what wasn't. ("Any self is constantly remaking the person from which it was cast to no end.")

Shelley once urged poets to imagine what they know, and that is an important way to write. It isn't the only way, and Shelley himself often wrote in other ways. In ways that are closer to the way of *Sight,* where we read poets trying, as another contemporary poet puts it, to imagine what they don't know. The dialogue of this text is the dominant sign of that effort. One poet writes and evolves a discovery of words. Then the other looks at that discovery and writes from what she saw what she comes to see. And that writing is then looked at, and the discovering gets replicated anew, from the other side of the dialogue. The chief figure of that endless dialogue, in this text, is "the wall." It is a figure that stands for the page bearing the text, for the spaces between the words and the characters, for the "double membrane" of the dialogue itself.

This text does not want its readers intimidated by what we don't know or understand. Socrates was judged a wise man because he knew he didn't know. So the text, in midst of other woe than ours,[5] says to us: read on, go on, keep your eyes open, watch what happens along the way, watch the changes. *Sight* is a textual condition that is imagining what it doesn't know. It means to include us in its revelatory passages.

And so does "Shenandoah" but in a very different way. Here's a poem carrying baggage, a poem facing backward, like Benjamin's angel. Its whole text bears remembering, "Shenandoah." And not just remembering either! Bernstein's "Shenandoah" seems a kind of travesty of the old song. Does it read like doggerel? It *is* doggerel. If that's a problem for the reader, it shouldn't be.

Many people, it's true, think doggerel's not poetry. But what's "poetry"? That old song? A famous poem by Byron or Pope? They're only documentary records; they have to be kept alive in the present. Do we want to imagine there are kinds of writing that would be, by definition, unpoetical. Pornography, perhaps? Well, Lord Rochester (among others) has shown us otherwise.

The truth is what Marianne Moore (among others) thought: that a poem might be better for including apparently unpoetical material, like business documents. Making poetry out of doggerel might be a good idea—just the sort of thing an ambitious poet could get interested in. Like choosing a difficult form arbitrarily. Browning, I seem to remember, said he always had a fascination for doggerel.

Or how do you make poetry out of all those poetical documents that come down to us—out of Yeats, or Crabbe, or "Shenandoah"? It isn't so easy; they've come to breathe such an official atmosphere. Far simpler to turn them into cultural objects—what Bernstein here calls "teeming valleys." Things of beauty that may be thought joys forever, images of the best that has been known and thought in the world. The old beautiful songs. But none of that "is" *poetry.*

Bernstein's "Shenandoah" sets about thinking through all those issues. So Bernstein begins with an old song he takes to be a pure product of America, at once figure and expression of its deepest desires. It's a sailor's song about a river that never reaches the sea. And he treats it emblematically, identifying the song, the river, and his own immediate writing, all of which have the same name. The name of a river that never reaches the sea.

The old song moves, like the new one, through incremental repetitions. It has only three stanzas, and each stanza has five lines: the first line gets repeated in the third line, while the second, fourth, and fifth lines get repeated in each of the three stanzas. This means that the song as a whole has only six integral linear units. Each stanza has one unique line, the first:

> Oh Shenandoah, I long to hear you
> Oh Shenandoah, I love your daughter
> Oh Shenandoah, I'm bound to leave you.

These three lines sketch the song's simple structure, which is a narrative of romantic longing. In Bernstein's "Shenandoah," however, romantic longing returns as impeded desire: "Bound to these stifling borders" and the "weaving" (wobbling, swaying) networks of this writing, as well as the writing on which it is written.

A kind of palimpsest, the poem is a "reading" of the old song. In this reading the impediments are seen as internal to the desire itself, functions of a song that is (contradictorily) "bound to leave." So when Bernstein's poem undergoes the old song, a revelation may develop that encompasses more than the elementary words of the text. But the revelation begins at that elementary level, as we see in the double meaning and paradoxes that Bernstein's text enforces: "I long to near you" (I long too near you); "to sway" ("enduring" as well as "wobbling" and "weaving"); "bound" (as in being doubly "bound away / Bound to these stifling borders"). The poem is constructed from these kinds of self-conscious replications of the old song, which undergoes a critical—even a satirical—visitation. But Bernstein's is no facile debunking, for the parody, like the parodies of Carroll and Lear, is every bit as sentimental as the original song—perhaps even more sentimental, its sentimentality being so self-conscious.

> Oh Shenandoah, let me forget you
> I want no image of your teeming valleys
> Oh Shenandoah, let me forget you
> Forget the promise, forget the promise
> Of your hollow heaving

But of course the poem cannot forget, the old song runs forever in the poem's head—as it must, by the rule of this undertaking itself. "The promise / Of your hollow heaving" is partly a social and partly an artistic promise, both of which Bernstein inherits (as an American, as a poet). It is the promise of loss:

Oh Shenandoah, why must I lose you?
To lose, to lose myself
Near, so near, your borders

These borders are the equivalent of the "wall" in *Sight*. They turn Bernstein's poem into a kind of political map whose subject is American history, the land of the lost and "hollow promise" whose failures (our failures) only regenerate the call to promise.

And doggerel is the poem's governing sign of this perpetuated loss and betrayal. Bernstein's doggerel returns to the sentimentality of the old song and makes a rhyme with it. Here is one (here are many) whose name is writ in water:

Oh Shenandoah, I'm only moisture
Only fog and fumbling shadows
Oh Shenandoah, I'm all deception
Astray, I'm bound to go
Midst these heaving waters

"Midst": the poetical archaism is perfect. "Engulf me in your weaving?" And so it does. Bernstein's burlesque and doggerel moments enact those engulfments, where poems are reborn—old songs, new poems—in a comical despair of their possibility.

III
It Must Give Pleasure

8

Marxism, Romanticism, Postmodernism
An American Case History

PROF. J: Then what can it mean, to practice a Marxist literary criticism?

PROF. M.: As an American issue in the post-Vietnam period, Marxism in literary studies has largely involved the appropriation of a set of interpretive tools of a sociological and historical character. Marxian models set a special privilege upon materialist analyses of culture and society. Investigations of literary and artistic products—even primarily formal or hermeneutical investigations—require, from a Marxian perspective, detailed study of the social and institutional determinant of cultural practice.

To the degree that Marxian thought has (historically) invested itself in a philosophy of historical determinism, its protocols for studying cultural works have tended to be coherently, sometimes even rigidly, organized. Marxian thought has always been closely tied to teleological, holist, and organic conceptions of human activity. This slant in Marxian thinking has proved significant so far as its Americanization is concerned. Its holism marries well with some of the synthetic critical trends of mid- and late-twentieth-century American aesthetic theory. I'm thinking here of all the various types of high formalisms—from Eliot's neoclassicism to New Critical, structuralist, and psychoanalytic methods.

PROF. J.: In a Marxist view, however, synthetic processes are structured as a dialectic of collisions and contradictions. Classical Marxist theory inclines to display cultural works—poems or novels—as reflections, perhaps even instances, of significant social instabilities or dislocations. There is a liberal American equivalent of those kinds of contradictions that the New Criticism called "ambiguity." And while a clear analogy may be seen between these two ideas ("contradiction" and "ambiguity"), in the end they are just as clearly quite different. Where the one—ambiguity—serves to fund stabilities and continuities via what we would call a liberal and pluralist imagination, the other—contradiction—has in view instabilities and more or less radical change.

PROF. A.: This all seems a fairly abstract way of coming at your initial question about the practice of, the praxis of, a Marxist criticism.

PROF. M.: Well, if I talk here about "ideas" and "conceptions," I'm trying to describe and partially explain actual institutional behavior. I'm thinking about the ideological practices of certain parts of the American academy and about specific books, essays, and the pedagogical strategies they've produced.

This is important to remember in the context of the American academic scene of the past forty years or so, when we saw the emergence of "deconstruction in America." For the conceptual self-representations of deconstruction often display remarkable congruities with important aspects of Marxian thought. In the period of deconstruction, "ambiguity" and "tension" gave way to "the hermeneutics of suspicion"—of "repressed contents," of "instabilities," of contradiction. Indeed, Marxian ideas and literary strategies flooded the American academic market in this very period. This is not to say that Marxian thought and deconstruction represent, or imagine themselves to be, congruent movements in recent American literary studies. On the contrary, in fact: for the social and historical orientation of Marxism has generally been despised by the subject-oriented procedures of deconstruction, while the latter has often been judged simply as a set of textual technologies, more or less useful as technologies, but utterly void of an activist social agenda. Ivory tower shoptalk fairly defined by that favorite and ludicrous word: *transgressive*.

This schematic history is familiar to all of us, I dare say. I give it here only to draw attention to a crucial element in Marxism that I've not yet emphasized and that your initial question clearly had in mind: Marxism's commitment to fundamental (as opposed to reformist) social change. This commitment is foundational in the precise historical sense that Marxism is a reflection upon capitalist society made from the point of view of people living alienated within that society. A Marxian view is that alienation is class based, that it is systematic, and that it can only be overcome by a radical transformation of political, social, and economic relations.

Permit me a brief but I hope not irrelevant digression. In the period since the Russian Revolution, the most important and influential Marxian thought did not emerge from that originary "Marxist" and socialist society, the Soviet Union. For the past eighty years Marxian thought has flourished, as it did from the first, in various pre- or parasocialist societies: the Western societies of Europe still dominated by capitalism or even by fascism, the third world, China. The exceptions to this rule—most spectacularly, the work of Mikhail Bakhtin and his circle—operated at the periphery of Soviet cultural life. Their work came into play only after the brief and blessed time of Mayakovsky.

Reactionary commentators observing this situation take it as the sign of a god that failed, definitive proof of the poverty of Marxian theory and practice. But a "Marxian"—as opposed to a "Soviet"—view of the matter would be, has been, very different. For it is arguable, and it has been argued (by New Left Marxists), that to the extent the Soviet Union organized itself—bureaucratized itself—against change and its own social contradictions, it had merely abandoned its revolutionary programs. Trotsky and Luxemburg stand at the head of a long and sometimes tragic red line that found its culmination in 1989.

In the late-twentieth-century emergence of a significant body of Marxian thought in America, then, an important question arises and must be faced: how does the Marxian critical imperative operate in the theater of American pluralism? Have Marxian ideas been appropriated to the American scene as a set of research tools and protocols for literary scholars, or do they involve a radical critique of the American theater of pluralism and perhaps even a program of fundamental social and institutional change?

PROF. J.: That's exactly my question. And the problem strikes particularly at the work of certain Marxist-influenced critics and scholars whose work focuses on the modern period (i.e., the period that saw the rise of the novel, the institutionalization of Kantian-based aesthetics, and the emergence of American culture). This is of the period of triumphant capitalist development, early to late (so-called). For Marxist criticism, in that context, necessarily finds itself in an acutely problematical relation to its own materials, subject matter, and procedures.

I can explain this best by instancing the rise of "new historicism" in literary studies. This general rubric locates a heterogeneous group of academics who operate in sociohistorical frames of reference. Marxist-influenced critics and scholars have sometimes been associated with this phenomenon, but to the degree that they embrace Marxist ideas and procedures, they have generally refused to be included in the designation. Marjorie Levinson explains this refusal by observing that "historicisms," whether the "old" nineteenth-century kind or the "new" types (like those associated with the journal *Representations*), do not characteristically make a problem of their own subject matter and critical procedures.[1] Historicism, new or old, is fundamentally a structural and formal set of operations; Marxist criticism, by contrast, is not Marxist if it is not dialectical.

Let's not forget: Marxism is a set of tools and ideas that emerged in a critical relation to its own immediate context (capitalism). Its founding years mark the period of its so-to-speak "happy consciousness," the period when Marxist studies underwrote themselves with the systematic formalisms appropriated from Hegelian categories. But Marxism, the critical method that included history in its procedures, would eventually find itself included in history—included in ways it had not been able to imagine and, least of all, foresee. As a consequence, Marxist thought from approximately 1930 to 1990 was driven to operate at a metacritical level. A set of descriptive, analytical, and problem-solving tools for studying human beings and societies in their historical relations, Marxist thought was "in the last analysis" forced to include itself in its own critical equations. Marxism, like its nemesis Christianity, turned out a variable value as much as any other.

PROF. M.: Yes, and this understanding was forced by Marxism's own most privileged category, the experience of history. Unfolding events brought profound theoretical crises to Marxism, crises that proved a theoretical boon to its subsequent New Left developments. From the heterologies of Bakhtin and the Frankfurt School to the (so-called) post-Marxism of Bourdieu, Baudrillard, and de Certeau, Marxian thought developed an astonishing range of critical skills for the study of cultural phenomena.

These tools and skills have been widely appropriated in American literary studies, and not only during the past forty years or so. American critical work in the 1930s and 1940s—the great period of the New Criticism—was far from abandoning Marxist ideas and commitments. F. O. Matthieson, Kenneth Burke, Francis Cornford: these dominant figures, as well as many others, achieved eminence because of the critical power of their Marxian inheritance.

Nonetheless, in America a question persists and never more so than in this continuing present of ours: has the implementation of Marxian critical strategies become a new kind a formalism, simply another "method" or "critical structure" in the market of literary studies?

PROF. J.: Clearly the answer must be yes. Look at the textbooks and anthologies used in "Literary Theory" classes! One finds a pluralist representation of the situation quite common now— in the way departments display themselves to prospective students and faculty, in the organization of courses in criticism and theory, in the eclectic (one might even say balkanized, or pragmatic) conceptualization of critical activities generally. Like feminism, reader response, deconstruction, new historicism, queer and ecological studies, and so on, Marxian studies represent a procedural option one may choose to identify with (as a move in one's personal goals within the educational institution) or a set of critical strategies one may decide to employ or not, depending on the circumstances. Indeed, as modern Marxism has deliberately underprivileged itself, as it has laid itself under its own historical critique, it has been opened to liberalizing processes.

PROF. M.: But in that event, as I've said, Marxist work in America has raised a difficult problem for itself. It is a serious question now whether the pluralization of Marxist thought is part of a self-critical investigative procedure, an opening of its own doors of perception, or whether such pluralization entails an abandonment of critical reflection altogether, a turning away from—even a tacit acceptance of—the real contradictions and disfigurements in American society, and a concentration upon merely formal and subjective matters (for example, the development of various technical skills and methods, or what we call literary criticism, and the pursuit of the theology of the text, or what we call literary theory).

PROF. A.: A particularly acute form of this problem emerges in the work of Professor Jerome McGann—an American scholar whose work centers in that pivotal modernist moment, the Romantic period. Unlike Fredric Jameson and/or Terry Eagleton—the one primarily a theoretician, the other primarily a critic of culture—McGann has never been anything but a critic and scholar in the narrowest sense.

PROF. M.: Given his editorial and bibliographical work, perhaps even a pedant.

PROF. A.: Indeed. His interpretive work characteristically gravitates around readings of particular texts, interpretations whose models come from the period of the New Criticism. These interpretations, moreover, are grounded in sets of detailed and often highly technical matters—scholarly, archival, not to say dryasdust materials drawn forth in order to highlight those sociohistorical aspects of a text occluded at the surface of its various illusions. Jameson and Eagleton generate literary interpretations, but they do not worry their documents with the often microscopic attention that McGann insists upon. That McGann is also a scholarly editor, an editorial theorist, and a textual scholar (in the technical sense of that technical term) is not surprising. Besides, if his work shows the marked influence of Bakhtin, Benjamin, and Habermas—seminal figures for all current Marxist studies—his scholarly face is revealed in two other unusual, but probably even more important, influences. The Italian Marxists Galvano della Volpe and Sebastiano Timpanaro are invoked at crucial moments in his work, and both of these critics are themselves, like McGann, distinctly scholastic figures—persons who used to be called, and who are still often called, philologians (at least in the traditional European university system, both Eastern and Western).

So McGann's work is often highly technical and specialized. Adorno might have scorned it as positivist. Yet because McGann unequivocally situates his work in Marxian terms, it's fair to ask in what its Marxism could consist.

This problem can be illuminated, I think, by beginning with one of his foundational ideas: his social theory of "the text." McGann's view here cuts sharply across, and against, the theory of the text that stretches from the New Criticism, on one hand, and Barthesian and deconstructive theory on the other. McGann does not move into an interpretive operation without having first analyzed "the text" into three distinct phases or aspects. As he puts it, one must distinguish "the text" (or the poem as a purely linguistic event) from the "version" (or the immediate and integral physical object "through which" the "text" is being executed) and make yet a further distinction of "text" and "version" from the "work" (this term to stand for some more global constitution of any writing activity).[2]

These distinctions arise from his documentary microstudies. The critical and interpretive exposures that flow from his procedures are clearly marked by these (dare I say old-fashioned?) philological pursuits.

Correlative with this "theory of the text" is a set of investigative methods designed to clarify the literary event even further. According to McGann, literary works are best conceived as events rather than as objects, as acts of representation rather than as representations. I shall return to this important idea later. For the moment we should observe that this eventual conception of literary works entails certain specific investigative procedures. Criticism is structured as a kind of double helix, an interconnected investigation of both the textual history of the work and its reception history. Interpretation begins as a set of extremely detailed descriptions of the literary work at every level of its structure and every phase of its development. For McGann, these would be, if they could be, exhaustive. To display the operations of this double helix—to observe the historical interaction of its two strands (textual history and reception history)—is to raise the literary work out of a historical amnesia.

These operations, according to McGann, always and inevitably reveal a Bakhtinian heteroglossia. The textual history imbeds different and often conflicting voices even at its most primitive

levels (at the linguistic level and at the level of the work's originary, "authorial" constitution). These "textual" voices only multiply further as the work moves through its later developments—
through its many subsequent material constitutions, its many
"versions" (as McGann calls them). A congruent and interactive
situation prevails in the work's reception history, which is marked
by a similar multiplicity of voices. For McGann, to expose these
complex and interacting sociohistories is in itself a critical act, an
act of remembering.

One last detail of this general project should be clarified. For
McGann, the complex dialectic of social subjects living and dead
is ideological at every point, with "ideology" here understood in
the classical Marxian sense of "false consciousness." As he puts it
in a recent formulation, "the body of literature is a body of falsehood" whose function is Blakean: to "Give a Body to Falshood
that it may be cast off for ever."[3] The phrase "for ever" is there understood as a process that goes on "for ever," *in perpetuum* rather
than *in eternum*. Thus if he says, after Arnold, that literature embodies "the best that has been known and thought in the world,"
he also says, after Benjamin, that "every document of civilization
is at the same time a document of barbarism."

Now, to the degree that this structure of thought confronts
Kantian-based conceptions of art and literature, it clearly represents a radical departure. In this view literary work (including those specific events we call "literary works") is not disinterested, is not aesthetic, is not only subjective. Furthermore, it is
not even integral and self-consistent. All such work is in every
case, in all such works, marked not merely by the classic Marxian "contradiction," but also displays random elements, as well
as patterns of congruence and incongruence, consequence and
inconsequence. The structure is much closer to what mathema-
ticians call "fractal," a form of "chaos" in the technical sense of
that term.

This imagination of works of imagination as "chaotic"—as
eventual forms marked equally, and contradictorily, by order and
randomness—institutes a radical critique of the dominant Western and capitalist ideas about art and literature over the past two
hundred years. It is a theory of literature, moreover, as we have
seen, deeply in debt to the entire history of Marxian thought.

But is it Marxist? The problem is not so much a theoretical one, that McGann's thought contravenes certain (apparently essential) Marxist ideas about the organic and dialectical structure of literary works, and about the historically determinate character of every social event, including that social event we call poetry or literature. These ideas are certainly contravened by McGann, whose subjects of study display at every point both determinacy and indeterminacy, organic form and arbitrary ornament, consciousness and nonconsciousness. Rather, the problem arises as a kind of metadeterminacy that appears to govern the immediate social subject, the specific current acts of critical reflection. This is not the Hegelian determinacy of the progress of the history of consciousness, so cherished by classical Marxist thought. It is rather the determinacy of atomization and randomness—the immobilization of the social subject in face of an indeterminacy (the multiply-voiced social text) that will never yield to consciousness. "Experience always outruns conception,"[4] he has observed. The thought might be Trotskyite, and Marxian to that extent, were it not that McGann discounts the interpretive adequacy of conceptual schemas far more than Trotsky himself ever did.

The question then arises—why does this remark not simply translate into Yeats's decadent reprise upon Shelley: "The best lack all conviction while the worst / Are full of passionate intensity"?

McGann argues frequently against that passivist (not pacifist) theory of literature which, in Auden's famous revisionist (and inaccurate) formulation, declares that "poetry makes nothing happen." On the contrary, for McGann "poetry is a deed of language" or in an alternative formulation: "poems are acts of communication." Consequently, critical reflection on poetry is an effort to declare not what poems mean, but "what they are doing in saying what they say."[5] But such a view surely contradicts McGann's correlative ideas about "Art as Experience," for poetic acts (including the acts of criticism) cannot possibly know what they are doing in saying what they say. They cannot because "experience always outruns conception," which is itself a condition predicated by the originary Bakhtinian insights into the multiplied voices and histories speaking through and occupying "the texts."

PROF. J.: Well if "contradiction" is to be the criterion by which we judge the adequacy of thought, then we will have to give up thinking.

PROF. A.: It's not the "contradictions" of McGann's work that present a problem, it's the atomized and indeterminate—the "chaotic"—situation that his kind of "contradiction" fosters. In classical Marxist thought, "contradiction" is a field of dynamic instabilities that develop linearly and progressively, in a synthetic operation. In McGann, contradiction appears as a set of unsolvable nonlinear equations, equations for which there are no integrals. McGann's theory therefore maps a field of dynamic change that exhibits determinateness but not determinability.

PROF. J.: I don't understand mathematics. Can you change your metaphor, can you speak in English?

PROF. A.: Within certain limits defined by the initial materials, literary works can mean—can be made to mean—anything. In more practical terms, the uses to which they are put, the tasks they perform in society, cannot be determined, for good or for ill. As they tell the truth, it is a truth that may or may not set you free.

PROF. J.: What is this, Neo-Kantianism? The work of art as "disinterested," as "the still point in the turning world"? The view that poetry and art are nonideological hardly seems to me a Marxist idea, and it's certainly not McGann's idea. To regard literary work as a praxis, a "deed of language"—which he does—clearly entails an ideological function.

PROF. M.: But *whose* deed is it? Your exchange here takes me back to what Ms. A. was saying about poetry as an act moaning round with many voices. The great American scholar Milman Parry once described how he proposed to deal with that kind of situation: "I make for myself a picture of great detail." I recall that McGann has appropriated Parry's graphical metaphor several times in his work. But I also remember that he makes an interesting alteration to it: he removes the first person syntax, thereby keeping the concept of the "picture of great detail" but refusing to declare the picture to be a purely subjective creation.[6] This refusal seems to define for him the objective status of literary activity. The literary work thus comes to appear not merely as an object, the thing "fixed and dead," as Coleridge once described the "object as object." It's rather a complex—a multiply-voiced—

subject of study interacting dialectically with immediate criticism, that other multiply-voiced subject engaged in the critical process of literary work. McGann makes me think of Robert Burns's "To a Louse," a favorite poem of his, as I recall. Everyone in the discourse field is seeing everyone else as others see them.

This seems to me the object of McGann's criticism: to represent, or remember, that social subject, to perpetuate its activity. His literary criticism, in particular the set-piece acts of interpretation focusing on specific works, seem to me allegories—extended figures—of his social subject, the social text. And I set before you here, by way of illustration, one of his classic interpretive allegories. We might call such works not "Allegories of Reading," after de Man, but "Allegories of Communicative Exchange."

Byron's "Fare Thee Well!"

by Jerome J. McGann

As is well known, Byron addressed this notorious poem to his wife at a volatile time during the marriage separation controversies that stretched over the first five months of 1816.[7] It descends to us largely through one line of interpretation, where it is read as a cri de coeur from a heartbroken husband. This is the way the poem was read by many people in 1816. Madame de Stael, for instance, Sir Francis Burdett, and various reviewers all read it this way and praised it extravagantly.[8] And Wordsworth read it this way as well, only he anticipated the common later judgment that the poem is hopelessly mawkish: "disgusting in sentiment, and in execution contemptible. . . . Can worse doggerel be written . . . ?"[9]

But another, very different reading sprang up when the poem began circulating in 1816, like tares among the wheat of that first reading. Byron's friend Moore—who would later endorse the sentimental theory of the poem—was at first deeply suspicious of "the sentiment that could, at such a moment, indulge in such verses."[10] Moore did not elaborate on his suspicions, but

---

This piece is excerpted from a longer essay, originally given as a lecture in London in 1987, titled "Lord Byron and the Truth in Masquerade." It has been collected in McGann's *Byron and Romanticism* (Cambridge, UK: Cambridge University Press, 2002).

others did. The reviewer of *The Prisoner of Chillon and Other Poems* in the *Critical Review* of November 1816 paused to reflect on the earlier "domestic" poem: "for many who disapproved most of his lordship's . . . publication of his "Farewell" address, as inflicting a parting and lasting pang upon his lady, thought that the lines were most delightfully pathetic, and wondered how a man, who shewed he had so little heart, could evince such feeling. They did not know how easy it was for a person of his lordship's skill to fabricate neatly-turned phraseology, and for a person of his lordship's ingenuity to introduce to advantage all the common-places of affection: the very excellence of that poem in these particulars, to us and to others, was a convincing proof that its author had much more talent than tenderness."[11]

As it happens, Anabella herself, the person to whom "Fare Thee Well!" was most directly addressed, read the poem in just this insidious way. It seemed to her yet another instance of Byron's "talent for equivocation . . . of [which] I have had many proofs in his letters."[12] On 13 February, a month before Byron wrote this poem, she explained this "talent" further and pointed out that she learned about it from Byron himself: "I should not have been more deceived than I was by his letters, if he had not pointed out to me in similar ones addressed to others, the deepest design in words that appeared to have none. On this he piques himself— and also on being able to write such letters as will convey different, or even opposite sentiments to the person who receives them & to a stranger." "Every day," she added, "proves deeper art" in her husband. What she most feared was "this ambiguity of Language in the Law," that it would give Byron an advantage over her in the separation proceedings.

Anabella went on to add two observations that are equally interesting and shrewd. Byron's skill in manipulating language reminded her of a passage in *Lara* (4–9) in which the deportment of that Byronic hero is exposed as a text of such ambiguity that, reading it, one cannot be certain if it signals a heart filled with "the calmness of the good" or with a "guilt grown old in desperate hardihood." And she added that this skill with words was one "he is afraid of" himself.[13]

In a good recent essay, W. Paul Elledge has revived a variant of this insidious reading of "Fare Thee Well!" The poem, he argues, is "a portrait of indecision, taut with antithetical tensions"; it "charts . . . the depth and configurations of the poet's ambivalence . . . toward reconciliation with his wife."[14] Although Elledge is, I believe, certainly correct in this reading of the poem, he does not go nearly far enough, either substantively or methodologically. In this respect the readings of both the *Critical Review* reviewer and Lady Byron seem to me more weighty and profound.

What Anabella and the *Critical Review* call attention to are the social contexts in which the poem was executed. Anabella was peculiarly alive to such matters because they touched upon her life in the most important ways. "Fare Thee Well!" was not simply a thing of beauty spinning in the disinterested space of a Kantian (or Coleridgean) theoretical world. It was an event in the language of art, specifically located, and she registered that event in particular ways. To her the separation controversy came to involve two primary matters. There was first the matter of the law, and who, in the complex legal maneuverings, would have power over the other to influence various decisions (Lady Byron feared, for example, that Byron would seek to deprive her of custody of their daughter Ada). And second there was the (closely related) matter of public opinion and who would enter into and finally emerge from the separation proceedings with what sort of public image.

When Byron sent her a copy of "Fare Thee Well!" soon after he wrote it, Lady Byron was quick to read it as a shrewd ploy to gain power over her in the context of those two areas of interest that most concerned her. At first she emphasized the "legal" reading, for she felt, as we have already seen, that Byron's various communications were designed to construct a sympathetic self-image in order to improve his bargaining position. "He has been assuming the character of an injured & affectionate husband with great success to some," she remarked in mid-February.[15] When Byron sent her a manuscript copy of the poem late in March, she wrote ironically to her mother of its apparent tenderness, "and so he talks of me to Every one."[16] But the poem did not disturb her greatly until she learned that Byron intended to print and distribute it privately in London society. This act, she feared, would turn "the Tide of feeling . . . against" her,[17] but she was dissuaded from her first impulse—to publish a rejoinder—by the counsel of Dr. Stephen Lushington.

The significance of all this becomes more clear, I think, if we recall that "Fare Thee Well!" was initially constituted as three very different texts, only two of which were manipulated by Byron, while the other fell under the coauthority of persons and powers who were hostile to him. The first of these texts is the one that originates in the manuscript poem addressed to Lady Byron and which Byron caused to have circulated in London in late March and early April. The second is the text privately printed and distributed in fifty copies on 8 April, at Byron's insistence and over the objections of his publisher, Murray. Byron's activities here are important to remember because they show that he was manipulating the poem, was literally fashioning an audience for it of a very specific kind. The original manuscript may have been addressed to his wife, but when copies of that poem began to be made and circulated, a new text started to emerge. The printed text in fifty copies represents the definitive emergence of that text, which was addressed past and through Lady Byron to a circle of people—friends, acquaintances, and other interested parties—whose "reading" and "interpretation" of the poem Byron wanted to generate and of course influence.

In the most limited sense, Byron wanted his poem to be read as the effusion of an "injured and affectionate husband." Moore's later report in his *Life,* that the manuscript text he saw was covered with Byron's tears, represents in effect such an interpretation of the poem. But the fact that Byron was also managing a certain kind of circulation for the poem set in motion other forces, and other readings, that were only latent (so to speak) in the manuscript text. The poem, that is to say, came to be widely seen—and read—as another event in Byron's troubled "domestic circumstances." It is this circulation of the verses that begins to change the meaning of the poem—indeed, that begins to change the poem itself. The words of the original manuscript do not significantly differ from the privately printed text; nonetheless, that first printed text has become another poem, one that sets in motion an urgency toward the production of yet another textual change.

This new change is definitive when the privately printed text finally makes its appearance in the *Champion* on 14 April and thence throughout the periodical press. This is a new poem altogether. In the first place, it does not appear alone but alongside "A Sketch," Byron's cutting satire on Mrs. Clermont that he had also put into private circulation in fifty copies several days before he began circulating "Fare Thee Well!" The editors of the *Champion* text so print and position "A Sketch" as to make it an exponent of the "real meaning" of "Fare Thee Well!" It is used partly for the light it sheds on "Fare Thee Well!" and hence exposes Byron's hypocritical malignancy. The farewell poem is accompanied in the *Champion* by a long editorial commentary denouncing Byron's character, as well as his politics, and explicitly "reading" the two poems as evidence of his wickedness.

The *Champion*'s text of "Fare Thee Well!" is, I would say, the definitive version of the hypocritical poem, just as the manuscript version sent to Lady Byron—which, interestingly, seems not to have survived—would be the definitive version of the sentimental poem. The "texts" that extend between these two versions dramatize this first, crucial stage in the poem's transformations. But they do not conclude those changes. Even as the *Champion* text is completing that first stage of the poem's transformations, it has initiated a new stage, the one in which the two faces of this poem are forced to confront each other. And it is in this next stage of its textual development that "Fare Thee Well!" becomes most rich and interesting. This is the poem whose meaning focuses and culminates the controversies among the readers in Byron's day. The question is gone over again and again: is this a poem of love ("sentimental") or a poem of hate ("hypocritical")?

The final contemporary text declares that in some important sense it is both. Byron himself produced the materialized version of this culminant text when he published the poem, with the telling epigraph from "Christabel," in his *Poems* (1816). This is the text that Elledge revived, a work full of painful and even frightening tensions and contradictions. And while I salute Elledge's success in rescuing Byron's poem from its impoverished sentimental readings, I must point out Elledge's insistence—it stems from his New Critical background—that his is not a reading of a work of poetry so much as an exploration of a set of tense personal circumstances: "my concern is less with the poem as poem than with the dynamics of the relationship between poet-husband and audience-wife as Byron represents them."[18] He makes this statement because his notion is that "the poem as poem" is an abstract verbal construct, a "text" that not only can be, but must be, divorced from the social and material formations within which the work was instituted and carried out.

Such an idea commits one to a certain way of reading poetry that seems to me intolerable. And it is a way that is particularly destructive for a poet like Byron, whose poetical language characteristically invokes and uses its available social and institutional resources. More, Byron's work insists that this is the way of all poetry, though some poets and apologists for poetry argue that it is otherwise, that poetry operates in a space of disinterestedness and autonomy. "Fare Thee Well!" is therefore, for us in particular, a kind of meta-poem, a work that foregrounds Byron's ideas about what poetry actually is and how it works.[19]

Byron himself seems to have recognized very clearly—that is to say, with pain and reluctance—the full significance of his poetic practice. In writing and circulating "Fare Thee Well!" he was the author and agent of the completed work, the one who finally would be responsible for all of the texts. Yet while Byron authored those texts, he could not fully control them—this, the fate of all poets, is sometimes called their "inspiration"—so that in the end he found that he too, like everyone else who would involve themselves with the poem, would have to trust the tale and not the teller. His discovery of this, a bitter revelation, would soon find expression in another of the "Poems on his Domestic Circumstances": the "[Epistle to Augusta]," which he wrote in the summer of 1816. Reflecting on that "talent for equivocation" that he flaunted before his wife, Byron would expose its equivocal character.

> The fault was mine—nor do I seek to screen
> My errors with defensive paradox—
> I have been cunning in mine overthrow
> The careful pilot of my proper woe. (21–24)

Which is as much to say of that most "cunning" of his poems to date, "Fare Thee Well!," that it tells more than one would have imagined possible, tells more than its own author wanted told.

I shall return to indicate what I believe this kind of analysis signifies for any concrete "reading" of "Fare Thee Well!" But first
I would ask you to reflect upon certain matters of general relevance for Byron's poetry. When we say that Byron's is a highly
rhetorical poetry we mean—we should mean—not that it is loud
or overblown, but that it is always, at whatever register, elaborat-
ing reciprocities with its audiences. These reciprocities, like all
social relations, accumulate their own histories as time passes
and more interchanges occur—and we then call these, as Donald
Reiman has called them, "the cumulative effect" of the work.[20]
New poetry is written—and read—within the context of those
accumulations. The development of the various texts of "Fare
Thee Well!" between March and November 1816 is a miniature
example of how these reciprocities can get played out.

I want to emphasize that Byron wrote this way throughout his
life. The masterpiece of *Don Juan* is a work of, quite literally, consummate skill, because the whole of his life and career is gathered into it. Without an awareness of, an involvement in, that poem's "cumulative effect" one will be reduced simply to reading its
words—as Eliot in this connection might have said—*not* to have
the experience *and* to miss the meaning.

Related to this rhetorical framework of the poetry is Byron's
habit of manipulating his texts. To present a work through a "cumulative" context is to open it to changes and modifications, in
fact, to new opportunities of meaning: not so much, as Coleridge
would have had it, the "reconciliation" of "opposite and discordant qualities" as their artistic and cultural exploitation. "Fare
Thee Well!" did not bring about any reconciliations, poetic or
otherwise; it raised a tumult of new discords and conflicts. Yet it is
those very tumults, and their artistic significance, that turned the
period of Byron's separation—from his wife, from England—to
a watershed in his career and in his understanding of what was
involved, for him, in his methods of poetic production.

To understand this better we have to retreat in time, to Byron's years at Harrow and especially Cambridge, when he took
his first lessons in the art of literary equivocation. Byron told his
wife that he had a talent for that sort of thing, and Louis Crompton's study of *Byron and Greek Love* has shown that it was a mode
of writing practiced by Byron's circle of Cambridge friends—a
deliberate and methodical set of procedures for saying one thing

and meaning something else. Briefly, they cultivated a mode of homosexual double-talk.

One of Byron's first epistolary exercises in this equivocal style was in his letter to Charles Skinner Matthews of 22 June 1809. Matthews's answer to this letter is important because of its explicit discussion:

> In transmitting my dispatches to Hobhouse, my carissime Buron I cannot refrain from addressing a few lines to yourself: chiefly to congratulate you on the splendid success of your first efforts in the mysterious, that style in which more is meant than meets the eye. . . . [B]ut I must recommend that [Hobhouse] do not in future put a dash under his mysterious significances, such a practise would go near to letting the cat out of the bag. . . . And I positively decree that every one who professes ma methode do spell the term wch designates his calling with an e at the end of it-methodiste, not methodist, and pronounce the word in the french fashion. Every one's taste must revolt at confounding ourselves with that sect of . . . fanatics.[21]

Byron's letter may in fact have been his "first effort" at writing in Matthews's particular dialect of "the mysterious," but it was a language he was already practiced in, one that would receive its apotheosis in the incredible display of puns and coded talk that constitutes *Don Juan*.

Matthews's letter is also interesting because it suggests that the use of this kind of style is a game that can be played with and that its practitioners should think of themselves as a kind of elite group with special gifts and powers. But it was also a style that ran grave risks for the user. Byron told his wife that he was afraid of his own skill with this method of writing. And well he might be, for it entailed the conscious deployment of duplicitous and hypocritical postures.

All of Byron's early tales are written in this equivocal style—which has become, in Byron's hands, a vehicle of immensely greater range and complexity than Charles Skinner Matthews would have imagined possible, had he lived to see Byron's displays. But the more Byron developed his talent for equivocation, the more he built a store of explosive and dangerous contradictions into his work. Those contradictions came to a head during the separation controversy, and in "Fare Thee Well!" they finally reached their flash point.

That the poem is not what the commonplace "sentimental" reading has taken it to be is exposed unmistakably for us in the initial period of its production and reception. Many readers were alive to its duplicities. The opening four lines signal the poem's method by installing a grammatical pun of fundamental importance:

> Fare thee well! and if for ever
>> Still for ever, fare thee well
> Even though unforgiving, never
>> 'Gainst thee shall my heart rebel.

The sense here urges us to take Lady Byron's as the "unforgiving" heart, but the grammar tells us that heart is Byron's own. The poem will operate under this sign of contradiction to the end. Noteworthy too is Byron's assertion that, though his heart is unforgiving, it will never "rebel" against hers: as if he were imagining their separation and mutual antagonisms succeeding to a second, darker marriage that would "never" be dissolved or put asunder. In fact, the poem is replete with this kind of complex doublespeaking. Ponder, for example, these four lines:

> Would that breast by thee glanc'd over,
>> Every inmost thought could show!
> Then thou would'st at last discover
>> 'Twas not well to spurn it so (9–12)

It is a nice question what the inmost thoughts of an unforgiving and yet unrebellious heart would look like. Blake wrote a great deal of poetry about just such a heart, and he always imagined it as dangerous and fearful. And if we merely "glance over" Byron's lines here we may easily fail to "discover" their full truth: that the passage does not merely tell about the dark truths of unforgiving hearts, but is itself executing them. "'Twas not well to spurn it so" is a warning of possible danger, but coming from this speaker it carries as well a threatening message and rhetoric.

Of course the poem delivers these kinds of messages obliquely, but in doing so it only increases the volatile character of the text. Because more is meant here than meets the eye directly, the censored materials exert enormous pressure for their freedom of complete expression. The parallel text in canto 3 of *Childe Harold's Pilgrimage* (st. 97) meditates the situation by comparing it to the fury of a storm breaking over the Alps:

> Could I embody and unbosom now
>> That which is most within me, could I wreak
> My thoughts upon expression.

And so forth: he longs for "one word [of] Lightening," one word of comfort that would "lighten" his heart of its weight of sorrow, one word of insight that would "enlighten" his understanding of his situation, and one word of power that would, like a bolt of lightning, "blast" and purify those places "where desolation lurk[s]."

Like Manfred—another creature of separation—who begs from Astarte "one word for mercy," Childe Harold's longings remain incompletely satisfied. In all these cases the very effort to achieve some kind of completion, to reconcile the various contradictions, only seems to install them more deeply and more firmly.

Charles Skinner Matthews wrote gaily of his "mysterious" style of discourse, but it was a style that Byron, its supreme master, came to fear as he developed it through his years of fame. And well he might have feared it since it was a style that forced into the open the hypocrisies of those who read and write poetry as if it were a beauty or a truth, as if it were something that could be controlled—enlisted to the purposes of either those who produce it or those who receive it. "Fare Thee Well!" is Byron's farewell to the illusion that he could be the master of the artistic powers that were given to him. Written in hopes that it would allow him to control the dangerous crosscurrents of his circumstances in 1816, the poem's bad faith—which is its genius—worked to undermine the actual despair latent in such petty hopes.

This interpretation of Byron's "Fare Thee Well!" involves an implicit critique of intrinsic, thematic, and text-centered hermeneutic methods that I want to make explicit. In the first place, important deficiencies follow when circumstances of production are not factored into the interpretive operation. At the most elementary level—at what Blake called "the doors of perception"— readers will be inclined to see, and hence to deal with, only the linguistic text. But the poetic event always comprehends a larger scriptural territory, one that is bibliographically (as well as linguistically) encoded. The physical forms within which poetry is incarnated are abstracted from an interpretive activity only at the price of a serious critical blindness, a blindness that brings with it little corresponding insight.

The problem emerges dramatically in the work of Blake, whose illuminated texts do not lend themselves to the kind of physical variabilities that are common in the case of typographical texts. I am speaking here of the variabilities that develop when texts are transmitted over time to later readers. That transmission history tends to erase not merely the bibliographical terms in which the texts—the meanings of the texts—were initially encoded, it tends to make us unaware of the presence and significance of bibliographical coding in general. People tend not to realize that a certain way of reading is privileged when "Ode on a Grecian Urn" is read in *The Norton Anthology of English Literature* and that it is a way of reading that differs sharply from what is privileged in Palgrave's *Golden Treasury* or in the *Oxford Book of Romantic Verse;* and when the poem is (or was) read in other kinds of formats—for example, in its first printing in the *Annals of the Fine Arts*—an entirely different field of reading is once again deployed. Furthermore, the work that descends to us descends through particular forms of transmission, and the work does not pass through those incarnations without having its meaning affected by them. We are able to discern patterns in a work's reception history because those historical influences have inscribed themselves in the works we receive.

The example from Byron, however, underscores yet another important matter. Poetic works are not autonomous in either of the senses that the academy has come, mistakenly, to believe. That is to say, poems are neither linguistically self-contained, nor are they simply the expressed forms of a single—an authorizing and integral—imagination. The actual production of poems is one part of that social dialectic by which they live and move and have their being, one part of the communicative interchange that they always solicit.

The Byron example is especially instructive, I think, because it shows how those interchanges can never be brought under the control of the author. Poems are produced, used, and read in heterogeneous ways; unlike informational forms of discourse, they require—they thrive upon—those diverse forms of life. Crucial parts of those interchanges are encoded in the bibliographical, productive, and reception histories of the poems we read. When we neglect those histories we simply condemn our readings to a culpable—because an unnecessary—ignorance.

PROF. A.: Surely whatever residual "Marxism" one may discover in that document has been so academicized as to have become a pure formality. An "Allegory of Communicative Exchange" indeed! What pretentiousness! The problem with that lecture of McGann's is the same problem with all his published critical works—they don't change anything essential in the way the academy goes about its business.

PROF. M.: But they make change possible. They postulate, and deploy, a communicative system where the terms of the communicative dialectic reflect each other in distorting, differential mirrors.

PROF. A.: That's simply what you say! Such a view would begin to be meaningful only if you could show that McGann's criticism is both true and false. In rhetorical terms, it would have to be a criticism we would want to accept and dismiss at the same time.

PROF. J.: Well then, consider this piece from his unpublished criticism. McGann has headed it "A Commentary on the Opening Passage of 'Stopping by Woods on a Snowy Evening.'" It seems a finished piece of work, though of course it has to be regarded as in some sense fragmentary, given the arbitrary limit it sets to its "commentary." There can be no question, I think, that the piece is authentic. The computer disk is clearly labeled and has many of his other works coded on it, some in draft forms. Furthermore, though the piece may appear in certain respects incongruent with his published work, its bibliographical preoccupations have a distinctively McGannian quality. Whatever, it seems pretty scandalous for a scholar to be writing this way.

"A Commentary on the Opening Passage of 'Stopping by Woods on a Snowy Evening'"

What comes to us as the title, the prefatory "Stopping by Woods on a Snowy Evening," is a set of words which, even if we regard them as a single word string, are by no means self-identical. An initial reading may legitimately ask, for example, whether the third word is a common or a proper noun, and hence whether the "stopping" referred to is a casual "stopping by" at the Woods's house or whether it is a "stopping alongside" a stand of trees. To say that the former reading is eliminated by the first line of the poem is merely to say that one has assented to the traditional formatting imposed upon the words of the poem. As we shall see in a moment, those words carry—fatally, as it were—many more signifying possibilities than the narrow range of significations so cunningly, and deceptively, specified by the received format.

But to return for a moment to the "title," or prefatory material. If we put a period after "Stopping by" the title changes; if we put "Stopping" on a line by itself, then place immediately below it, centered, "by Woods," and then on a third line, centered, put "On a Snowy Evening," another set of possible signifiers opens up for us (one much closer, perhaps, to what one could find in verse published in certain periodical formats).

Finally, of course, the words may be imagined to have been so arranged as to set all these (and perhaps other) signifying chains in motion, along with the corresponding diversity of signifiers as well as the contextual referents that they evoke. A multiplied text is latently present in these words, a text that reaches out to the equally multiplied textual codes that are socially dispersed in the audience of readers.

But let us move into the body of the poem's text, specifically, into what the traditional poem sets down as the first two lines, which thus appear thus:

Whose woods these are I think I know,
His house is in the village, though.

If we ask, once again, whether the final word of this couplet is a common or a proper noun, we begin to see how arbitrary is the traditional text of these words. Furthermore, if we take "though" to be the name of the village where "His house" is located, we may find ourselves inclined to construct a wholly different poem here, a wholly different set of signifiers. If a village may be called "though" we may have found ourselves pitched into a world where "concrete realities" are to be imagined as parts or operations of language. If "though" is imagined as a village in that "world," that fact may be taken to signify that subordinate clauses are to stand metaphorically for certain types of subordinate political entities, like villages (with the corresponding analogy to be understood as operative—that sentences are "cities," and so on up (and down) the grammatical hierarchy).

This metaphorical structure will incline one to "read" the text very differently from the reading under which the couplet has traditionally functioned as a couplet. These other readings emerge if, following the lead of the work's traditional arbitrary formulae, we arbitrarily shift the punctuation—for instance:

Whose woods? These are, I think. "I know! His house is in
the village
Though!"

or:

Who's woods? These are "I think," "I know,"
"His house" is in the village Though.

In the latter case, the text calls attention to the fact that certain words that are arbitrarily arranged to act as points of reference to an extralinguistic field (the place of forests and villages, the place where a man named Woods may be imagined to be living) may equally and at the same time function as parts of a system of pure signifiers. In such a case, what has been set in motion is an allegorical work entirely analogous, for example, to the opening of Charles Olson's "In Cold Hell, In Thicket" or to the opening of Olson's more famous precursor text, the *Inferno:*

> Nel mezzo del cammin di nostra vita
> mi ritrovai per una selva oscura

This resonant text calls out to the "woods" in Frost's work, an equally "dark and deep" woods of a self obscured from itself. (And how appropriate it now seems that the text of "Stopping by Woods" should be attached to an author named Frost!) We may name the woods of the modern poem "I think" and "I know" on the Dantean allegorical analogy, and we add the distinctively postmodern touch by noting that this woods exists in purely linguistic space, near a village here named "Though."

But the power hovering most immediately over Frost's work, it seems to me, is probably not Dante. It is the late Romantic Dante Gabriel Rossetti, whose great and nightmarish work *The House of Life* seems to be glanced at in Frost's word "house." The house of Frost's text is partly Rossetti's poetical house, where one frequently encounters a discourse analogous to one that could name a stand of trees "I think" and, alternatively, "I know." One recalls, for instance, Rossetti's sonnet "Superscription":

> Look on my face; my name is Might-have-been;
> I am also called No-more, Too-late, Farewell.

The Rossetti text, where the "house of life" is at all points the house of language, a house of pure (and impure) signifiers, allows us at last to appreciate fully the signifying labyrinth into which the Frost text has led us. So bound are we to positivist structures of reading that we initially overlook entirely the strength of the wordplay being carried, and carried out, in those key terms in the poem's title and first line, "Woods" and "woods." The words are metaphors, but they are metaphors imbedded in a metonymic wordplay that conceals the correspondent (and purely linguistic) signifier, "Woulds" and "woulds." "Stopping by Woulds" is a poem about subjunctive states of desire and of the darkness and cold with which they seduce and threaten us. To stop by this "selva oscura" is to confront the promise and the threat of all that we "would" or "would not" encounter and understand.

More than that, however, the text is about how texts signify in the first place. Poetry is the discourse that lays bare, that makes it possible to understand, how all texts—including the text we call "the world"—function. Thematizing the work's textual operations (for example, saying that the poem is about desire and subjunctive states) tends to conceal the more important and powerful communicative exchange executed through the poem. "Stopping by Woods on a Snowy Evening" is a display of the heteronomy that Bakhtin, for example, postulated of fictional discourse. That heteronomy is itself a tool, a signifier, by means of which human beings, as individuals and as groups, define the possibilities of their lives.

And do we not also hear in Frost's "woods," besides "woulds," "words"—at the meta-level called out by the language games? Whose words are these anyway?

PROF. M.: This cannot be an authentic text. It's a travesty of criticism, a travesty of scholarly criticism.

PROF. A.: Perhaps it's authentic. The absurd frivolity unmasks the hidden face of McGann's spurious Marxism. The whole thing is a game—a game of academic scholarship whose correspondent breeze is this shameless personal *jeu*.

PROF. J.: Perhaps it's a serious travesty, or even a travesty of seriousness, or both. The piece reminds me that McGann extolled, in *The Romantic Ideology,* the deconstructive ironies of Heinrich Heine. In fact, that book seems to me plainly set on a strange series of self-contradictions. Most apparent, I suppose, is the collision between the book's authoritative—not to say imperious—prose style and its commitment to the program (dare one say the ideology?) of the romantic ironist.

PROF. A.: I recall that several reviewers have associated McGann's middle-age work with postmodern and even de Manian positions. Of course he did produce a studied critique of de Man, but it seems to me a critique carried out from a position of sympathy. How could it be otherwise? McGann is after all an open supporter of weird experimentalist writing.

PROF. M.: But his allegiances emphasize the socially activist orientation of that writing. He repeatedly discusses not "texts" but what he calls "textual events" involving multiple agents. This is why experimental writing seems to him nothing more or less than a contemporary instance of Marxian expression.

PROF. A.: Does it really matter what he *says*? The point is that these kinds of contradiction undermine the seriousness of the work—as if it were all finally inconsequential.

PROF. J.: Contradictions seem of great consequence, as all Marxists think and have always thought. Only when they're not real contradictions, even shameful ones, are they inconsequential. Isn't that one of the implicit points of the discussion of Byron's "Fare Thee Well!"? Perhaps the short piece on Frost comes to underscore the point, perhaps its meaning rests in the way it scandalizes the ground of meaning—as if meaning had to seek its renewal through paths of falsification. If there is pretentiousness and shamelessness within

[Here the document breaks off, leaving readers with various problems and with what seems one overriding question: is this a case of multiple personality disorder, or is it a social text? If so, is it a "Marxist" text? And what is "this" anyway?]

9
Looney Tunes and Unheard Melodies
☺ An Oulipian Colonescapade, with a Critique of
"The Great-Ape Love Song Corpus" and Its Lexicon

It is not sufficient to be elsewhere in order not to be here.
—St. Thomas Aquinas,
Summa Contra Gentiles

Abstract: The ultimate aim of this paper is to raise the consciousness of colonized scholars—to free us from the colonic obstruc-
tions that have become a rampant academic disease. This is a
colonescapade and not a colonoscopy for two reasons: first, we
are investigating the waste regions of the linguistic and not the
biological body; second, our "escapade" is not an "oscopy" because it seeks to go beyond diagnosis and operate on the disease directly. The procedure is radical, arguing by example, not
precept. It operates under the eleventh thesis of Feuerbach: "In-
tellectuals have only tried to understand the world in various
ways; the point is to change it." May there be no more colonic ob-
structions in our lives! This is my hope and fervent wish.

Some fifteen years ago an essay appeared in Paris in a marginal publishing venue that altered forever the practice of trans-phylogenic linguistics. Jacques Jouet's paper did more than translate an Obliterature[1]
that had been to that point complete terra incognita. His modest—
traditionalists call it his *bestial*—essay shook the foundations of language study in the West. So radical were its implications that it remains
either ignored or treated as a kind of looney tune by academicians;
and beyond that tight little professorial island, the essay is unheard. To
specialists the essay appears even more suspect than Saussure's early
researches into the anagrammatics he discovered in Silver Age Latin
poetry.[2] Saussure, as we know, turned his back on his own disturbing
discoveries and proceeded to his fame and glory. Jouet, by contrast, has
stood game and steadfast.

Now, fifteen years later, the situation has changed, in no small part because of what Jouet's work accomplished for the study of language, especially poetical language. All humanists owe an unpayable debt to his little paper on "Great-Ape Love-Songs" and in particular to the example his practice set for those of us who came after him. So in this examination of Jouet's work I come like Marc Antony to the corpse of Caesar—I come to bury Jouet, not to praise him. He more than most would appreciate this precisely because he is still living near Paris.

I shall spend much of my time recapitulating Jouet's original work. Its deficiencies are inseparable from its virtues, so that we cannot examine the former without first being clear about the latter. Besides, if his paper falls short of the definitive, as we shall see it does, it remains, like Newton's *Principia* and Ptolemy's *Almagest,* a perpetual source of inspiration to creative intelligence.

We must begin a little before the beginning marked by Jouet's essay, however, with a man who was Jouet's most formative influence, Raymond Queneau.[3] I confine myself to one small but crucial section of Queneau's seminal 1976 *Foundations of Literature,* an axiomatic treatise on poetical forms drawn out of David Hilbert's equally seminal mathematical treatise of 1899, *The Fundamentals of Geometry.* The relevant passage is theorem 3 and its natural consequent theorem 7, both of which Queneau derives from the third of the second group of his foundational axioms, the so-called "Axioms of Order."

According to theorem 3, "Where two words are present, the sentence in which they appear includes at least one word between these two words." Consequently, theorem 7: "Between two words of a sentence there exists an infinity of other words." Anticipating the "surprise" that these two theorems can occasion, Queneau adds the following comment: "To overcome his astonishment and understand these theorems [the reader] need only admit the existence of what we shall call . . . 'imaginary words' and 'infinitesimal words.' Every sentence contains an infinity of words; only an extremely limited number of them is perceptible; the rest are infinitesimal or imaginary." Or, we must further add, "transcendental."

Queneau went on to say, in the same commentary, that this theorem would prove a great boon to students of rhetoric and linguistics. In fact, however, the treatise itself remains almost as little known as Jouet's essay or Aristotle's treatise on comedy. Jouet is one of a small band of angels who would grasp its import and build upon it.

How he did this is best told by himself. In what follows I quote in extenso from his remarkable work *The Great-Ape Love-Song. An Unappreciated Lyric Corpus, collected, translated, and annotated by Jacques Jouet*. As will be very clear, where Queneau is a theoretician and philosopher, Jouet is an empiricist and field-worker. (Note: In these translations, the Great-Ape poetical texts come as Jouet's phonetic transcriptions from the oral originals, and the scholar's explanatory prose comes in its English semantic equivalent. The form of the former—the prosodic and auditory form—is of course crucial to preserve, as much as we can, whereas the latter is simply informational academic prose and presents no particular aesthetic difficulties.)

> *Zor boden tanda*
> *Kagoda bolgani*
> *Rak gom tand panda Yato*
> *kalan mangani Kreegh-ah yel*
> *greeh-ah Kreegh-ah zu-vo*
> *bolgani Greek-ah tand pogo*
> *Ubor zee kalan mangani*

The preceding poem is written in great-ape language. And here is a translation:

> *Where are you going, gorilla,*
> *In the dark forest?*
> *You run without a sound*
> *Seeking the female ape.*
> *Beware of love*
> *Watch out, gorilla*
> *A lover dies of hunger*
> *Of thirst, of hoping for the leg of the female great-ape.*

The great-ape language has the peculiarity of being composed of a lexicon of less than 300 words. In the absence of any information, it must be deemed that the syntax is according to the user's preference, as are the pronunciation and the prosody.

The French-Ape and Ape-French lexicon is to be found in Tarzan, by Francis Lacassin, Collection 10–18, Paris, 1971. In it, Francis Lacas-

sin clarifies as follows: "This lexicon, drawn up by Edgar Rice Burroughs himself after the compilation of his own works, was published under his own auspices in 1939 in the now unobtainable booklet The Tarzan Clans of America.

"Since then it has become the guide of the well-informed amateur and the official style-manual of successive artists and authors of strip-cartoons.

"It is published here for the first time in French, by special permission. Copyright, Edgar Rice Burroughs Inc., 1971."

According to Edgar Rice Burroughs the great apes are comparable to the gorilla in terms of strength, but far more developed on the level of intelligence.

It is at the breast of a great-ape (a great-ape with a great-ape's great heart) that little Lord Greystoke, orphaned of his father and mother, humans come to grief somewhere in equatorial Africa, acquired the strength of his species of adoption, while his British and innate intelligence was to sprout within him like an indestructible reed. That, at least, is more or less what Burroughs says.

Tarzan, born in the jungle, lived for a year with his human mother, whom he heard speaking to him in English, no doubt telling him English stories. He lived for a year with his English mother and father, and when his English mother died of boredom and unfamiliarity, he lived for a night and half a morning with his father, still English but completely desperate. Adopted by Kala (in great-ape language, she who has kal, milk), Lord Greystoke became Tarzan, Tar-zan, which signifies, precisely, "white skin"—but I have no intention here of retelling the hackneyed story of that equatorial baron-in-the-trees.

Here, rather, is another love-song. I begin with the translation. It will be seen that, this time, the poem is addressed to the human, thus, unless I am mistaken, to the reader himself.

> *Black cousin of the great-ape, my friend,*
> *Halt under the tree to be wed.*
> *Your heart is in tatters for having killed too much,*
> *Steep it again in the forest's black nest. The river is wet,*
> *The river that devours truncheon,*

Wet too the tongue in its hut.
Come now, abandon your dryness and abandon your gun.

Gomangani yo
Dan do par kalan den
Thub tul bundolo Vo
wala go vo hoden
Gom-lul eho-lul
Gom-lul popo balu-
den Eho-l'l lus wala
Aro tand-lul pand-balu-den

As the title of this paper, The Great-Ape Love-Song an Unappreciated Lyric Corpus, indicates in a very insistent way, the essential themes of great-ape poetry are amorous. But we also find an appreciable number of songs of food-gathering, the great-ape being, by nature, somewhat pacific and a vegetarian. Nor will I conceal the fact that certain of these love-songs are concerned with various carnivore perversions, trans-specific zoophilias, and are indeed sadly xenophobic and exterminatory. Let no one expect that I should paint an unduly idyllic picture of the great-apes. If they are not, on the whole, either cannibals or Calibans, either good angels or nasty brutes, let us never forget that they are capable of everything, since they are capable of poems. But let us return to love-poems and, by way of example, to the following:

Voo-voo to
Voo-dum red tand Zee
Yo kalan sheeta
Zu-kut koho gu zu zee
Bzan for tand-utor
Bzan for to pal rand-ramba
Tand-utor gugu zut
Eho-nala to tand amba

I sing at the top of my voice
Because I am not really sure of myself.
I love the female leopard
Her warm grotto, and her belly, and her leg.
A hair of the beast makes one brave
The hair of my beast I pluck from her mons.

I take my courage from within and without
And from the highest summits I shall never again return.

It is clear that this is a very beautiful love-poem which sets nothing higher than love. It is also a poem which is fairly forthright in its approach to the sexual relationship between species that are generally ill-assorted; something of value, above all if we consider that the literary text is a mirror, albeit a distorting one, carried along the road of languages and of passions, basic or marginal. With the next poem, which is a poem of food-gathering, one will readily be drawn to conclude that the great-ape food-gathering poems are not very different from great-ape love-poems, to the degree that it is perhaps pointless to have created this sub-category in the general typology of great-ape poetry. The food-gathering songs are also songs of a quite different quest.

I draw attention to the composite word balu-den greeh-ah, which I have translated, word for word, as "love-truncheon."

Gu pan-vo manu
Yar vo-o-vo rea
Tand kree-gor sopu
Iro balu-den greeh-ah
Pan-lul tand cho-lul
Pan-lul galul she-eta?
Gu tand-vulp dum dum
At dan-sopu tand tand-ramba

Weak stomach of the little small ape,
Listen to this poem, which is made only of words.
What use is there in crying for the fruit?
Rather rear up your love-truncheon.
You weep like a madeleine . . .
Does she weep, the bleeding panther?
Your stomach will sound hollower than the drum
If your stick does not rise up to the nuts.

Quite obviously the great-ape lyric has no great cause to be jealous of the highest topics of reference in the history of the literatures which have existed from the very beginnings of time and the first morning. If the poem sings only of love, it sings of it to some extent by more often—but without underrating, in its turn, the spiritual dimension—putting in the fore-ground its formidable physical vigour. Thus it is true that the "raw" of in-stinct will always, tragically (at all events among the great-apes), precede the "cooked"—or the rehashed—of sentiment. Franz Kafka has already said it: "Apes think with their bellies." (A Report to an Academy)

We cannot therefore completely rule it out that, in great-ape poetry, the recourse to a vocabulary as rich in vitamins as the leaves of the wild cel-ery they greedily devour, does not come close, with the hearer of the poem, to the expectation, indeed the near reflex quest of a Pavlovian erection (or Pavlova-style juiciness, as we may certainly evaluate in the next ex-ample, which is a ritual nursery-rhyme of copulation, moreover incestu-ous, which I prefer not to translate, especially as, with the aid of Bur-roughs' lexicon (op. cit.), the curious reader will be able to attempt his own translation:

Kut za-balu
At zot at gugu
Kut za balu
At zot at gugu
Sord b'wang kali
At zot at gugu
Kut sato kali
At zot at gogo

It must be said that, among the great-apes, there is a great deal of lov-ing going on, time and time again, left, right and centre, and non-stop, without for all that misjudging the anarchic power of that particularly widespread activity, without ignoring its fundamentally tragic charac-ter which on occasion renders the matter as daunting as the filling of the barrel by the Danaids.

But since I fear I am being wearisome with these very abstract considera-tions, and certainly to provide the reader with a little amusement, I shall now speak of poetic technique.

All the poems I have quoted, with the exception of the last, are written in accordance with a great-ape fixed form, the bzee-bur, which means, word for word, "cold foot."

It will have been observed that each poem is an octave with a metric schema 5 6 5 7 5 7 5 8. The very movement of the syllabic count (or, if you prefer, the count of feet) presents a picture of a body making ready for a bath. When you venture your feet in cold water, you do it one at a time. It's cold; you withdraw the first, but if you try again, you try both.

The bzee-bur is a poem rhymed a b a b a b c b, or sometimes a b a b c b d b, or sometimes differently. The fifth line is characteristic, since it must be formed around two words in rime riche, or near paronyms, possibly around a pivot—"Kreegh-ah yelgreegh-ah," in the first poem quoted. These two words of line 5, taken up again at the beginning of lines 6 and 7, constitute the semantic core of the bzee-bur. In this instance, "love," and "watch out."

It will have been observed that the food-gathering song is a sort of slovenly bzee-bur since, at the beginning of the 7th line the repetition of "cholul," "wet," is lacking.

The following bzee-bur is entitled "Love-song of the great powerful knee." The poem is addressed to the great-ape lambda. It is a poem which expresses the violent rivalry between the drive towards love and the drive towards feeding.

Where are you projecting your desire?
Here, or there? the leg, or the courgette-flower?
The leaves, or the buttocks?
Under the warm rain
Are you going to get something good, or something brilliant?
Are you going to get the muscle, or the forest-larder? Is all that universe in a celery-stick Better than a lusty thigh?

Yel? yeland? aro
Po-ubor? zee rota?
Wa-usha? goro?
Eta-koho meeta
Gando vando tu?
Gando vo popo hoden?
Vando ben abu
Hohotan popo-baluden?

Why knee? . . . It must not be expected that I, at the expense of the great-apes, should involve myself in the slightest ethnographic type investigation. That I became acquainted with the great-ape language in a book—which I readily agree is as unbelievable and inadequate as the way in which the little Lord Greystoke learned to read English in a spelling-book, and all on his own, without ever being able to speak it, to the point that, in a few years he was perfectly capable of reading, for example, a letter addressed to him, but did not recognise the same words read out loud, so much so that a certain character in the novel thought him deaf and dumb—is rather comical when, page after page, one has heard Tarzan's famous cry of victory echoing throughout the deep and generally terrified forest.

And the extraordinary character of that learning-process does not end there, for when his new friend, the naval lieutenant D'Arnot, who is French, realises that Tarzan can read (English), and not speak it, he decides—an initiative of inspired stupidity—to teach him to speak . . . French, better still to have him pronounce a unique species of Franglais which raises to its highest point the arbitrary nature of the sign, seeing that if Tarzan sees the written English word MAN, D'Arnot teaches him to pronounce the word HOMME, if he sees the word APE, he reads it SINGE, and the word TREE, ARBRE!

It appears that, using the great-ape language from the age of a year and a day (can we go so far as to say that it is a question of his mother-tongue?), Tarzan has, as it were, no particular attitude towards the plurality of languages and the arbitrariness of the sign, not the faintest pre-babelian and inveterate nostalgia for THE unitary language—which, for my part, I find rather attractive.

All of this is of course quite unexceptionable, at once thorough, meticulous, and imaginative. But consider the following. After a critical digression on Mary Shelley's *Frankenstein* and the linguistic proficiency of Frankenstein's monster, Jouet returns, as he says, "to the Great-Ape poems, and to a few thoughts about the lexicon":

Less than three hundred words, I said . . . One might suppose that there are grave deficiencies. Thus, in the great-ape language, you appear not to have the word "categorilla," you lack the word "allegorilla," you do not have the word "fantasmagorilla" (or, what is more, the utterance "ha-

ha") . . . *and many others are equally lacking. But, in the long run, you can always manage with a paraphrase. My own conviction is that, from the point of view of poetry, languages are equal among themselves (at all events virtually equal), just as the words of a language are equal among themselves (at all events potentially equal in so far, that is, that, in that language, poets have a feel for those words.)*

When I first read this passage I scarcely noticed the *aporia* concealed within. Jouet's rhetoric is after all very persuasive. But recently, on re-visiting the essay, the deficiency appeared with the force of a revelation.

Jouet missed his error, I believe, because of his empirical turn of mind. Had he more of Queneau's theoretical rigor, he would have grasped the problem. Of course it is perfectly true, in an empirical view of the matter, that the words "categorilla," "allegorilla," and "fantasmagorilla" do not appear in the Great-Ape lexicon. They do not appear because they cannot appear. They are among the lexicon's "infinitesimal" words theoretically determined—indeed, theoretically *fore*cast—by Queneau's theorems 3 and 7. Only Jouet's 300 words are perceptible. The rest are infinitely distributed.

I have not the occasion here, nor perhaps you the patience, to pursue all of the deficiencies in Jouet's work. Let me cite just a few telling examples.

First of all, consider another imperceptible word of the same class as those cited by Jouet as nonexistent: *Godzilla*. Apparently far removed—at least in a field-worker's purview—from the world of Great-Ape Love-Songs, nonetheless it is clear, on Jouet's own showing, that this word must be another infinitesimal linguistic presence secretly inhabiting, like Keats's unheard melodies, those distichs recovered for us by Jouet:

Atan kalan yat yato yat
Kudu   yat yut yato   tand tand

How many godzillas, categorillas, allegorillas, and fantasmagorillas live and move and have their being—how many are propagating to this day—between the eleven words of that incomparable Great-Ape distich. The hills are alive with the sound of logorillas, the prancing and pawing of all their little cold feet.

Jouet also says, in that misbegotten paragraph, that the expression "ha-ha" is also absent from the Great-Ape lexicon. We know, of course, that he calls attention to this particular supposed absence in order to make an amusing reference to Queneau's master, Alfred Jarry, and in particular to the Great-Ape who is the sidekick of Dr. Faustroll, the hero of Jarry's visionary fictional narrative *The Life and Opinions of Dr. Faustroll, 'Pataphysician*. But in this case Queneau and Jarry have the laugh on Jouet, for it is clearly the case that "ha-ha" *is* part of the Great-Ape lexicon—even though the expression is not entered in the lexicon drawn up by Edgar Rice Burroughs and published in Francis Lacassin's *Tarzan*. And so we stand in wonder that this great empirical scientist could have been so naïve as to assume the positive accuracy of a document forged at two removes from the living language of Tarzan and his animal friends.

Let me add that Jouet's mistake here is in many respects a kind of felix culpa. Not only does that error lead us back to re-found our thinking in core first principles, it has stimulated the discovery—the empirical discovery—of some of the heretofore unknown words concealed in the interstices of the Great-Ape lexicon. Working from the newly exposed "Godzilla" and "ha-ha," for example, one can see what is involved in the two-word lexicon that underpins the whole series of *Road Runner* cartoons that Chuck Jones created between 1948 and 1964. Wile E. Coyote never speaks, and Road Runner's only utterance, like Bosse de Nage's "ha-ha," is "Beep, Beep". But metastasizing between those two words is a nano-order of imaginary and infinite words that would crash the capacities of a quantum computer. The cartoons themselves are merely the hem of that transcendental garment known to the ancients as the Veil of Maya and in our own day named with a name we no longer find odd or mysterious: Mozilla.

I must not close in a way that could be thought disrespectful of Jouet and his breakthrough scholarly work. Indeed, one of the most important parts of his essay is the translation he makes of the Great-Ape creation myth. As Jouet observes, this mythopoeic document gives us "a great-ape version of the evolution of species."

> *A grotto on a mountain. The grotto is inhabited by a strange creature; it is a chimera with the head of a zebra, the forefeet of a crocodile, the back wheels of a Land Rover, and the splendid breasts of a great-ape. It is a female chimera.*

> *Outside the grotto, a queue.*

In the queue there are any number of people: Den, Tongani, Balu, Gorgo, Skree, Tanbalu, Gimla, Tantor, Kando, Omtag, Bolgani, Tarmangani, Gormangani, Duro, Dango, Nene, Sheeta, Numa, Sabor, Kali, Pizza, Klu, Buto, Horta, Za-balu, Kalo, Ska, Pacco . . . and, of course, Mangani.

One must absolutely, on pain of death, answer a question. A particularly unexpected question. It is a riddle: "Which animal is it that walks in the morning on four legs, at midday on two, and in the evening on three?"

Mangani gives his answer. He doesn't want to get himself eaten up. Mangani gives his answer "That animal is Mangani," (i.e. the great-ape answers: "That animal is the great-ape." "Why is that?" the Chimera says, turning pale. "Because, in the morning of the world, the great-ape was the white-man: Tar-man ga-ni (four feet). By the midday of the world, he had become an ordinary ape: Man-nu (two feet). In the evening of the world, finally, he has become great-ape: Man ga-ni (three feet).

And the Chimera rushes off, hotfoot, to throw herself into the abyss.

To humanists like ourselves, that narrative must come as a sobering revelation. The riddle of the sphinx, a foundational myth of enlightenment, here comes in a version that questions the very ground of Western enlightenment. And so we begin to wonder: what if the riddle had another answer—an answer like the Great-Ape answer? What if it had an infinitude of other answers?

The following curious fact, which shall close my presentation, suggests the riddle in fact did, or rather *does*, have an infinitude of answers. As we all know, the first of the *Road Runner* cartoons to appear was "Fast and Furry-ous." The title is allegorillical, for all of these cartoons are about "us": "fast" us (Road Runner) and "furry" us (Coyote). But we now also know that a (so-to-speak) pre-historigorillical cartoon antedated that famous work. It was called "Uns-table" and it involved, as the prefix of its title indicates, an inquiry into "our" general human(?) condition.

Posing as the sphinx, Road Runner sets up a portable bridge table on a plateau in very high desert tableland. Road Runner's pose is a device to lure Coyote to his everlasting and ever-recurring doom (the myth of the eternal return). Seeing the large sign ACME COMPANY behind the disguised Road Runner and the bridge table, Coyote goes up and hopes to purchase an infallible death and destruction machine. *Vanitas vanitatis.*

At Coyote's approach Road Runner poses the Sphinx's first question, "Beep Beep," and Coyote responds with the word "Coyote." Appearing satisfied, Road Runner then asks, "Beep Beep" and Coyote again responds, this time with the answer "Road Runner." Unflustered by that second, clearly correct answer, Road Runner finally demands "Beep Beep" and Coyote makes his last astonishing reply: "Coyote." The riddle being solved in this truly unheard of fashion, a great sucking sound takes away the entire illusion of desert table plateau and sphinx and ACME COMPANY, with Road Runner racing into a vanishing point in the cartoon and drawing from the visual field everything but Coyote. For Coyote, the infallible death and destruction machine *is* the answer to the sphinx's riddle—an answer he never should have given in the first place since one of the infallible rules of the Chuck Jones universe is that Coyote must never speak. In that universe are only two words, *Beep Beep*, and they belong to Road Runner.

Consequently, having given the correct but literally *unheard of* answer, Coyote must be left—as ever—hanging in an empty space where once there had been solid bridge table and tableland. He hovers for a brief but touching moment and then plunges away, like the Monk at the end of Lewis's immortal story. And the cartoon closes with a tight shot of Coyote limping across the desert on three legs, his front right being broken and useless. And we hear offscreen, simply: "Beep Beep."

Beep Beep. Two little words with infinity between—and, I strongly suspect, not only between. Beep Beep.

All together now: Beep Beep.

And not only between or around *words*. Think of the infinitudes belonging to the characters!

M, N, O, P—
I could go on all day.
Q, R, S, T—
Alphabetically speaking,
We're OK.

Coda. I have to report a certain uncertainty I have begun to entertain, since completing my investigations, about the reliability of my primary documentary evidence. I am troubled by the odd coincidence in orthography of the French words *signe* and *singe*. Phonetically one would never confuse those words, but orthographically they have a troubling likeness. It then occurred to me that "Jacques Jouet" may be a name to conjure with, so to speak. *Faire le Jacques* in French slang means to "try to be funny," and of course *jouet* in French means "toy" or "trick." None of this would count for anything were it not for the fact that I have never actually *met* Jacques Jouet except in his bibliographical body. That is, thank Somebody, a material existence, so we know at any rate that human purpose and intention have brought that body into being. Still, it is not exactly flesh and blood. DOES M. Jouet live today in the suburbs of Paris? It is an important question. So I close this paper today by pointing out this slightly disturbing situation, in case some scholar might help to throw light on the matter. Perhaps one of you has been to Paris lately?

Thank you for your attention.

Page 14: The hills are alive with the sound: *The Sound of Music*.
Page 14: the prancing and pawing: "'Twas the Night Before Christmas."
Page 17: a great sucking sound: Cf. Ross Perot.
Page 19: thank Somebody: This was the prayer of thanks that Swinburne liked to intone.

IV
Continuing Present

10

The Evidence of Things Not Seen
A Play

Scene 1

STUDENT: I wonder, is the professor embarrassed by that essay of his from 1987—"Contemporary Poetry, Alternate Routes"?[1]
PROFESSOR: Should I be?
STUDENT: Well, it seems pretty dated, no? And dare I suggest that it also seems *wrong*.
PROFESSOR: Why?
STUDENT: It sets up a distinction between experimental writing and, well, everything else. That's bad (let's say, *loose*) enough. It also buys into Barrett Watten's idea about how to "test for a 'politics of poetry.'" Worst of all, it decides that L=A=N=G=U=A=G=E writing, that exemplary experimentalism, has passed the test.
ANGEL: It did pass the test.
STUDENT: Really?
ANGEL: No, surreally. According to Watten, "The test of a 'politics of poetry' is in the entry of poetry into the world in a political way." Poetic action is successfully political when it executes "a self-conscious method." For Watten, surrealism exemplifies such a method.
STUDENT: You're joking.
ANGEL: Just trying to be literal. Surrealism succeeded, Watten succeeded, the project of L=A=N=G=U=A=G=E Writing has clearly succeeded. The professor himself succeeded.
PROFESSOR: I did?
STUDENT: How?

ANGEL: The professor succeeded in showing that Watten possessed the "self-conscious method" that he called for. This wasn't the surrealist method he made the exemplary type of a "politics of poetry." It was something better still . . .
PRINTER'S DEVIL:

> something better still, so surreal,
>   That the sweet model must have been the same.

STUDENT: Huh? What's he saying?
PROFESSOR: He's quoting Byron—to be precise, misquoting.
ANGEL (frowning and then resuming his remarks): . . . a meta-method for identifying any occurrence of self-conscious method. And the professor also succeeded in showing how the experimental work of L=A=N=G=U=A=G=E Writing passed Watten's "test" with, as they say, flying colors.
PRINTER'S DEVIL: Flying to or from the field?
STUDENT (to the Devil): Huh? (to the Angel): Go on.
ANGEL: Didn't the professor succeed in showing the "self-conscious method" of L=A=N=G=U=A=G=E Writing?
STUDENT: So what? The whole point of the showing was to argue something else: that a self-conscious poetic practice could intervene in the world in a practical, revolutionary way. This is what the professor argued: "[Ron] Silliman calls poetry "the *philosophy of practice in language*" because it . . . represents the 'social function of the language arts' as a liberating rather than a repressive structure: 'to carry the class struggle for consciousness to the level *of* consciousness' " ("If by 'Writing' We Mean Literature" *131*). Because *"all meaning is a construct"* ("Disappearance of the Word, Appearance of the World" 168); however, this self-transparency of the word is not an idea or a priori form that the poem tries to accommodate. Self-transparency, like social justice, is a practical matter—a form of accomplishment rather than a form of truth. It has to be carried out.
ANGEL: Right.
PROFESSOR: Right.
STUDENT: Wake up, get *real*. Since 1989, when the Soviet Empire broke apart and the United States assumed a position of unrivaled military power, all this theoretical talk looks like, well,

theoretical talk. The politics of L=A=N=G=U=A=G=E Writing reads very differently now. A poem like *The Alphabet*, no less than Pound's *Cantos*, has become "a poem including history"—the history of a capitalist imperialism grown in wisdom, age, and grace.

ANGEL: Oh dear. Not grace, I think.

PRINTER'S DEVIL: My text reads "disgrace."

STUDENT: So where's all that critical self-consciousness got to? The "transgressive" writing of the literary academy? I'm changing my major. Even the prose has gone bad.

PRINTER'S DEVIL: Myself, I'll take the cold eye of your X-Generation. A plague on all your houses. Kathy Acker's the girl for me. Did you see her picture in those *New Yorker* ads?

PROFESSOR: But was my essay successful then?

STUDENT: Meaning *when* or meaning *in fact*?

ANGEL: Indeed it was.

PRINTER'S DEVIL: I *loved* it.

STUDENT: *Ceci ne pas une pipe.*

ANGEL: That's a horse of a different color, and I don't have anything to do with them. I don't even think they exist, or could exist.

PRINTER'S DEVIL: Or should exist?

ANGEL: They go against natural law, it's true. And I don't know anything about unnatural law. I don't even approve of unnatural law. It's completely immoral. Like unnatural acts.

PROFESSOR: But was I *right*?

Scene 2

DAWN INGMENS: It's not important, Professor. And don't pay attention to all that silly talk; they're just trying to confuse things. I found your essay very interesting, especially the part where you discussed how Silliman and John Hollander use the device of a Fibonacci number sequence to organize an important poem that each had written.

> In *Tjanting* . . . Silliman deployed a numerically based rule for generating his materials, which clearly held something more than a procedural interest for him. The work, he has

said, grew out of a problem he had been pondering "for at least five years: what would class struggle look like, viewed as a form. Would such a form be usable in writing?" The answer was that it would look like the Fibonacci number series—that is to say, the series in which each term is the sum of the preceding two.

What initially attracted me to the series were three things: (1) it is the mathematical sequence most often found in nature, (2) each succeeding term is larger, and (3) the quantitative difference between terms is immediately perceptible, even when the quantities are of syllables or paragraphs.

Such a sequence came to embody for Silliman an *objectively based* dialectical process:

The most important aspect of the Fibonacci series turned out not to be those gorgeous internal relationships, but the fact that it begins with two ones. That not only permitted the parallel articulation of two sequences of paragraphs, but also determined that their development would be uneven, punning back to the general theory of class struggle.

But what must be noted is that *Tjanting* does not tell the/a "story" of "class struggle." It does not reflect the operation of "the general theory of class struggle" in a projected "fiction" (first person or otherwise). Rather *Tjanting* is a localized instance of class struggle itself: not merely Silliman's personal act of struggle, but his deployment of an artistic occasion within which such struggle may take place. In the end, as [Charles] Bernstein observed [in a discussion of the poem], it is the reader in the poem who "counts."

But what might a reader today note in the accumulating Fibonacci numbers? A figure of Marxian dialectics? Or a figure of capitalist accumulation? What if a reader were to demonstrate that *Tjanting* exemplifies a kind of linguistic or poetical pyramid scheme?

PROFESSOR: Yes, you could do that. But why would you want to? It's not reading in the same spirit that the author writ, I think.

DAWN INGMENS: No, but it still might be interesting, or even important. Anyhow, let's leave that aside for a minute and think about the politics of this kind of "procedural writing." Here's something else you wrote that I find interesting.

> Of *Ketjak* Bernstein has acutely noted that "the narrative rules are not taken to be of intrinsic interest." Indeed, these are not "narrative rules" at all, but generative ones. Furthermore, they do not occupy the reader's attention as such; they provide the framework within which acts of attention are carried out. Therefore Bernstein observes, in a brilliant turn of critical wit, that "definition is a posteriori" in Silliman's work, "arising from a poetic practice in which the reader is acknowledged as present and counting." What "counts" are the multiple perspectives processed through the text along with the reader who takes part in that processing. This is why Bernstein says that a Silliman poem is "not reductive to a single world view" but is "participatory, multiple."

But if the writing makes "a poem including history," it includes a lot of readers who won't read in the same spirit that the author writ, won't it?

PROFESSOR: That would be wrong. You can't make words mean anything you like (or don't like). *Tjanting* was published by the distinguished imprint of late twentieth-century experimental and political writing, The Figures. No one would read a book published by The Figures in the way you imagine.

DAWN INGMENS: But *Tjanting*'s figures, like all poetical figurations, like all of the books published by The Figures, may be subjected to a Humpty Dumpty reading. "The question is, who is to be master, that's all."

PRINTER'S DEVIL: And does anyone doubt who the economic and political masters of public discourse in 2005 *are*?

STUDENT: And as Bernstein says, it's the reader in the poem who *counts*.

DAWN INGMENS: But there's a lot more interesting stuff in your essay, Professor.
PROFESSOR: Good. Tell me about it.
DAWN INGMENS: Well, how about this passage:

> The special character of Silliman's nonnarrative texts is nicely dramatized if we set a work like *Tjanting* beside an academic text like John Hollander's *Reflections on Espionage* (1976). This may seem an odd comparison, but it is in fact quite apposite. In the first place, both poems are fully conscious of their placement within the sociohistorical field of cold war America. Correlatively, both imagine and reflect upon the function of poetry within such social circumstances. Finally, both resort—in an extraordinarily odd conjunction of purposes—to the Fibonacci number sequence as an important procedural device within which their poems' meanings are carried out.
>
> *Reflections on Espionage* is a narrativized text made up of a series of code messages sent by the spy Cupcake to various other persons in his espionage network. The poem tells the story of Cupcake's increasing psychic disaffection—partly concealed even from himself—with his work as a spy. Eventually Cupcake comes under the surveillance of his own organization's internal security apparatus, and at the end—his reliability as a spy hopelessly compromised—the organization calls for his "termination."
>
> The story involves an elaborately executed allegory in which "spying" is equated with "being a poet," and vice versa. The text is full of coded references to American poets and writers, mostly Hollander's contemporaries. Its distant progenitor—Robert Browning's "How It Strikes a Contemporary"—underscores, by contrast, the special character of *Reflections,* for Hollander's story—like his hero—is dominated by nostalgia and a pervasive sense of ineffectuality. The poem's world is graphed along an axis of "them" and "us" that reflects both the political situation of the cold war and the typical antagonisms and divi-

sions between "schools" or groups of poets. All this would merely be amusing were it not that Hollander's hero continually reflects upon the social function of poetry. From these reflections he draws the most mordant and disheartening conclusions. In fact, *Reflections* argues—or rather demonstrates—that poetry under the social circumstances "reflected" in this poem has, like spying under the same circumstances, only an alienating effect. This poetry of "reflection" preserves, and ultimately reifies, the world-as-alienation, and it does so by failing to imagine that poetry might struggle with, rather than merely reflect (upon), its world.

Cupcake's meditations on his work as spy/poet lead him to a sharp sense of his own isolation. In his loneliness he calls into question the whole enterprise to which he has given himself:

> What kind of work is this
> For which if we were to touch in the darkness
> It would be without feeling the other there?
> It might help to know if Steampump's dying
> Was part of the work or not. I shall not be
> Told, I know.
>
> —*R*, 3–4

Cupcake's question is rhetorical and will not—cannot, in his imagination of the world—be answered. This social alienation mirrors a correspondent crisis of the personality:

> Names like ours leave no traces in
> Nature. Yet what of the names they encode, names
> One's face comes in time to rhyme with, John or James?
> The secret coded poem of one's whole life rhymes
> Entirely with that face, a maddening
> Canzona, every line of which sings in the
> Breaths we take and give, ending with the same sound.
> As with the life, so ridiculously, with

The work. But, after all, which of them is the
Enciphered version of the other one, and
Are we, after all, even supposed to know?

—*R*, p. 28

In the end Hollander's "master spy" will watch the system
he has served send out a broadcast order for his execution. His final coded transmission is a frightening poem
constructed partly on the use of the Fibonacci number series. Its principal message, secreted away in the poem's initial and terminal syllables, is revealed by using the Fibonacci number sequence as an index to those syllables. It
is a plea for death, and it is answered in the poem's final
line—a generation of Xs that, decoded, translate: TERMI-
NATE CUPCAKE.

Silliman's imagination, as we have seen, thought to discover in the Fibonacci numbers an image of class struggle
and social dialectics. In 1981 the numbers confirm his
search for signs and modes of social dynamism. But when
Cupcake uses the Fibonacci series in his final transmission, he interprets his own usage in these terrible terms:

and I have sat watching
Key numbers in their serial dance growing
Further apart, outdistancing their touching,
Outstretched arms.

—*R*, p. 71

Hollander's alter ego "editor" of Cupcake's story supplies
a gloss to Cupcake's final transmission. The exegesis remarks on the desperation of the passage but can only rep-
licate the master spy's own sense of helplessness: "This disturbing and disturbed transmission seems to be a kind of
cry for help. But to whom?" (*R*, p. 75). The interpretation here is congruent with the poem's self-conception.
Hollander characterizes cold war America and its poetry
as a world of desperate (rather than rich) ambiguities. It
is a poetic world whose own highest value—close interpersonal relations—is contradicted by the social struc-

tures and practices it takes for granted. To Hollander, the march of the Fibonacci numbers is the apocalypse of such a world, the prophecy of its desperation and its even more fragmented future.

PROFESSOR: I really got going there, didn't I.

DAWN INGMENS: You sure did. And what I find interesting is the way you make Hollander's academic exercise read like a work of sharp political critique. Your comment recalls a passage from Silliman that you quoted earlier in your essay: "Repression does not, fortunately, abolish the existence of the repressed element which continues as a contradiction, often invisible, in the social fact. As such, it continues to wage the class struggle of consciousness" (126).

STUDENT: It's the reader who's present and counting, as usual. In this case, the professor who also, in this case, isn't reading in the same spirit that Hollander writ.

Hollander's poem imagines what it knows (or thinks it knows) about poetry and society alike. Such an imagination, however, can mount no effective resistance against its own terrible revelations: vacancy in luxurious words, dismemberment in the way we live now. It is all mirror and meditation, a story and a set of reflections on the story. In this respect the contrast with writers like Bernstein and Silliman is striking and unmistakable. In them antinarrative and nonnarrative continually work against and move beyond the enchantments of what has been given and what is taken to be "real." They are the true inheritors of Blake's early attempts to dismantle the prisons of imaginary beauties: social and personal life in its cruel apparitions, and art as what reflects upon such things. Hollander's poem is a work of decadence in that it refuses to press the charges called for by its own investigation. Pleading "no contest," it is properly found guilty. *Reflections on Espionage* is far from a trivial poem. Its analogues are, for example, besides various works by Tennyson and Browning, Edward Fitzgerald's *Rubáiyat* and Dante Gabriel Rossetti's *House of Life,* and all those works which deliver us over to

luxurious and unlivable things. The highest form of such
poetry is reached in the work of artists like Baudelaire, the
mayor of the City of Pain over whose gates is written the
legend "Anywhere Out of the World."

So what is it, professor? A good poem or a bad poem? Calling it
"a work of decadence" and "far from a trivial poem" just slips past
the issue, doesn't it?

PROFESSOR: It's a good poem. A very, very good poem.

STUDENT: Why didn't you say so in the first place?

Scene 3

PRINTER'S DEVIL: He didn't say so because he was being good,
professionally speaking. There were two roads diverging in his
yellow wood—those "Alternate Routes" he mapped out in the
first place. With their alternate roots.

STUDENT: Jesus.

PRINTER'S DEVIL: I don't think he's got anything to do with it.

ANGEL: Oh no? How about "he who is not with me is against
me"?

PRINTER'S DEVIL: Right. And the professor was working along
the left road. So he did the right thing and stayed to the left.

. . . [The exchange continues in dumb-show at a level that can be
heard but not understood.]

Scene 4

DAWN INGMENS: They can go on like that for hours, professor. Let's try something else. What if I say this: that the artist and
writer—you too, professor, and me—are always complicit and
must be so.

PROFESSOR: Well, it's true that if you survey the history of poetry you very quickly realize that the most important figures are
often the least "oppositional": Homer, Aeschylus, the biblical authors, Virgil, Shakespeare, Austen, Proust, etc. And the figures
of opposition—Dante, say, or Milton, Blake, Byron, Swinburne—
are only oppositional in highly equivocal ways. Or P. B. Shelley,
Charlotte Bronte, Emily Dickinson, Virginia Woolf, Gertrude

Stein. That exemplary critic of our administered age, Harold Bloom, has always pointed this out, as have many others from Arnold to the present.

DAWN INGMENS: I've no doubt you're right; you've been around the poetical block, that's for sure.

PROFESSOR: "Much have I traveled in the realms of gold / And many goodly states and kingdoms seen."

DAWN INGMENS: Whatever. I was trying to make a different point. You do have a lot a poetry stuffed in your head.

PROFESSOR: Too true.

DAWN INGMENS: It's ok, I like it, I like to hear it. Anyhow, last night at home I was reading an essay by Stephen Spender where he remarks that "the basic contradiction of life of every contemporary is that he is involved in the guilt of the society in which he lives." He wrote that to explain the error of what he calls "escapist" art.

PROFESSOR: Some would say that all art is disengaged from politics and ideology. That it *must* be. Famous people. Kant, for instance. Marx himself said that art wasn't among the ideologies.

DAWN INGMENS: Because "ideology" for him meant "false consciousness," right? And he thought art escaped that condition.

PROFESSOR: Yes.

DAWN INGMENS: But that's not what I'm trying to say. I'm thinking that this escaped condition would be politically engaged through its escapism.

PRINTER'S DEVIL: Brave new girl!

DAWN INGMENS: . . . and that it would have the privilege of its ideological backwardness.

ANGEL: Am I hearing correctly? The artist sinks into complicity— decadence, escapism, whatever!—and comes out smelling like a rose.

PRINTER'S DEVIL: A rose is a rose is a rose is a rose.

STUDENT: Why not? What is it some poet or other said once upon a time: "Of its own beauty is the mind diseased, / And fevers into false creation."

PRINTER'S DEVIL: That was in another country. And besides, the guy is dead.

STUDENT: Well, as Bernstein says, don't be Saussure. Criticism too gets infected with its moral commitments. How could it be

otherwise? Writer and reader both work from within, sympathizing with the contradictions and complexities they half perceive
and half create.

PROFESSOR: Remember plate 21 of *The Marriage of Heaven and
Hell*, where Blake separates the sheep of philosophy and criticism
from the goats of art and poetry?

STUDENT (to DAWN INGMENS): Is he kidding?

PRINTER'S DEVIL: And where he takes his stand with the devils cast out by angelic characters like that prig Plato: "Morality [is]
not Poetry but Philosophy the Poet is independent and Wicked
the Philosopher is Dependent & Good"!

DAWN INGMENS: Not "independent", *complicit*. Maybe we should
stop trying to be devils, or pretending to be angels.

STUDENT: Or the other way round.

PROFESSOR: So was I *right*?

STUDENT: Let's say you left things out. Let's say you were trying
to write in the same spirit that the authors writ. Let's say you forgot that other readers were counting too.

DAWN INGMENS: We're all working from inside. "After all, the
world is around me, not in front of me." Only the "wisdom pro-
fessions" imagine otherwise, cherishing their fantasies of perfection.

ANGEL: Set a thief to catch a thief. Those fantasies are part of
an economy of grace.

PRINTER'S DEVIL: Rubbish. In a looking glass world, which is
where we are, friends, who are the thieves, who the police? And
who decides? What is truth here anyhow?

DAWN INGMENS: Could Wordsworth tell the truth that Byron
knew? To him it wasn't truth at all. So he told the truth as he
imagined he knew it—just like Silliman did, and Hollander, and
you too professor. "In a dark time the eye begins to see."

STUDENT: To see *what*? The eye or the I?

ANGEL: Say, rather, to see *how*! To see and think beautifully, in-
effectually, angelically. To see like this:

> Writing in inhibiting. Sighing, I sit, scribbling in ink
> this pidgin script. I sing with nihilistic witticism,
> disciplining signs with trifling gimmicks—impish

hijinks which highlight stick sigils? Isn't it glib?
Isn't it chic? I fit childish insights within rigid limits,
writing shtick which might instill priggish misgiv-
ings in critics blind with hindsight.

—Bök, 50

DAWN INGMENS: So "which blind spirit is whining in this whistling din? Is it . . . with ill will in its mind, victimizing kids timid
with fright?" (Bök 54)
STUDENT: "If it is—which blind witch is midwifing its misbirth?"
(54)
DAWN INGMENS: "Is it this thin, sickish girl, twitching in fits,
whilst writing things in spirit-writing?" (54)
STUDENT: "If it isn't—it is I; it is I . . ." (54)
PROFESSOR: "Christ, this ship is sink-
ing." (53)
ANGEL: "I find bliss in this primitivism. Might I mimic it in
print?" (52)
PRINTER'S DEVIL: "The business of Art as I tried to explain in
Composition as Explanation is to live in the actual present, that is
the complete actual present, and to completely express that com-
plete actual present." (Stein, *Lectures in America* 104–5)
DAWN INGMENS:

   Diving in, I swim, fighting this frigid swirl, kicking, kicking, swimming in it till I sight high cliffs,
rising, indistinct in thick mists, lit with lightning. (53)

Scene 5

ANGEL: She's a sweet girl, but really—what an *idea*!
PRINTER'S DEVIL: *Which* girl do you mean?
ANGEL: Both of them of course. Or all four.
PRINTER'S DEVIL: I think there are only three, not four. One
is just imaginary, the other is both real and imaginary. So that
makes three, not two or four.
ANGEL: Alright then, three saints in four acts.

PRINTER'S DEVIL: Don't you think it's time to stop playing and start playing?

ANGEL: What an idea? What do you mean?

PRINTER'S DEVIL: The philosophers have only tried to interpret the world. The point is to change it. So here's a riddle: "The business of Art . . . is to live in the actual present, that is the complete actual present, and to completely express that complete actual present."

ANGEL: I thought that was a statement. Pontifical and impossible.

PRINTER'S DEVIL: No, it's a riddle and its problem is this: How could you do that?

ANGEL: As I said, it's impossible. It might even be a contradiction. Or a couple of contradictions.

PROFESSOR: Actually it's just a trick question.

STUDENT: Why is it impossible?

DAWN INGMENS: Why is it a trick question?

ANGEL: It's impossible because nobody could do it.

STUDENT: Maybe not, but everybody does.

PROFESSOR: That's the trick. You'd be doing it if everybody was doing it. Otherwise you wouldn't be.

Scene 6, The Continuing Present

HOLY GHOST: But you are, because everybody is. Only it's hard to see because it looks as if somebody else has already done it. But they haven't; we're all living in the complete actual present in order to completely express its beginning again and again.

SAINT ALICE: You need a looking glass to help you see what's being seen.

ANGEL: A mirror up to life?

PRINTER'S DEVIL: Nothing's up to that.

ALL: Nonsense.

> The Bible of Hell
> Maldoror.
> Pataphysics

SAINT TERESA: None of that patriarchal poetry. I want a hero.

PRINTER'S DEVIL:

>   an uncommon want,
>   When every year and month sends forth a new one.

SAINT TERESA: . . . a hero in eclipse, a noble rider rescuing the sound of the words. Like Ivanhoe.
WALTER SCOTT: Not *my* Ivanhoe!
THE BLESSED VIRGIN: Of course not. The point is to change it. *My* IVANHOE.
HOLY GHOST: Once upon a time there was a Printing House in Hell whose business plan was to print only works that were "dictated from Eternity." Imitating God and Gutenberg, it announced its first publication to be "The Bible of Hell." Because this book could not be found in the Goblin Markets that flourished in those days gone by, a legend grew that it was never made.
IVANHOE: And of course it never was.
THE BLESSED VIRGIN: Correct. This book is also called "The Book that Never Was."
ALL: Why?
THE BLESSED VIRGIN: Because it never was.
IVANHOE: A book.
ALL: A wonderful book.
SAINT TERESA: But a difficult work, written in strange codes. What does it mean?
IVANHOE:

>   Have you practiced so long to learn to read?
>   Have you felt so proud to get at the meaning of poems?
>   Stop this day and night with me and you shall possess the
>   origin of all poems

HOLY GHOST: A book to be read to be read to be read to be read to be.
THE BLESSED VIRGIN: A device for reading again and again, a textual composition of human characters.
GERTRUDE STEIN: Typeset?
DAWN INGMENS: Autopoietic.
ALL: Does it have a name?

THE BLESSED VIRGIN:

> In the world unknown
> > Sleeps a voice unspoken,
> By thy step alone
> > Can its rest be broken,
> > > Child of Ocean!

DAWN INGMENS: Here lies one whose name is writ in Java.
IVANHOE: Once upon a time its name is Legion. Before the many bibles were, I VAN.

11
IVANHOE
A Playful Portrait

DAWN INGMENS: It's something we made for the professor who spends too much of his time thinking about thinking. We thought he should be doing something about it.

ANGEL: About what?

MARY MARGARET O'MALLEY: About thinking of course.

GIRL POET: What happened?

JENNIFER: Well, first we got him to understand The Alice Fallacy.

DAWN INGMENS: That was critical.

MARY MARGARET O'MALLEY: Thinking.

JENNIFER: It started with Geoffrey's Gen-X questions about Keats, but we all got in on the act—Chris, Margaret, me. The games began soon enough.

DAWN INGMENS: And what's *he* doing now? Lecturing again. Hopeless. You give him something to play with and he can't help *talking about* it.

IVANHOE. Education in a New Key
by Jerome McGann, in collaboration with Johanna Drucker and Bethany Nowviskie
IVANHOE (http://patacriticism.org/ivanhoe) is a research and pedagogical project for humanities scholars and students working in a digital age like our own, where books are only one among many cultural sources and objects of critical reflection. It is designed within the framework of the traditional goals of humanities education: to

promote rigorous as well as imaginative thinking; to develop habits of thoroughness and flexibility when we investigate our cultural inheritance and try to exploit its sources and resources; and to expose and promote the collaborative dynamics of all humane studies, which by their nature both feed upon and resupply our cultural legacy.

IVANHOE emerged in the spring of 2000 from a conversation between Jerome McGann and Johanna Drucker on the subject of literary-critical method and their shared dissatisfaction with the limitations of received interpretive procedures. They were interested in exploring forms of critical inquiry that moved closer to the provocative freedom of original works of poetry and literature.

McGann suggested that Walter Scott's famous romance fiction *Ivanhoe* contained within itself many alternative narrative possibilities, and he added that this kind of thing was characteristic of imaginative works in general. Scott's book epitomizes this situation in the many continuations it spawned throughout the nineteenth century—versions in different genres as well as other kinds of responses, textual, pictorial, musical. For example, when many Victorian readers complained about Scott's decision to marry Ivanhoe to Rowena and not Rebecca, they were clearly responding to one of the book's underdeveloped possibilities. In our own day readers often react to other unresolved tensions in the book—for example, to the complex ways it handles, and mishandles, the subject of anti-Semitism. "Everyone knows that an anti-Semitic strain runs through the novel," McGann said. "The question is: 'What are you prepared to DO about it?'" Victorians rewrote and reimagined the book. Why are we so hesitant to do the same thing?

The concept of criticism as "a doing," as action and intervention, is a founding principle of IVANHOE. Traditional interpretation is itself best understood as a set of reflective activities and hence as something that lays itself open to active responses from others. It is not so much that "all interpretation is misinterpretation," as Harold Bloom observed some twenty-five years ago, as that all interpretation pursues transformations of meaning within a dynamic space of inherited and ongoing acts of interpretation. Interpretation is a dialogical exchange and, ultimately, a continuous set of collaborative activities.

This critical vantage point necessarily resists the traditional assumption about the self-identity of a particular text or cultural work. Various factors and agencies so impinge on the textual condition that the field of textuality, including all the objects we locate in that field, are in a perpetually dynamic state of formation and transformation. This view of textuality implies that any textual object—what in IVANHOE we call "the source text"—has to be encountered within a dynamical "discourse field" (i.e., the extended network of documents, materials, discussions, and evidence within which the work is continually being constituted). Approaching textuality in this way, we concluded that a digital environment would provide IVANHOE with an opportune and useful playspace.

When we began playing IVANHOE these initial premises were a somewhat loosely held set of intuitions. The actual gameplay transformed them into clear and governing ideas. Not surprisingly, it also drove us to rethink the whole process of interpretive method and theory. As a result, we began to see that IVANHOE could be designed and developed as an environment for the study and encouragement of critical practices that would make self-awareness pivotal to the whole enterprise. IVANHOE is what Coleridge might have called "an aid to reflection": a machinery for making explicit the assumptions about critical practice, textual interpretation, and reading that remain unacknowledged, or irregularly explored, in conventional approaches to literary studies.

In IVANHOE, the idea is that interpretation should no longer be imagined as proceeding from a subject grappling with a transparent object. By contrast, IVANHOE discourages players from assuming that there is something to be called, say, "The Poem Itself." Perhaps even more crucially, it routes the acts of an interpreting agent back into the material being studied. Players and their moves are continually returned to the ongoing process of collaborative investigation for further critical reflection, both by the agent herself and by the other players. All players thus move in that Burnsian space where each is repeatedly drawn "to see ourselves as others see us." Based on economies of expenditure, deficit, and gain, with winning conditions and costs, IVANHOE's underlying game model urges the player—the thinker—to a continuing process of measuring and assessing his or her moves in relation to everyone else's. IVANHOE has been dominated from the start by a ludic spirit. This attitude is reflected in the name of the project, IVANHOE, which references a cultural work now rarely taken "seriously," though it once reigned as perhaps the most popular and seriously influential work of fiction in nineteenth-century Europe and America. We took that avoidance as a sign of a poverty of criticism, which goes broke by following a gold standard of value. IVANHOE would encourage, instead, as much circulation and exchange as possible.

From the initial provocation, IVANHOE quickly spun itself into life. Playing with Scott's novel generated new practical design features, the most important of which was the idea that the game would have to be played "in" a role, or *en masque,* under an explicitly assumed conceit of identity. Players would make their moves only through that role. This device would introduce into IVANHOE another vehicle—in addition to the dialogic form and performative procedures—for encouraging critical self-reflection. We also began to see that a robust environment would only be built if we tested our ideas in as many kinds of gameplay as possible.

STUDENT (to DAWN INGMENS): What was *that* all about? I had the experience but I think I missed the meaning.
DAWN INGMENS: That's High Theory getting translated when you cross the bar. We're talking about *transgression* here!
PROFESSOR: Cross the bar? As in Tennyson?
DAWN INGMENS: You've heard of passing the bar? This is *crossing* the bar, as in "don't cross me, man!" Poets often talk about that bar in funny ways. "On those infinite mountains of light now barr'd out by the Atlantic sea, the new born fire stood before the starry king!"

PROFESSOR: It's true. Poets cross the bar and live in Eternity, in that actual present that is the complete actual present and where they completely express that complete actual present.

PRINTER'S DEVIL: Thrilling, isn't it?

STUDENT: Complete actual present or complete actual nonsense? And "Eternity"? That's not *my* "Actual Present"!

GIRL POET: It's a figure of speech, dummy.

STUDENT: Dumb me and dumber you. If we're talking about the actual present, I *still* think it's the reader who's present and counting. Are you living in Eternity, Professor?

PROFESSOR: I'm thinking about it. Give me time.

DAWN INGMENS: But this time let's play another game. Let's call it going back to the present.

PRINTER'S DEVIL: Let's.

PROFESSOR: How do you play?

DAWN INGMENS: In this game, that's a question nobody can answer. I mean if you really want to *play*. And if you don't want to play—well, you wouldn't want to know how.

PROFESSOR: But I do want to play.

DAWN INGMENS: But *everybody* who wants to play knows how to play, Professor.

PRINTER'S DEVIL: Some people don't want to play, they just want to join.

STUDENT: But they're no fun.

DAWN INGMENS: People can forget how to play, the way people forget how to read poetry.

GIRL POET: Or why.

STUDENT: So if they joined in they might remember how.

ANGEL: But first they need to learn the rules.

GIRL POET: Yikes. "Dost thou think, because thou art virtuous, there shall be no more cakes and ale?"

PRINTER'S DEVIL: "Bring out number weight and measure in a year of dearth."

GIRL POET: Rules? That's not how anyone learns to play anything. It's not even the way kids learn to talk. If you start with a book of rules you're sure to get into bad habits. Wanting to do things right.

MARY MARGARET O'MALLEY: We could cross the bar again a different way.

STUDENT: Huh?

MARYMARGARET O'MALLEY: Let's run and fetch something from the professor's realms of gold. Way back when, somebody fetched this:

> A thing of beauty is a joy for ever:
> Its loveliness increases; it will never
> Pass into nothingness; but still will keep
> A bower quiet for us, and a sleep
> Full of sweet dreams, and health, and quiet breathing.
>
> —*Endymion*, bk. 1, 1–5

Now, let's take that and run it through an algorithm:

> In play, there are two pleasures for your choosing,
> The one is winning, and the other, losing.

STUDENT: What happens next?
DAWN INGMENS: Whatever.
GIRL POET:

> A thing that shocks us is like Dawn (whatever),
> Diseasingly increasing, she will never
> Pass into common day, but slyly keep
> A ludic freeway for her dark and sleep
> Less angels watching o'er our heavy breathing.
> Therefore, in what we borrow, we are wreathing
> This uncompleted actual present dearth,
> As gift and klupzy crowning for her mirth . . .

DAWN INGMENS: (blushing slightly) How sweet.
GIRL POET: I could go on.
PROFESSOR: I can't go on.
DAWN INGMENS: You must go on.

12

Modernity and Complicity
A Conversation with Johanna Drucker

JM: Let's talk about complicity.

JD: Not the first word usually associated with modernity. But the conjunction of modernity and complicity had become a focal point for each of us independently. I had been thinking about this conjunction within modern visual art, particularly among American modernists such as Winslow Homer, Philip Evergood, and Thomas Hart Benton, because of their relation to popular culture. Because I've been so struck by the exclusion of American art from the critical paradigms that grew in the soil of European modernism. I came up against the impasse that that critical tradition meets in facing contemporary art's relation to the culture industry. The premises of opposition and radical criticality foundational to that tradition felt utterly inadequate as a framework for understanding contemporary artists and their work. The concept of complicity began to take shape in response. But you arrived at this idea from your work within the tradition of Romanticism, English poetry, and in particular, Rossetti—didn't you?

JM: Actually, Rossetti came as a way to see through the immediate contradictions—though he also illustrates the issues in a distinctive way. The problem appeared many years ago when I was reading some American poets in the '60s, in particular Berryman, Dugan, Sexton, and Plath. The poets of a savage god, as Alvarez called them at the time.[1] I'd grown up under the influence of certain Romantic ideologies, not least of all the Late Romantic ideology of "radical critique."

JD: I think that the concept of radical critique is the crux of the matter. The practices that have been carried out under that rubric are premised on blindness to complicity. Certainly the art historical assessment of visual modernism from Romanticism to the present is created in a denial of the ways fine art practice functions within, rather than outside of, mainstream culture. But art historical discourse is deeply attached to the idea that a radical critique legitimates fine art and that aesthetics has an agenda of opposition.

JM: As in the discourse of literary and critical studies in general. I now see that constellation of ideas as an enlightenment version of Keats's radical sentimentalism—remember his famous "a thing of beauty is a joy for ever"? Those American poets utterly corrupted that Romantic inheritance in all its variant forms of thought: that poets are the unacknowledged legislators of the world (Shelley), that poets are men [*sic*] speaking to men [*sic*] out of more endowed moral insight and sensibilities (Wordsworth), that imagination is the mark of a quasi-divine creativity (Coleridge). So on the High Romantic end—because I didn't know Burns then— I was left pondering Blake, for whom imagination was a specifically uncreating faculty, the power to build the building of Los(s). And with Byron, the master of the spoiler's art: "In play there are two pleasures for your choosing, / The one is winning and the other losing." On the modern and contemporary end I grew interested in poetries of bad faith and especially in so-called workshop poetry where the writing is so heavily administered and professional.

JD: But can we understand modernism differently if we take a different stance? What if we allow that Homer's work as an illustrator is central to the way he creates images? His commercial work is not the expression of day-job labor to be bracketed out of our understanding of his aesthetics. Instead the techniques and methods, the approaches to composition and communication, the thematics and treatments of figures, scenes, sentiment, ideas—in brief, everything in those illustrations forms a structural foundation for his work as a whole. He thinks in terms of vignettes that border on cliché, trying to make of experience a set of recognizably familiar views. You have seen this before, he says in making of experience an image that strikes a receptive chord in the viewer. Recognition depends upon shared understanding (as opposed to shock, which presumes novel invention). The standard *epater le bourgeoisie* of conventional radical modernism (and its critical acolytes) dismissed such work (and its attitude) as formulaic, uninteresting, worse than academic—unthinking and uncritical. As if they wouldn't see the extent to which the elaboration of such imagery was an expert act, deft in its ability to crystallize collective perception into a representation of a shared experience. Not surprisingly, such works (I'm thinking of Homer's Civil War images, produced when he worked as a reporter) are journalistic and meant for reproduction and wide circulation. Disdain for the popular has so debased these works that neither their modernity nor their aesthetic precepts have been given credible reading. Does this discussion resonate with your interest in a poetics of "bad faith"?

JM: Yes, in a couple of respects. In literary terms the issue arises with the advent of a poet like Felicia Hemans, a late Romantic who became the most published poet in the nineteenth century in England and America. (I bring her in here as an exemplary case only—many others could be cited, including figures of greater substance, like Tennyson, Christina and D. G. Rossetti, or Hemans's contemporary, Letitia Elizabeth Landon). Hemans was a jingoist writer, completely committed to the most central British imperialist ideas, as well as a good craftsperson (in this respect more accomplished, for example, than Landon, who is a more complex writer). Hemans was also a mature sentimental poet(ess)—the term *sentimental* meaning here a person who deployed the conventions of that method of writing. Her ideology and her style made her immensely popular—until the coming of the pre-Modernist aesthetic movement and then Modernism itself, when she became an emblem of everything a writer should NOT do or think or be. And an emblem of bad art.

Most interesting to think about here is the vigorous comeback Hemans has made in the past ten years or so in the wake of the academic interest in women Romantic writers. This comeback rides, typically, on an argument that Hemans is actually a poet of "radical critique," with her true meanings inflected in disguised or oblique ways because of the presence of various censoring mechanisms, some psychic, some institutional. But the truth is that her work promotes—consciously as well as unconsciously—

the most conservative political ideas and attitudes: conservative by the measure of her contemporaries, that is to say, and for the most part by our own measures as well.

The problem, as you suggest, lies not in the writers and artists—Winslow Homer, Felicia Hemans—but in the standards of judgment that weigh upon and control our own critical procedures. It is as if, in order to permit an artist or writer into the canon of serious art, a case must be made for that person's work as "radical critique."

Now let me put down a (perhaps controversial) position from which to restart this discussion of making critical judgments about art. It would be this: that the artist and writer is always complicit and must be so. Complicity comes, however, like the society it engages and reflects, in many types and forms. The measure of the effectiveness of artistic work—its significance and power as art—is not per se related to the degree of its "oppositionality," so-called. When one surveys the history of poetry one sees very quickly that the most important figures are regularly the least "oppositional": Homer, Aeschylus, the biblical authors, Virgil, Shakespeare, Austen, Proust, etc. And figures of opposition—Dante, say, or Milton—are only oppositional in highly equivocal ways. This equivocalness marks even the greatest saints of the oppositional brotherhood and sisterhood: Blake, Byron, P. B. Shelley; Charlotte Bronte, Emily Dickinson, Virginia Woolf. That exemplary critic of our administered age, Harold Bloom, has always—and correctly—pointed this out, as have other exemplary critics from Arnold to the present.

JD: I agree that artists and writers are "always complicit," and I also agree that an artist can occupy a considerable range of positions in relation to the celebration or criticism of their age's accepted cultural values. The definition of complicity also raises questions about the extent to which artists are self-conscious about their alignments. This awareness even varies within a single artist's oeuvre. Homer as an illustrator knows he is attempting alignment with certain norms of legibility—for instance, for the sake of communicative efficacy. Later he paints the canvases that are always awarded the label *heroic*—those images of the Maine coast. Because he becomes focused on a contemplative struggle of natural forces, that work can be read in opposition to the modernizing effects of industrialization in all sectors of American life in the late nineteenth century. While in no sense posing a radical critique, his late work lends itself to validation on terms that are much more in conformity with the values of a modernist stance that embraces these oppositions. Here I am largely thinking of the ways that T. J. Clark's discussions of nineteenth-century French modernism perform peculiar acts of selectivity upon the object of his inquiry. To make his case for an oppositional modernism, he singles out the "good" objects of Impressionism as those paintings that suggest an awareness of the ravaging effects upon the working class being wrought by transformations in the Parisian landscape. But he brackets out the way the work of Monet, Degas, Renoir are primarily always bourgeois paintings (paintings of and by and for an affluent middle class created by industrialism). Impressionist paintings figured "beautifully" the images of sun-dappled leisure beloved of the American middle class (who receive them rather differently than Clark does); they were not incitements to revolutionary action. The attempt to recuperate Impressionism as a radical movement seems perverse, the product of an academic Marxist wish-dream. Whatever position the artists might have espoused, the reading presumes a critical stance, obviously for its own purpose.

But to go back to Homer and his illustrations, early paintings, and his Maine coast works—is he equally "complicit" or differently complicit in these different instances? Illustration and isolated painting, commercial work in a journalistic context, and fine art produced by an artist at the end of his life are different undertakings. My argument is that we should not try to regard the entirety of his oeuvre within the terms of his later aesthetic. And, in fact, those Maine paintings don't conform to the terms of radical critique either. Instead, they are aligned with another primary element of modernist rhetoric—the idea of autonomy.

I'm going to leave the question about the differences between these two aspects of Homer's work hanging for the moment, because I think the case might be more clearly made—or more daringly (because of his unacceptability) brought to the fore—by a discussion of the work of Thomas Hart Benton. Benton is much despised by the modern art history establishment—as is almost all of early-twentieth-century realist American art. This fact is very telling in itself—that the devotees of modernism, the generation of critics who strove to recast the midcentury discussion of the avant-garde in neo-formalist dialectics refused (still refuse) to even *look* at early-twentieth-century American art. From their perspective, the work is beneath notice since it offers nothing to their formalist premises. Benton is outside the pale of critical attention, a figurative, illustrational painter of popular work. His imagery (and his methodology) are conceived on terms that cannot be made to align with the avant-gardist critique that forms the unquestioned core of modernist studies. And if Benton is problematic, then Reginald Marsh, Grant Wood, John Steuart Curry, Elizabeth Bishop, and other realist artists of the 1930s are as well. Ashcan School painting, much of which remains closely linked in subject matter and approach to the illustrational base of training from which it sprung, only receives attention insofar as its practitioners can be aligned with radical causes. Thus John Sloan is the "good" Ashcan painter because of his work with *The Masses,* but Everett Shinn, who is a dazzling virtuoso painter of effects, is persona non grata at the table of high modernist criticism.

This act of excising entire movements from the history of modern visual art and culture strikes me as unconscionable on many fronts—since by the violence of this exclusion one risks the most perilous ignorance of the period and all that follows from it. And worse, to my mind, this ignorance supports a grotesque misconception of the way modernism works. The fact that so many contemporary critics flounder in the face of work by John Currin or Lisa Yuskavage, which takes so much of its imagery, aesthetics, and even ideology from the mass culture domain of illustration and popular press sensibility, is in part due to the lacuna left by the academic establishment in its historically lopsided conception of what constituted modernism. Artists are sometimes, fortunately, less doctrinaire, being rather more eclectic in their appetites for whatever strikes them as useful. But to establish the foundation for a discussion of *their* complicity requires some backtracking into the earlier period of modernism, at least as a point of reference for the way the critical stance we both find problematic (a polite way of putting it) came to have the form and limitations we are trying to rethink.

This leads me to a question about your last remark—because

I don't think that within the art historical context I can point to such an example. Do literary critics really acknowledge complicity? And if so, how? On what terms? What is meant by it?

JM: I was reading an essay by Stephen Spender last night in which he observes that "the basic condition of life of every contemporary is that he is involved in the guilt of the whole society in which he lives." He wrote this to try to help explain the error of what he calls "escapist" art. Now you and I would say, I think, that an "escapist" art might easily represent a form of social/cultural involvement, even economic involvement. Blake's art, in my view, is radically escapist, and we'd have no trouble marching out many other examples. Escapists are "involved" through and in their escapism, surely. So why does Spender make this distinction, and what might we think from the fact that he makes it? Does an escapist stance vitiate or weaken the grounds of representation? Is that what he means? And then there is this question: what art ISN'T escapist? Of course one can draw lines between forms of escapism—between Zola and Huysmans, or between Courbet and Rossetti.

But then what?

JD: Don't you think that Spender would argue that Courbet is *not* an escapist artist? From my perspective, Courbet's purported political engagement through his art has as much escapism in it as Rossetti's apparent non-engagement (and vice versa—Rossetti's seemingly unpolitical imagery and mode of working are intrinsically and absolutely encoded with ideological value). One lineage of avant-garde radical rhetoric takes its cue from Courbet—with an urge to refute the "guilt" Spender attributes to us all through a claim to action, a conviction that a radical resistance, manifest through visual or aesthetic form, contains a potential for transformation of consciousness that can bring about social change. But I'm always reminded by this of the irony, the sad pathetic paradox, of El Lissitzky's modern graphics in their place on a wall outside a Russian/Soviet factory in the late 1910s. Who among those workers read that arrangement of triangles, circles, and dynamic compositional elements as a call to action? As a platform for their own activist self-determination?

Most of what follows in the rhetorical claims of twentieth-century art/artists belongs to either a false claim (radical form =

radical politics of resistance), a hollow salve to conscience (do some good and thus make a change), or some other denial of the complicit role of aesthetics as ideological support for the status quo. At the same time, however, I don't want to deny the need for independent and alternative culture, for imaginative work, for creative life, or for progressive and radical thought. Where, if not in aesthetic imagination, are we to find the capacity to "imagine otherwise"? Or is that concept fraught with self-delusion for artists and critics alike?

JM. Whatever Spender might think, contemporary criticism sees Courbet as you have said. But Courbet and Rossetti, or Hemans and Tennyson, are not the problem. The problem lies with our critical measures and standards. Criticism is infected with moral commitments, left, right, center. It is as if the only sine qua non of art—that it deliver to us acute revelations of experience— were not enough. We want those revelations to be something more—something moral, something uplifting. But the ancients had it right: the business of art is to hold a mirror up to life in all its complexities and complicities, in all its beauty and ugliness. Clarity, precision, and truth of representation. The *aesthetic* experience is the recognition of the presence of that kind of truth, the recognition that an agent has been assiduous in bringing it about and that the process of its realization can also be realized as we engage with it. Remember what Blake said about philosophy and criticism, on one hand, and art and poetry on the other? On plate 21 of *The Marriage of Heaven and Hell* he calls the one a class of angels and the other a class of devils. When the angel brings his critical observations to the works of the artist he simply "holds a candle in the sunshine." Why is this? Because to Blake's view "Morality [is] not Poetry but Philosophy the Poet is independent and Wicked the Philosopher is Dependent & Good."

We've got to stop trying to be angels, or pretending to be devils.

JD: "Peut être," as a character in the Waugh novel I'm reading says when he disagrees ever so slightly with something in conversation. Critical modernism (and its later extensions into postmodern and deconstructionist debate) would, of course, take issue with the theological tenor of even Blake's perverse cosmology. Revelation and truth are quaint concepts, much bracketed and qualified in our day. I could get sidetracked here into a discussion of the way religious art, or even, to put it more usefully, an art of faith, is completely excised from consideration in serious critical terms. And where faith is an integral part of a modernist's work, it has to be bracketed out. The critical treatment of Mondrian is a perfect example of this phenomenon. Theosophy? Religion? "No, no" protest our most esteemed and lauded critics, Mondrian's work is the pinnacle of abstraction without words, beyond language, reference, faith, or thematics, the ne plus ultra of a formal system in love with its own calibrated capacity for perfect articulation. I find such a critical stance reprehensible. Not because a critic is obliged to embrace the faith (or lack thereof) of any artist, but because such a reading of the work is incomplete and provides a limited understanding.

JM: You misunderstand me when I said that acuity and revelation are the sine qua non of art. I'm not suggesting that artwork might not have serious moral or religious views or commitments. Obviously it does, and (equally obviously) it can impress us and move us in those frames of reference. But as we know, in the world, as in art, thousands of different kinds of moral and religious flowers bloom. This is why the proverb *Nihil humanum alienum a me puto* applies to each. Beliefs, commitments, faiths: all their contradictions and strange diagonals are held in the space of art in a special way—indeed, just in the ways you described when you talked about that marvelous Benton picture. Probably the chief function of art is to be able to represent those contradictions as thoroughly and acutely as possible—in order to give us a chance to *see* and reflect on them in all their remarkable differentials.

JD: I didn't think you were really proposing truth and revelation as essential to artistic practice in any prescriptive sense. I just got a little worried about all those angels and devils.

JM: But I *like* talking about angels and devils. They put a ludic tilt into our critical seriousness!

JD: As I say, "peut être." But we know that artists *do* think beyond these critical categories, frequently. If the imperative for art to serve the role of moral conscience of the culture is such a straitjacket for critical thought, it has not, fortunately, constrained the production of aesthetic works. I'll be specific. Take Benton's *Persephone*, an American figurative work of the late 1930s. Benton's image serves Persephone up on a half shell of foliage that looks like an overgrown cabbage, the harvest of the fertile heartland, while a farmer looks on. Persphone is modeled on the Hollywood starlet of her era, with a long torso and marcelled hair, and she is vignetted into the image according to a spatial rhetoric taken right out of movie poster design. Cold and inaccessible, she barely merits our sympathy, portrayed as a strumpet of commerce herself, already fallen, though within the terms of the story her innocence has to be maintained as a convenient fiction. The unappealing farmer doesn't get our sympathy either. He is the more cruelly treated of the two—a caricature of the rough provincial gawking with drop-jawed lascivious lust even as he condemns our professional Persephone.

The complexities of this image, and of its citations and borrowings, span a range of contradictory positions. Is Benton sympathetic? To whom? Accurate? Revelatory? Or descriptive, problematic, and presentational? More these latter, and thus his use of mass culture thematics and motifs can't be taken critically— he doesn't savage the young woman, nor does he suggest that the culture industry fate that has caused her to fall from purity renders her hopelessly tainted. Her strong body looks primed for its natural cultural purpose of reproduction within the very terms of American-ism that places her in the landscape of the farmer's gaze. Benton doesn't provide a single standpoint. He presents a set of conditions and uses the aesthetic conventions that are themselves complicit in ways I could detail exhaustively. My point is that to deal with this image requires an analytic method that isn't premised on exclusionary binarisms or misrepresentations, but works descriptively through the apparent and real contradictions of Benton's simultaneous enthusiasm for and distrustful judgment on a range of mainstream values. Morals, seductions, pleasures, work ethics, entertainment values, voyeurism, exploitation, and so forth all are present in this image. Critics on the right find Benton celebratory. Are they just not looking? And those on the left condemn him for his regionalism and seemingly devout nationalistic provincialism. They don't seem to be looking either. But I think that Benton's work presents visual contradictions that, fortunately, can't be reconciled into the categories of modern art or its critical legacy.

I could bracket all this and say, OK, let's revisit Benton's work and American realism, but then no one would pay attention to the critical issue any more than they have through responding to your work on Rossetti. In both instances, the issue is that these figures show the need to rethink the critical premises on which modernism has been received. The most pressing aspect of the legacy such premises bequeath is for contemporary art and criticism, I think. Or, in any case, I see no separation between the creation of a viable critical framework for assessing historical figures of modernism and their work and discussion of contemporary work.

JM. "Benton doesn't provide a single viewpoint." Precisely. Philosophy and criticism work toward clarity by pursuing cognitive simplification. Art does not. And of course when certain philosophers recognize the limits of their procedures they veer into and exploit the methods of the artist.

Rossetti is an especially interesting case here because his explicit theory rested in what he called "an art of the inner standing-point." He referred to this idea twice, once when he was just beginning and again at the peak of his career when he wrote to answer the critical attack on his work by Robert Buchanan, who charged Rossetti with artistic immorality. Rossetti's position, however, was that the artist could not approach his representations "from without," as if he might have or aspire to gain (or give) some objective or "single" viewpoint. The artist works from within, sympathizing with the contradictions and complexities. More than that, this inner standing-point means that the artist and poet's own practice is engulfed in the process of representation, becomes itself part of the subject being represented.

"Art is not among the ideologies," Marx once—famously—said. And critics left, right, and center regularly want to put works of art in some uninfected and transcendental place. Beyond "the world's slow stain," beyond complicities. But this is the dream and desire of the philosopher cherishing fantasies of perfection. When artwork cherishes the same fantasies, as it often does, it draws them down to earth so that we can see them for exactly what they are—dreams and desires spinning out the Veil of Maya where all our complicit and contradictory stories are forever unfolding.

JD: The question of ideology is a difficult one. Clearly works of art participate in ideological formations. Highly fraught with symbolic potency, an image can be a lightning rod for the most powerful of polarized responses, as we know from the long history of iconoclasm, censorship, outrage, adoration, and so on. If art is not "among" the ideologies in Marx's sense, is that because it is unstable? Independent? Of a different order of cultural expression? In what does ideology inhere, through what means do systems of belief find form?

I ask because the dominant orthodoxy (I use the term deliberately, with all its religious associations) of contemporary art is grounded in a paradox of beliefs. The artist's role is to make work that reveals ideological tenets, redresses the wrongs wrought by bad faith or worse abuses of power in the structure of social relations, and yet be both in and outside of those relations. As if fine art were not itself an industry arm of culture, as you say, critics and artists want to "put works of art in some uninfected and transcendental place." So if I read you correctly, above, you think Marx is wrong. Yes? I do. Though precisely how is he wrong?

JM. Yes, Marx is/was wrong. Art is made by human beings, who live and work in the fields of ideology (false consciousness, veils of Maya). What Plato called *eros* is the affect signaling our desire—vain, insistent, perpetual—to break the spells of illusion. Criticism's "paradox of beliefs" is at best a struggle in those illusions and at worst—alas, too commonly—a way of standing upright and enlightened, armed with method and theory. Art, by contrast, is a drunken boat, in constant danger of shipwreck from that freight it carries about—its own "dead thoughts" as Shelley called them. It skirts the disaster it courts by its own processes of constant flight and pursuit. Being constructed at an inner standing-point, the intelligence of art lies in its action—in a thinking it sustains—and not in some thematic constellation of truth or idea. As a poem of Alan Davies once wonderfully put the matter: "Truth is lies that have hardened."

Criticism likes to set art under its microscopes but too often fails to see the ironic eye staring back. The complicity of art? Let Baudelaire bring us all down to earth: "Hypocrite lecteur, mon semblable, mon frère." Think about Paul de Man, that exemplary critical intelligence. Surely it's clear that his greatest critical legacy emerged from his failure to deconstruct the *aporias* of his own work. He left unwritten the one book that would have set his work at an inner standing-point: his reflective memoir.

JD: I agree that the most obvious lapses are always the grandest, greatest gaps. We always see everything except what lies within our blind spot. Thus the usefuless of dialogue—don't you think?

JM: Yes. Hermeneutic circles and aporias—the snares that wait for every ivory tower, like ourselves. The only chance to get free of them is to have someone push you into thinking in a different way.

JD: Well, then, let me try to get you to rethink Plato's concept of *eros*. Two contemporary artists whose work raises hackles in different ways are Vanessa Beecroft and Lisa Yuskavage. Both are women whose work finds little favor among feminists, the first because she stages performance events that exploit women as objects in the terms of mainstream consumer industry—seminude fashion models interspersed with young male cadets in military uniform, all in a formal pattern, standing without moving, a kind of photo-op human sculpture in Busby Berkeley mass-ornament mode. The second because she uses the visual tropes of exaggerated illustration-style kitsch to create somewhat grotesque images of women with enormous nipples, baby-doll faces, vinyl hair. Weird exaggerated big-eyed creatures all suffused in a kitsch luminosity. You get the idea. Beecroft is beloved of the art world writers for whom fashion is now conceived of as a critical practice, whatever that means. She gets celebrated—wrongly, I think—for proposing a critique of that world. I see no critique. I see engagement with illusions. Thus my echo of your citing of Plato—because in both instances my conviction is that the artists themselves are quite enthralled with the illusions they use to seduce an audience that wants to pretend to a moral superiority. The complicity with pleasure in both instances, the exploitative and the grotesque, provided by these artists is a major transgression of oppositional correctness. They have no desire at all to dispel their illusions.

JM: That's art working at our inner standing-point, it seems to me. And it works—it unsettles us—just because it lets us see how deliberately it has chosen to act this way. Let's us see that in our culture, art cannot escape an involvement with codes of fashion. JD: But isn't art always much involved with fashion? Isn't that another lesson Baudelaire bequeaths us? The ephemerality of reference, the passing condition of awareness, all that fleeting-ness that characterizes perception, awareness—aren't these bound up in modernity with a notion of fashion? Isn't art, in that sense, most complicit with such an idea? And in the case of Yuskavage, the obvious flirtation with kitsch forms, even tacky painting, ugly illustration, has a junk food for the eye unholy unhealthiness to be sure. But she is working opportunistically, without any self-aware criticality. Like Beecroft, she is aware that any attempt to reconcile these forms to a position of critique will be pretty well fraught with illusion. And so we're left without a critical oppositional position to keep us from falling into the crime of simply looking at work we "know" is "bad" in all kinds of ways. I don't particularly love this work, but I think the way in which it succeeds in unsettling the familiar ground of comfortable opposition is useful in showing the perverse pleasures of complicity.

Specific instances like these abound in contemporary art and its critical reception. But the continual sorting into "good" objects of critique and "bad" objects of transgression against sacred tenets of critical opposition still goes on.

JM: How about going back to and through all those early figures of modernity who plunged themselves into popular forms: Burns, Byron, Poe, Rossetti. The Modernist history of modernity regularly skirts past them. But in a high culture shaped by Enlightenment and critical theory, popular forms are singularly fertile ground.

That we have largely forgotten Burns, for instance, is simply a scandal—that charmer who takes no prisoners. Think of applying our code word of genteel critique, *transgressive,* to such a person! But Burns is a special case because there is simply no one like him in the past two hundred years of British-American art and culture. Byron and Poe are characters we can understand because their complicity is so familiar to us in the work of Warhol, say, or Robert Altman, Cindy Sherman, Kathy Acker. And then there's Rossetti, a writer and artist more for this imperial time of ours than almost anyone else from the last century I can think of. Because all his work is fixated on the very subject we've been talking about: artistic bad faith. Not fixated with Byron's cold and aristocratic eye, which gave him some protection from his self-searching gaze; but with an addictive and erotic sensibility whose closest contemporary analogue is probably William Burroughs. Rossetti's art is—like his culture, like ours—a soft machine.

JD: Bad faith? But also intense investment—wouldn't you say? Rossetti seems to appeal to you because of the complexity of this combination—he doesn't really think of himself as an artist of bad faith—does he?

JM: Well, yes he does. Explicitly. And before that, when he imagined he might be a part of a revolution in the practice of art, he asked this premonitory question through one of his surrogate creatures: "May one be a devil without knowing it?" Think of the failed revolutionary in *Amoresperros* and the strange desire spawned from his bad faith. Rossetti came to know that he could be, that he was, such a devil. What Blake, one of Rossetti's mentors, called an angel. And out of that came England's painter of modern life, the artist of bad faith, painting and writing about what he sees in himself and in the culture that nurtured and rewarded him.

JD: What interests me, finally, is what an artist's "take" is. Odd construction that, with its suggestion of appropriation or possession when in fact it is the giving back through that specific view that really matters. The world is so complex. I have so little faith that our ways of describing it are in any way adequate to that complexity. Quite the contrary. Most of what passes for art, commentary, literary work is a mere commentary upon the social construction of reality in representational conventions—criticism being one of the most narrow, policed, and disciplinary among them. My largest frustration is with just that—the ways the categories of criticism subsume works under the already known. Roger Fry talked about this almost a century ago—suggesting that once we think we know (or can name what we know) we cease to look. Reading is the same, really. And all these prescriptions for how we are to know things—by their virtues as "political" or "social" or "enlightening" works—what use is this?

What if, instead, critical interpretation were a way to write about what is NOT known—as you are fond of saying—and to show something else to us, some record, embodiment, instantiation that shows us our experience again. Well, that is quite utopian, isn't it? But, at least, the goal is not to circumscribe perception or behavior as if images, poetry, aesthetic works of any kind were outside their circumstances. The condition of art is in some ways its innocence—complicity cannot be fully encompassed by the knowing artist. But denial of that condition is what I cannot countenance. Too absurd to imagine we are otherwise (not complicit and/or not innocent). Don't you think, really, that complicity is a kind of desiring condition? One that admits its impurity of purpose without sacrificing nobility of insight or selfish motive? Or is that too lofty a way to defend/define the relation to popular culture modes of presentation and aesthetic expression?

If you asked me, at this moment, to say why I think the concept of complicity is worth bringing into a discussion of modernity from a critical perspective I would say because it provides a more interesting way to think about what it is we do, and see, and read—and a more flexible way to describe the artifacts of aesthetic expression—than the modes of radical critique and oppositional aesthetics on which so much of twentieth-century criticism was premised.

JM: "Complicity as a kind of desiring condition?" It might be, but it usually isn't, unfortunately. When our poets laureate start writing satires against the institutions of culture, or when they start turning against their art—like Laura Riding, like J. D. Salinger. Maybe there we see examples of unusual desires.

You ask us to look again at that wonderful Benton painting, that shocking and parodic odalisque. And so we should. But look again at those late Rossetti oils—*Monna Vanna,* for example. Shocking and parodic as well. An image of a soul—that is what Rossetti thought a painting should be—that has lost everything but its last ditch of desire: truthfulness. What do you think? Is it bleak? Beautiful? Whatever, it's definitely "something else to us, some record . . . that shows us our experience again."

Notes

Chapter 1

1. William Blake, *The Marriage of Heaven and Hell*, plates 25, 26.
2. John 8:58.
3. Swinburne, "Anactoria" 102.
4. Coventry Patmore, *Mystical poems of nuptial love; The wedding sermon, The unknown Eros, and other odes*, ed. Terence Connolly (Boston: H. Humphries Inc., 1938).
5. Gerard Manley Hopkins, "That Nature is a Heraclitean Fire and of the Comfort of the Resurrection."
6. Theodore Roethke, "In a Dark Time" 1.
7. William Blake, "Auguries of Innocence" 127–130.
8. "Lost in Translation": see James Merrill's poem and Sofia Coppola's film.
9. Shakespeare, *The Tempest*, act 2, scene 1.
10. John Keats, "On First Looking into Chapman's Homer."
11. St. Paul quoting the Greek pagan poets Epimenides and Aratus in Acts 17:28.
12. William Wordsworth, "Lucy Gray" 63–64.
13. Wallace Stevens, "Sunday Morning."
14. See especially Isaiah.
15. Alexander Pope, "An Essay on Criticism" 234.
16. William Hazlitt, "On Going a Journey."
17. See Marianne Moore's "Poetry" (text of 1921).
18. Percy Bysshe Shelley, "A Defence of Poetry."
19. Transquoting Tertullian's De Carne Christi, chap. 5.
20. Gertrude Stein, "Composition as Explanation."
21. C. K. Ogden and I. A. Richards, *The Meaning of Meaning.*

22. Karl Marx, "Theses on Feuerbach," 11.

23. Lyn Hejinian, *My Life*.

24. Rob Pope, *Textual Interventions* 1.

25. IVANHOE (http://patacriticism.org/ivanhoe).

26. The word *Ducdame* calls fools in a circle in Shakespeare, *As You Like It*, act 2, scene 5.

27. Swinburne, *Atalanta in Calydon* 314–17.

28. William Blake, *The Four Zoas, Night the Second*.

Chapter 2

1. I quote from the *Notebooks* excerpts printed in *Code of Signals: Recent Writings on Poetics,* ed. Michael Palmer (Berkeley, CA: North Atlantic Books, 1983), 172–84. The other quotations from Coolidge are taken from *Space* (New York: Harper and Row, 1970); *The Maintains* (Berkeley, CA: This Press, 1974); *Mine* (Berkeley, CA: The Figures, 1982); *Solution Passage* (Los Angeles: Sun & Moon Press, 1986); *The Crystal Text* (Great Barrington, MA: The Figures, 1986); *Melencolia* (Great Barrington, MA: The Figures, 1987).

2. Williams's classic statement on objectivism insisted that "the poem, like every other form of art, is an object that in itself presents its case and its meaning by the very form it assumes." What he meant was that poems were not to be thought of as mimetic of something else but as integral and self-declarative. In the jargon of language philosophers like J. L. Austin, poems would be "performative utterances."

3. It seems clear that Coolidge's title is making an oblique reference to Zukofsky's "Poem Beginning 'The.'"

4. "Maintaining Space: Clark Coolidge's Early Works," reprinted from *Stations* 5 in Charles Bernstein's *Content's Dream: Essays 1975–1984* (Los Angeles: Sun & Moon Press, 1986), 261.

5. One must not fail to see that the "reader" is very specifically imagined here as a North American living at a particular period in time. Indeed, "the developed world" is itself being imagined as an "American" world—with all that such an imagination necessarily implies.

6. See Jean Baudrillard, "The Precession of the Simulacra" and "The Orders of Simulacra," the two essays printed in *Simulations,* trans. Paul Foss, Paul Patton, and Philip Beitchman (New York: Semiotext(e), 1983).

7. This is Bernstein's extended *ars poetica* first printed in *Paper Air* 4, no. 1 (1987); the poem comprises the entire issue. It was published as a book the same year by Singing Horse Press.

8. Melville is a dominant presence in all of Coolidge's work. In "Homage to Melville" (*Solution Passage,* 130–31) the central themes of Coolidge's Melville are set down. Melville is the figure of the person who is always:

Setting out, putting forth, drawing down,
toppling measure, drawing on, escaping
the yard, unfurling the tooth,
having a go, leaving off, launching
sentence. The land sheers away.

An implacable voyager with an equally implacable eye for concrete detail and practical activities, Melville bends his worldliness upon the beyond: "He averted his head, and gazed back / beyond all humanity."

9. *Aesthetic Theory,* trans. C. Lenhardt, ed. Gretel Adorno and Rolf Tiedemann (London: Verso, 1984), 279, 472.

Chapter 3

1. *Longpoem* is the word that Silliman prefers to use, as in his "Statement for the Guggenheim." The following Ron Silliman titles appear throughout this essay: *Lit* (Elmwood, CT: Potes and Poets Press, 1987); *The New Sentence* (New York: Roof, 1987); *Paradise* (Providence, RI: Burning Deck, 1985); *What* (Great Barrington, MA: The Figures, 1988); *The Age of Huts* (New York: Roof, 1986); and *ABC* (Berkeley: Tuumba, 1983). For Silliman's important theoretical and historical essays on these topics, see *The New Sentence,* especially parts 2 and 3.

2. Silliman, *New Sentence,* 23.

3. Ibid., 25.

4. Our text for *Oz* is a typescript sent by the author. Various parts of the work have been published in different magazines.

5. Silliman, *Age of Huts,* 45.

6. Silliman, *What,* 28, 26. As shall be seen more fully later—when we discuss Silliman's verse techniques in some detail—this poetical "statement" is so scripturally organized (by the play of line endings against syntax) as to be readable in amusingly different ways/directions. For example, do we translate the line break after "romantic" as a comma, or not?

7. Silliman, *New Sentence,* 142.

8. Ibid., 143.

9. Silliman, *What,* 72.

10. This quotation is from Silliman's 1988 "Statement for the Guggenheim," which he was kind enough to send to us.

11. Quoted from a letter to us, 27 August 1988.

12. Silliman, *ABC,* [1]. The title "Albany" names the place where Silliman lived (in California, not New York).

13. Silliman quotes this passage from Adorno's *Aesthetic Theory* in a letter of 15 August 1988.

14. Silliman, *What*, 117.

15. Ibid., 28–29, 125. The text's remarks on distance and absorption constitute a specific critical commentary on Charles Bernstein's ars poetica, "The Artifice of Absorption" (see chapter 6). *What* is dedicated to Bernstein, and it opens with an implicitly critical allusion to Bernstein's signature poem "The Klupzy Girl." Needless to say, since critical interaction is one of Silliman's most privileged activities, the engagement with Bernstein is imagined as part of a cooperative intellectual event.

16. In interpersonal terms, what Silliman proposes is a particular enactment of Blake's famous proverb: "Corporeal friends are spiritual enemies."

17. Both are reprinted in *New Sentence*, 63–108.

18. Ibid., 92.

19. Silliman, *Paradise*, 30.

20. Silliman, *What*, 90.

21. Silliman, "Demo," *Temblor* 3 (1986): 146, 148.

22. Silliman, *What*, 83. Oral sex and homosexual eroticism both appear frequently in Silliman's texts. They are used with great rhetorical self-consciousness—as instances of behavior understood by the writing to be textually (rather than humanly) deviant. This kind of rhetoric is especially effective in a poem like "Sunset Debris" (printed in *The Age of Huts*). As in the present case, such texts function as signs of a certain (limiting) convention of reading (and writing). The breach of the conventions constitutes a revelation of the existence of the conventions: laying bare (for examination) certain forms of thought and language and social behavior (both the deviant and the conventional).

23. We have in mind here particularly the thought of the Buddhist philosopher Nagarjuna. See Frederick L. Streng's study of Nagarjuna's thought, *Emptiness: A Study of Religious Meaning* (Nashville: Abingdon Press, 1967), including the two appendices (which contain translations of key works by Nagarjuna). On the matter of Silliman's use of line endings and spatial breaks, see the interesting set of essays collected in *The Line in Postmodern Poetry*, ed. Robert Frank and Henry Sayre (Urbana: University of Illinois, 1988).

24. From Silliman's letter of 27 August 1988.

25. Silliman, *Lit*, 67.

26. Ibid., 66.

Chapter 4

1. "Constitution/Writing, Politics, Language, the Body," in L=A=N=G=U=A=G=E 4, "Open Letter" special issue (1981), 154–65; "Equals What?," in *Manifestoes*, ed. Douglas Messerli, *Washington Review of the Arts* (1983); "Four Poems from *I Dont Have Any Paper So Shut Up (or, Social Realism)*," *Temblor* 4

(1986), 67–74; *Give Em Enough Rope* (Los Angeles: Sun & Moon Press, 1987); *Getting Ready to Have Been Frightened* (New York: Roof Books, 1988); "I Knew the Signs by Their Tents," *Avec* 2, no. 1 (1989): 63–7; "Poetry as Explanation, Poetry as Praxis," in *The Politics of Poetic Form,* ed. Charles Bernstein (New York: Roof Books, 1990); "Paradise and Method," in *Paradise and Method Poetics and Praxis* (Evanston, IL: Northwestern University Press, 1996).

2. The quotations from Byron are taken from *The Oxford Authors Byron,* ed. Jerome McGann (Oxford: Oxford University Press, 1986).

3. See Serge Fauchereau, "Three Oppen Letters," *Ironwood* 5 (1975): 78–87.

4. See Lyn Hejinian, "Hard Hearts," *Poetics Journal* 2 (1982): 42–48.

5. The quotations from Shelley are taken from *Shelley's Selected Poetry and Prose,* ed. Donald H. Reiman and Sharon B. Powers (New York: Norton, 1977).

Chapter 5

1. See *The Truth and Life of Myth: An Essay in Essential Autobiography* (Fremont, MI: The Sumac, 1978). Peter Quartermain devotes a couple of excellent pages to this subject in relation to Duncan's work in his *Disjunctive Poetics: From Gertrude Stein and Louis Zukofsky to Susan Howe* (Cambridge: Cambridge University Press, 1992), 163–65. Other Duncan texts quoted here are *Derivations: Selected Poems 1950–1956* (London: Fulcrum, 1968) and *A Selected Prose,* ed. Robert J. Bertholf (New York: New Directions, 1995).

2. The texts for these examples are taken from: William Blake, *The Complete Poetry and Prose,* ed. David V. Erdman (Berkeley: University of California Press, 1986); *Lord Byron: The Complete Poetical Works,* ed. Jerome McGann (Oxford: Oxford University Press, 1980–1992); *William Wordsworth: The Oxford Authors Text,* ed. Stephen Gill (Oxford: Oxford University Press, 1984).

3. E. C. Mayne, *Byron* (London: Metheun, 1924), 177; *Byron: The Complete Poetical Works,* vol. 3, 416.; Paul West, *Byron and the Spoiler's Art* (London: Chatto and Windus, 1960).

4. *Byron: The Complete Poetical Works,* vol. 2, 340.

5. For a more complete account of this interesting case see my *Byron and Romanticism* (Cambridge: Cambridge University Press, 2002), 188–92.

6. These quotations are from Pound's *Drafts and Fragments* cantos.

7. See discussion below of Duncan's "This Place Rumord to Have Been Sodom."

8. For a more detailed discussion see my "Laura (Riding) Jackson and the Literal Truth" in *Critical Inquiry* 18 (Spring 1992): 454–73.

9. Laura Riding Jackson, *The Telling* (New York: Harper and Row, 1972).

10. For the text of Burns's poem see *Burns: Poems and Songs,* ed. James

Kinsley (Oxford: Oxford University Press, 1969. Further discussions of Yearsley and Cristall can be found in my *Poetics of Sensibility: A Revolution in Literary
Style* (Oxford: Clarendon Press, 1998).

11. See Kathy Acker, *Blood and Guts in High School* (Grove Press: New York,
1978).

Chapter 6

1. This is the last poem in the first section ("The Riddle of the Fat Faced
Man") in Bernstein's *Rough Trades* (Los Angeles: Sun & Moon Press, 1991). It
was first published in *Conjunctions* in 1987.

2. The texts parodied are Byron's "She Walks in Beauty," Rossetti's "The
Sonnet" (the opening text of *The House of Life*), and the nursery rhyme that
begins "Star light, star bright."

3. See Bernstein's *Content's Dream: Essays 1975–1984* (Los Angeles: Sun
& Moon Press, 1986), 55, 351; hereafter cited in text as CD.

4. I quote from Bernstein's *Artifice of Absorption*, his extended ars poetica published as a single issue of *Paper Air* 4 (1987): 8; hereafter cited in text
as AA. The futurist influence is most evident in, for example, works like *Dis-
frutes* (Needham, MA: Potes and Poets Press, 1981) and *Veil* (Madison, WI.:
Xexoxial Editions, 1987). For a good introduction to futurism see Marjorie
Perloff, *The Futurist Moment* (Chicago: University of Chicago Press, 1986).

5. Charles Bernstein and Tom Beckett, "Censers of the Unknown: Margins, Dissent, and the Poetic Horizon," *Temblor* 9 (1989): 126; hereafter cited
in text.

6. In a prose note to "Dysraphism" Bernstein observes that the word is
"used by specialists in congenital disease to mean a dysfunctional fusion of em-
bryonic parts—a birth defect . . . so dysraphism is mis-seaming—a prosodic
device!" (*The Sophist*, [Los Angeles: Sun & Moon Press, 1987], 44) But this
"prosodic device" is simultaneously a thematic element—"Content's Dream,"
as it were. The title of "Ambliopia" is another medical term, in this case a disease of the retina that results in a dimming or blurring of vision. For Bernstein, the dysfunction is a trope that offers the possibility of engaging with
the world on an entirely new footing. Bernstein in fact hears in "Ambliopia" a
word play to "ambliopia-multilevel seeing, which is to say, vision repossessed"
(see Bernstein and Beckett, "Censers of the Unknown," 127).

7. Charles Bernstein, "Ambliopia," in *The Sophist*, 115; hereafter cited in
text.

8. See Ron Silliman's essays collected in *The New Sentence* (New York:
Roof, 1985) and his Wittgensteinian poetical meditation on writing, "The Chi-
nese Notebook," in *The Age of Huts* (New York: Roof, 1986). See also Barrett
Watten, *Total Syntax* (Carbondale, IL: Southern Illinois University Press, 1985),

Alan Davies, *Signage* (New York: Roof, 1987), Susan Howe's great study *My Emily Dickinson* (Berkeley: North Atlantic Books, 1985), and Nick Piombino, *Boundary of Blur* (New York: Roof, 1993).

9. Charles Bernstein, "An Interview with Tom Beckett," *The Difficulties* 2, no. 2 (1982); the present text is taken from the one reprinted in *Content's Dream*, 391.

10. Charles Bernstein, "The Klupzy Girl," in his *Islets/Irritations* (New York: J. Davies, 1983), 47; hereafter cited in text as KG.

11. Charles Bernstein, "The Simply," in *The Sophist*, 7. For an extended reading of this poem see the appendix to the present chapter.

12. It is perhaps worth remarking that the kiwi fruit actually grows on "vines" rather than trees. Bernstein takes his poetic license here, presumably, because the word "tree" is important to his book in a general way—as one observes, for example, in the pair of important poems printed later: "Reading the Tree: 1" and "Reading the Tree: 2." The latter are textual reimaginings of Ron Silliman's recent anthology of language writing, *In the American Tree* (Orono, ME: National Poetry Foundation, 1986).

13. That is to say, in a journal widely known as a regular outlet for "Language Writing."

14. The other poems are "The View from Nowhere," "Catabolism," and "Force of Feeling." The poems are introduced by an eight-page discussion (by the editors), "On Language Poetry." See *Rethinking* MARXISM 1 (1988): 69–84.

15. See Alan Davies, "Private Enigma in the Opened Text," in *Signage* 70–74.

16. Charles Bernstein, "The Lives of the Toll Takers," in *Rough Trades* (Los Angeles: Sun & Moon Press, 1991). The ellipses are not Bernstein's: they indicate the absence of some text.

17. Charles Bernstein, "The Lives of the Toll Takers." The ellipses are not Bernstein's: they indicate the absence of some text.

18. Bernstein quotes from Silliman's longer critique—a private correspondence—in a note at the end of "Thought's Measure" (CD 85–86n).

19. "The Simply" is printed as the initial poem in Bernstein's collection *The Sophist*. I quote here from that text.

20. I take this phrase from Ron Silliman's "The Chinese Notebook" in *The Age of Huts*, 54, 63.

Chapter 7

1. See *The Bellingham Review* 20 (spring 1997): 38–43.

2. *Nous sont une autre:* Arthur Rimbaud, "Je suis une autre."

3. "we who love to be astonished": Lyn Hejinian, *My Life*.

4. "an adequate mode of expression is senseless": Kathy Acker, *Empire of the Senseless.*

5. "in the midst of other woe than ours": Keats, "Ode on a Grecian Urn."

Chapter 8

1. See Marjorie Levinson, introduction to *Rethinking Historicism: Critical Readings in Romantic History* (Oxford: Basil Blackwell, 1989).

2. Jerome J. McGann, "Theory of Texts," *London Review of Books* 18 February 1988, 21.

3. Jerome J. McGann, *Towards a Literature of Knowledge* (Oxford: Clarendon Press, 1989), ix. (See also chapter 2 of this book.)

4. Ibid. The book *Towards a Literature of Knowledge* comprises McGann's Clark Lectures, delivered at Trinity College, Cambridge, in February 1988.

5. Jerome J. McGann, *Social Values and Poetic Acts* (Cambridge, MA: Harvard University Press, 1987), viii.

6. *Social Values,* 122.

7. The essential critical discussions of the poem are the following: *The Works of Lord Byron: Poetry,* ed. E. H. Coleridge (London: John Murray, 1898–1904), vol. 3, 531–35; David V. Erdman, "'Fare Thee Well!'—Byron's Last Days in England," in *Shelley and His Circle: 1773–1832,* ed. Kenneth Neill Cameron (Cambridge, MA: Harvard University Press, 1970), vol. 4, 638–65: W. Paul Elledge, "Talented Equivocation: Byron's 'Fare Thee Well!'" *Keats-Shelley Journal* 35 (1986): 42–61; *Lord Byron: The Complete Poetical Works,* ed. Jerome J. McGann (Oxford: Clarendon Press, 1980–1993), vol. 3, 493–94.

8. See Mayne, *Byron,* 256; and Erdman, "'Fair Thee Well!,'" 642 and n.

9. See *The Letters of William and Dorothy Wordsworth,* ed. E. de Selincourt (Oxford: Clarendon Press, 1970), vol. 3, 304. Wordsworth's reading is given in a letter to John Scott, who put out the unauthorized printing of Byron's poem.

10. Quoted in Mayne, *Byron,* 256.

11. *Critical Review* (December 1816): 577–78.

12. Quoted in Malcolm Elwin, *Lord Byron's Wife* (New York: Harcourt, Brace, 1962), 394.

13. Ibid., 400.

14. Elledge, "Talented Equivocation," 43.

15. Elwin, *Lord Byron's Wife,* 409.

16. Ibid., 448.

17. Doris Langley Moore, *The Late Lord Byron* (London: John Murray, 1961), 164.

18. Elledge, "Talented Equivocation," 44n.

19. It is in many ways a rehearsal for what seems to me its clear companion piece, *Manfred*. See McGann, "Byron and Wordsworth," in *Byron and Romanticism*.

20. *The Romantics Reviewed, 1793–1830: Contemporary Reviews of British Romantic Writers*, ed. Donald Reiman (New York: Garland, 1972), part B, vol. 4, 1979.

21. Quoted in Louis Crompton, *Byron and Greek Love* (Berkeley: University of California Press, 1985), 128–29.

Chapter 9

1. This term (and the genre it names) is the invention of Randall McLeod. See his essay "Where Angels Fear to Tread," in *Marking the Text: The Representation of Meaning on the Literary Page*, ed. Joe Bray, Miriam Hadley, and Anne C. Henry (Ashgate: Aldeshot, 2000), 144–92.

2. See Jean Starobinski, *Words Upon Words: The Anagrams of Ferdinand de Saussure* (New Haven: Yale University Press, 1979).

3. Jouet's work was originally published as no. 62 in the *Bibliothéque Oulipienne*. Queneau's work, cited above, appeared as no. 3 in the same series. My quotations from both works are taken from the reprint in the *Oulipo Laboratory*, trans. Harry Mathews and Iain White (London: Atlas Press, 1995).

Chapter 10

1. Jerome McGann, "Contemporary Poetry, Alternate Routes," *Critical Inquiry* 13.3 (Spring 1987), 624–47.

Chapter 12

1. Alfred Alvarez, *The Savage God: A Study of Suicide* (New York: Random House, 1972), a study of the confessional suicidal poets like Plath and Berryman.

Bibliography

Note: The footnotes in the chapters devoted to the poetry of Bruce Andrews, Charles Bernstein, Clark Coolidge, Robert Duncan, and Ron Silliman give the bibliographical information about the various works dealt with in each case.

Adorno, Theodore. *Aesthetic Theory*. Trans. C. Lenhardt. London: Verso Books, 1984.

Allen, Donald, ed. *The New American Poetry*. New York: Grove Press, 1960.

Allen, Michael. *Poe and the British Magazine Tradition*. Oxford: Oxford University Press, 1969.

Arnold, Matthew. *Essays in Criticism*. 1st ser. London: Macmillan, 1865.

———. *The Poems*. Ed. Kenneth Allott. 2nd ed. London: Longmans, 1979.

Barfield, Owen. *Saving the Appearances: A Study in Idolatry*. London: Faber and Faber, 1957.

Barthes, Roland. *Critical Essays*. Trans. Richard Howard. Evanston, IL: Northwestern University Press, 1972.

———. *S/Z*. Trans. Richard Howard. New York: Hill and Wang, 1975.

Bennett, Tony. *Formalism and Marxism*. London: Methuen, 1979.

Bernstein, Charles. *Islets/Irritations*. New York: J. Davies, 1983.

———. *My Way: Speeches and Poems*. Chicago: University of Chicago Press, 1999.

Blake, William. *The Complete Poetry and Prose*. Ed. David V. Erdman, commentary by Harold Bloom. Rev. ed. New York: Random House, 1988.

Bloom, Harold. *The Anxiety of Influence*. New York: Oxford University Press, 1973.

Bök, Christian. *Eunoia*. Toronto: Coach House Press, 2001.

Byron, Lord. *The Complete Poetical Works*. Ed. Jerome McGann. 7 vols. Oxford: Clarendon Press, 1981–1993.

Coleridge, Samuel Taylor. *Biographia Literaria*. Ed. James Engell and W. J. Bate. 2 vols. Princeton, NJ: Princeton University Press, 1983.

Coolidge, Clark. *Now It's Jazz: Writings on Kerouac and The Sounds*. Albuquerque, NM: Living Batch Press, 1999.

———. *Sound as Thought: Poems 1982–1984*. Los Angeles: Sun & Moon Press, 1990.

Crawford, Donald W. *Kant's Aesthetic Theory*. Madison: University of Wisconsin Press, 1974.

Crews, Frederick. *The Pooh Perplex: A Freshman Casebook*. New York: Dutton, 1963.

———. *Postmodern Pooh*. New York: North Point Press, 2001.

Davies, Alan. *Signage*. New York: Roof Books, 1978.

Della Volpe, Galvano. *Critique of Taste*. Trans. Michael Caesar. 1860. London: New Left Books, 1978.

Eagleton, Terry. *The Ideology of the Aesthetic*. Oxford: Oxford University Press, 1990.

Eco, Umberto. *The Limits of Interpretation*. Bloomington: Indiana University Press, 1990.

Eliot, T. S. *Selected Essays*. New ed. New York: Harcourt Brace, 1950.

Forrest-Thomson, Veronica. *Poetic Artifice: A Theory of Twentieth-Century Poetry*. Manchester, UK: Manchester University Press, 1978.

Golding, Alan. *From Outlaw to Classic: Canons in American Poetry*. Madison, WI: University of Wisconsin Press, 1995.

Hejinian, Lyn. "The Rejection of Closure." In *Writing/Talks*, 270–91. Carbondale: Southern Illinois University Press, 1985.

Hoffman, Daniel. *Poe Poe Poe Poe Poe Poe Poe*. Doubleday: Garden City, 1972.

Hollander, John. *Reflections on Espionage*. New York: Athenaeum, 1976.

Hopkins, Gerard Manley. *The Poems*. Ed. W. H. Gardner and N. H. Mackenzie. 4th ed. London: Oxford University Press, 1990.

Howe, Susan. *My Emily Dickinson*. Berkeley: North Atlantic Books, 1985.

———. "These Flames and Generosities of the Heart: Emily Dickinson and the Illogic of Sumptuary Values." In *The Birth-Mark: Unsettling the Wilderness in American Literary History*. Hanover, NH: Wesleyan University Press, 1993.

James, Henry. "The Art of Fiction." In *Henry James: Literary Criticism*. New York: The Library of America, 1984.

Johnson, Galen A., ed. *The Merleau-Ponty Aesthetics Reader: Philosophy and Painting*. Trans. Michael B. Smith. Evanston, IL: Northwestern University Press, 1993.

Kant, Immanuel. *The Critique of Judgment*. Trans. James Creed Meredith. Oxford: Clarendon Press, 1952.

Keats, John. *John Keats: The Poems*. Ed. Miriam Allott. London: Longmans, 1977.

Lang, Cecil Y. *The Pre-Raphaelites and Their Circle*. Chicago: University of Chicago Press, 1975.

———, ed. *Swinburne: Letters*. 6 vols. New Haven, CT: Yale University Press, 1959–1962.

McGann, Jerome. *The Beauty of Inflections: Literary Investigations in Historical Method and Theory*. Oxford, UK: Clarendon Press, 1985.

———, ed. *The Complete Writings and Pictures of Dante Gabriel Rossetti: A Hypermedia Research Archive*. *http://jefferson.village.virginia.edu/rossetti/*.

———. *The Textual Condition*. Princeton, NJ: Princeton University Press, 1991.

McGann, Jerome, and Lisa Samuels. "Deformance and Interpretation." In *Radiant Textuality: Literature after the World Wide Web*, 105–36. New York: Palgrave/St Martin's, 2002.

McKenzie, D. F. *Bibliography and the Sociology of Texts*. London: The British Library, 1986.

———. *"Making Meaning": Printers of the Mind and Other Essays*. Amherst: University of Massachusetts Press, 2002.

Merleau-Ponty, Maurice. "Eye and Mind." In *The Primacy of Perception*. Evanston, IL: Northwestern University Press, 1964.

Merrill, James. *Divine Comedies*. New York: Athenaeum, 1976.

Moore, Marianne. *Complete Poems*. New York: Viking Press, 1981.

Nagy, Gregory. *Poetry as Performance*. Cambridge: Cambridge University Press, 1996.

Nelson, Cary. *Repression and Recovery: Modern American Poetry and the Politics of Cultural Memory, 1910–1945*. Madison, WI: University of Wisconsin Press, 1989.

Ogden, C. K., and I. A. Richards. *The Meaning of Meaning*. New York: Harcourt Brace and Co, 1925.

Perloff, Marjorie. *The Dance of the Intellect: Studies in the Poetry of the Pound Tradition*. Evanston: Northwestern University Press, 1996.

Pichois, Claude, ed. *Baudelaire: Oeuvres Complètes*. Paris: Gallimard, 1976.

Poe, Edgar Allen. *Essays and Reviews*. Selected and with notes by G. R. Thompson. Literary Classics of the United States. New York: The Library of America, 1984.

———. *Poetry and Tales*. Selected and with notes by Patrick Quinn. Literary Classics of the United States. New York: The Library of America, 1984.

Pope, Alexander. *An Essay on Criticism*. Ed. E. Audra. London: Methuen, 1961.

Pope, Rob. *Textual Interventions: Critical and Creative Strategies for Literary Studies*. London: Routledge, 1995.

Pound, Ezra. *The Cantos of Ezra Pound*. 4th ed. London: Faber, 1986.

Quartermain, Peter. *Disjunctive Poetics: From Gertrude Stein and Louis Zukofsky to Susan Howe*. New York: Cambridge University Press, 1992.

Riding, Laura. *Anarchism Is Not Enough*. Ed. Lisa Samuels. Berkeley: University of California Press, 2001.

———. *Progress of Stories*. With new material and a new preface. New York: Persea Books, 1994.

———. *The Telling*. New York: Harper and Row, 1973.

Roethke, Theodore. *Collected Poems and Selected Prose*. Ed. Stanley Burnshaw. Austin: University of Texas Press, 2002.

Rossetti, Dante Gabriel. *Dante Gabriel Rossetti: Collected Poetry and Prose*. Ed. Jerome McGann. New Haven, CT: Yale University Press, 2003.

Shelley, Percy Bysshe. *The Major Works*. Ed. Donald Reiman. Oxford: Oxford University Press, 2003.

Showalter, Elaine. *The New Feminist Criticism: Essays on Women, Literature, and Theory*. London: Virago, 1986.

Silliman, Ron. "Disappearance of the Word, Appearance of the World" and "If by 'Writing' We Mean Literature . . ." In *The L=A=N=G=U=A=G=E Book*, 167–68, 121–32. Ed. Bruce Andrews and Charles Bernstein. Carbondale, IL: Southern Illinois University Press, 1984.

Soderholm, James, ed. *Beauty and the Critic: Aesthetics in an Age of Cultural Studies*. Tuscaloosa: University of Alabama Press, 1997.

Sokal, Alan D. "What the Social Text Affair Does and Does Not Prove." In *A House Built on Sand: Exposing Postmodernist Myths about Science* Ed. Noretta Koertge. New York: Oxford University Press, 1998.

Stevens, Wallace. *The Collected Poems*. New York: Alfred A. Knopf, 1967.

———. *The Palm at the End of the Mind: Selected Poems and a Play*. Ed. Holly Stevens. Alfred A. Knopf: New York, 1972.

Swinburne, A. C. *Swinburne: Major Poems and Selected Prose*. Ed. Jerome McGann and Charles Sligh. New Haven, CT: Yale University Press, 2004.

Tennyson, Alfred, Lord. *Tennyson: The Poems*. Ed. Christopher Ricks. Harlow: Longmans, 1969.

Todd, Mabel Loomis, and Thomas Higginson, eds. *The Poems of Emily Dickinson*. 3 vols. New York: Little Brown, 1891, 1892, 1896.

Wittgenstein, Ludwig. *Philosophical Investigations*. 3rd ed. Trans. G. E. M. Anscombe. New York: Macmillan, 1958.

Wordsworth, William. *Selections*. Ed. Stephen Gill. Oxford, UK: Oxford University Press, 1984.

———. *The Poems*. Ed. John O. Hayden. 2 vols. Harmondsworth, UK: Penguin, 1977.

Zukofsky, Louis, ed. *An Objectivists' Anthology*. New York: Objectivist Press, 1932.

Index